THE HAIRY BIKERS'
MEAT FEASTS

SI KING AND DAVE MYERS

THE HAIRY BIKERS'
MEAT FEASTS

— SI KING AND DAVE MYERS —

W&N

WEIDENFELD & NICOLSON

We'd like to dedicate this book to the farmers, producers and butchers who care about the meat we all eat, and to our mams who taught us how to cook it!

First published in Great Britain in 2015
by Weidenfeld & Nicolson, an imprint of the
Orion Publishing Group Ltd
Carmelite House
50 Victoria Embankment
London EC4Y 0DZ
An Hachette UK Company

10 9 8 7 6 5 4 3 2 1

A CIP catalogue record for this book is available from the British Library.

ISBN: 978 0 297 867371

Photographer: Andrew Hayes-Watkins
Food director: Catherine Phipps
Food stylists: Lisa Harrison, Anna Burges-Lumsden
Designer and prop stylist: Loulou Clark
Prop stylist: Rebecca Newport
Project editor: Jinny Johnson
Proofreader: Mary-Jane Wilkins
Indexer: Vicki Robinson
Technical artworker: Andy Bowden
Photographer's assistant: Kristy Noble
Food stylists' assistants: Jane Brown, Lou Kenny

Printed and bound in Germany

The Orion Publishing Group's policy is to use papers that are natural, renewable and recyclable and made from wood grown in sustainable forests. The logging and manufacturing processes are expected to conform to the environmental regulations of the country of origin.

www.orionbooks.co.uk

by
BOOK
or by
COOK

COOKING
EATING
SHARING

For lots more delicious recipes plus articles, interviews and videos from the best chefs cooking today visit our blog
bybookorbycook.co.uk

Follow us

 @bybookorcook

Find us

 facebook.com/bybookorbycook

CONTENTS

MEAT FEASTS

There's something about the smell of meat cooking that signals a feast – it's savoury, comforting and tempting. A steak on the grill, a roast in the oven, a casserole bubbling – they make your mouth water. You have a sense of anticipation that something tasty is on the way. Of course, we love all things veggie too, but this book is for the carnivore – it's an unashamed celebration of meat.

When we were kids, a meal wasn't a meal without meat. It might have been just a bit of mince, a sausage or two or a cheap cut in a stew, but meat was at the heart of it. We had meat pies and suet puds, nourishing lamb hotpots in winter, a nice ham salad in summer. We ate plenty of offal – liver and bacon, steak and kidney – and soups made with beef bones, trotters and oxtail. Si's mum had a tongue press, which looked a bit like an instrument of torture, but she would layer the tongue meat with fresh rosemary to make an Easter treat – and very good it was too.

There were things we didn't care for, of course. My dad ate honeycomb tripe and that was where my meat tastes stopped (Dave). My granddad insisted on cow heel soup being on the menu regularly (Si).

Nowadays, as well as cooking roasts, chops and stews, we like to use small amounts of meat in lighter dishes such as stir-fries and fresh Asian salads. We cook up the less tender cuts in spicy curries and tagines, and experiment with more unusual morsels such as pig's cheeks. With the cosmopolitan nature of our country now, we have the most extraordinarily eclectic range of food. Put our great produce with that multicultural inspiration and you have something very special.

British meat really is good. The climate here is perfect for grass and perfect grass makes for great meat. Our traditional cattle produce beef without equal – in fact, we were the first people to breed cows for beef rather than dairy, and beef cattle such as Hereford, Longhorn, Galloway and Aberdeen Angus are among the best in the world. Our lamb and pork is fantastic as well. There are more than 60 breeds of sheep, including Herdwick, Kendal Rough Fell and Swaledale, and there are many traditional pig breeds, such as Gloucestershire Old Spots, Tamworth, Saddleback and Berkshire to name but a few.

When we did our *Food Tour of Britain* telly series a few years back, we discovered that home cooks like us are becoming more and more interested in the quality of the meat we buy and where it comes from. We want to cook better meat and get the best from it. We want meat from animals that have been properly reared, fed decent food and allowed at least some time to roam. And it's not just a moral thing – meat from animals that have had time to grow and roam tastes better! It's a win-win situation.

Many producers have responded to this interest. Our bacon is the best in the world, in our opinion, and sausages are now a gourmet item. Customers are rediscovering the value of a good butcher's shop and supermarkets are offering a similar experience by providing butchery counters as well as shelves of prepacked meat. There are farm shops too and farmers' markets, where you can often buy direct from the suppliers.

Most diet experts would agree that we shouldn't be eating large quantities of meat every day. This is all the more reason to choose carefully and make sure that what you do eat is good and tasty so you enjoy it to the full. What's more, good doesn't have to mean expensive. Often the cheaper cuts such as shin, shoulder, neck and so on have a better flavour than your prime cuts. And you don't have to buy big quantities of meat to make an interesting meal. In this book we have recipes for everything from roast rib of beef and prime steaks to meatballs, sandwiches and burgers. And check out our A Little Goes a Long Way chapter for loads of great ideas for making a small amount of meat feed the family.

Meat is one of the best sources of protein and protein keeps you feeling satisfied for longer than carbs or fat. This means that meat is good even if you're watching your weight. Red meat is also a source of iron and B vitamins, which are important in a balanced diet. Good meat is tasty, moreish and sustains you.

SOMETHING FOR EVERYONE

Cooking meat is about more than roasts and chops. It's about making use of the less familiar cuts too. As a mark of respect to the animals and the farmers who raise them it seems only right to use as much of the beast as possible.

This book is about meat, not chicken and other poultry. Most of the recipes are for pork, lamb and beef, but we have included some for veal and for wild boar, venison, goat and rabbit. We've divided our recipes not by types of meat but by styles of cooking, so we have chapters on Salads and Starters, Soups and Broths, Fast Meat, Roasts and Pot Roasts, and Slow Cooking. As well known pie lovers, we had to have a chapter on pies and suet puds. We look at mince dishes and we've a chapter on hot curries. We also have a chapter on offal – it's good to make use of every bit of an animal – and one on using up any leftovers. Something for everyone.

In these recipes we want to show that meat is not just for high days and holidays. We've included loads of ideas for mince, stews, sausages and so on – the sort of things we all want to cook and eat. And we've taken a fresh look at some classics. For instance, we've shared our recipe for Lancashire hotpot with you before, and we think it's the best. When we put together this book we knew we couldn't better it, but on the other hand – a book on meat without a hotpot? No way. So we came up with a new version – a sausage hotpot that we know everyone is going to love.

OUR TOP TIPS

Shop wisely. People say that 90 per cent of great cheffing is great shopping and we'd go along with that where meat is concerned. Strike up a good relationship with your butcher or the people on the supermarket meat counter and ask questions about the meat and where it comes from. They should know their stuff and can be really helpful. Be adventurous; try different cuts and ways of cooking them.

Marinate. Marinating meat adds flavour and helps to tenderise cheaper tougher cuts of meat. In most cases you will need to leave the meat for several hours or overnight and it's best to keep it in the fridge. Don't marinate your meat in a metal bowl, as the acid ingredients in a marinade, such as lemon or vinegar, can react with the metal and spoil the flavour. Use a plastic, glass or ceramic bowl or easier still, pile everything into a freezer bag and seal it well.

Don't cook meat cold. For best results, take your meat out of the fridge and allow it to come to room temperature before you cook it. Cooking fridge-cold meat lowers the oven temperature and it then takes a while to build up again. And if you're grilling or frying the meat, you risk overdoing the outside while not cooking it properly on the inside. If meat is near enough at room temperature it will cook more evenly.

Let your meat rest after cooking. Recipes always say this but, believe us, it is really important. During the cooking process the juices in a piece of meat go towards the centre. When it is removed from the heat and allowed to stand for a while, these juices are redistributed through the meat, making it more tender and better to eat. Leave a roast joint for 15–20 minutes or a smaller piece such a steak or chop for 5 minutes or so.

While the meat is resting, place it on a board or a warm plate and cover it very loosely with a piece of foil. Don't wrap it or cover it tightly or it will sweat and that's not nice.

CARVING

Most important is to have good sharp knives. You can't carve a piece of meat properly with a blunt knife. Always have a steel or sharpener to hand.

Use a carving fork too, so you can keep the meat steady as you carve.

Let the meat rest before you start to carve and carve against the grain of the meat. This is particularly important with cheaper cuts, as if you carve them with the grain the meat can be stringy.

And lastly, if you've slow cooked your meat until it's falling off the bone, rejoice in that and don't try to carve it. Just give in to your inner caveman and pull the meat apart in chunks.

A FEW LITTLE NOTES FROM US

- Peel onions, garlic and other veg and fruit unless otherwise specified.
- Use free-range eggs whenever possible.
- Stock features in lots of recipes and we've included guidelines for making your own stock at the back of the book – it's not difficult, honest. Otherwise, use the good fresh stocks available in the supermarkets now or use the little stock pots or cubes. Many are pretty good these days.
- We've made oven temperatures and cooking times as accurate as possible, but all ovens are different so keep an eye on your dish and be prepared to cook it for a longer or shorter time if necessary. A meat probe thermometer is a really useful bit of kit if you want to be sure of perfectly cooked meat every time.

THE SUNDAY ROAST

Everyone loves a Sunday roast, with gravy, lots of veg and all the trimmings, and we've proved it once and for all. The roast dinner was voted the nation's favourite meal in a poll conducted for a television show we did recently. It's a meal we remember fondly from childhood and something we will always continue to cook.

And roasts don't have to be expensive. Lamb shoulder and beef topside are much cheaper than leg of lamb and sirloin and just as tasty. Have a look at our recipes in the Roasts and Pot Roasts chapter of this book for more ideas.

'We always had a Sunday roast, never failed, and it was the meal of the week that the whole family gathered to enjoy. If we'd had beef on a Sunday my mum would do a leek and onion suet pud on the Monday. She'd put it in a clootie bag, steam it for hours and serve it up with the leftover gravy and beef. Nothing better. Later on, when my brother and sister and I were living away from home, we still went back on Sundays because no one makes a roast dinner like your mum. Now we do the same for our kids, but I'm not sure my roast dinners will ever be as good as my mum's.'

— SI —

'In my family there was always a roast on Sundays. It was chicken, lamb, beef and pork in rotation, never changed. There were just the three of us – me and my mum and dad – so we had a small joint and it did for three meals: Sunday dinner, then with bubble and squeak on Monday and perhaps a broth on Tuesday. Nothing was ever wasted. We always had the right accompaniments, such as mint sauce with lamb, apples with pork and so on – and by golly it was good. I can still remember the anticipation I felt, hearing Two-Way Family Favourites on the radio and smelling the meat roasting.'

— DAVE —

CHAPTER ONE
STARTERS AND SALADS

PARMA HAM WITH GINGER-MARINATED MELON

Parma ham and melon is a classic combo for a good reason – they're great together. We like charentais and cantaloupe melons, but any kind other than watermelon should be fine. Fresh root ginger packs a punch and brings this dish bang up to date.

SERVES 4

1 melon, peeled, deseeded
  and sliced into 12 thin
  wedges
20g fresh root ginger, peeled
juice of 1 lime
12 slices of Parma ham
small handful of basil leaves,
  very finely shredded
flaked sea salt
freshly ground white pepper

Put the melon wedges in a bowl. Grate the ginger into a small bowl, then squeeze it through a small sieve, discarding any fibrous bits and reserving the juice. Mix this juice with the lime juice and season with salt and white pepper. Add 2 tablespoons of water, then pour the mixture over the melon. Turn the melon over with your hands until all the wedges are coated.

Leave the melon to stand while you arrange the slices of Parma ham on 4 plates. Add the wedges of melon, then toss the shredded basil leaves in any ginger and lime juices left in the bowl and sprinkle them over the melon and ham. Serve immediately.

COARSE COUNTRY TERRINE

Terrines are dead impressive and this one is a real show-off dish that looks like it comes from a posh deli. It's a lot easier to make than you think, though, and if we can do it so can you. Once cooked, the terrine needs to be chilled overnight so make it the day before you want it. You'll need a one-litre terrine mould, ideally one with a lid, although you can cover it with foil instead.

SERVES 10

300g rindless pork shoulder, chopped into small pieces
300g rindless pork belly, chopped into small pieces
150g rindless unsmoked streaky bacon rashers, chopped into small pieces
225g pig's liver, rinsed and patted dry with kitchen paper
2 garlic cloves, crushed
juice and zest of 1 orange
6 tbsp brandy
3 tbsp chopped fresh sage
1 tbsp chopped fresh thyme
1 tbsp black peppercorns
1 tbsp juniper berries
400g rindless smoked streaky bacon rashers
200g cornichons, drained

Put half the pork shoulder, half the pork belly and half the unsmoked bacon rashers in a food processor with the liver and garlic and blend until smooth. Add the remaining shoulder, pork belly and bacon, then pulse until roughly chopped and well mixed.

Tip the mixture into a bowl and stir in the orange juice and zest, brandy and herbs. Grind the peppercorns and juniper berries with a pestle and mortar, then stir them into the mixture. Cover the bowl with clingfilm and chill in the fridge for 1–3 hours.

Place the smoked bacon rashers on a board and stretch them, one at a time, with the back of a knife. Line the terrine mould with the rashers, placing them across the width so that some of each rasher overlaps the edge of the mould.

Preheat the oven to 150°C/Fan 130°C/Gas 2. Spoon a third of the meat mixture into the lined terrine and place half the cornichons neatly on top. They need to run lengthways down the terrine, so that when the terrine is cut, they form a row of green circles in the centre.

Spoon another third of the meat mixture on top of the cornichons and press until the surface is smooth and firm. Cover with a second layer of cornichons and finish with the remaining meat. Bring the ends of the bacon rashers up and over the meat mixture, then put more strips of bacon over the top so it is all covered.

Cover with the lid or some foil and place the mould in a small roasting tin. Add enough just-boiled water to come 2cm up the sides of the mould. Bake in the centre of the oven for 1½ hours.

To check if the terrine is ready, remove it from the oven and insert a skewer into the centre. Hold it for 10 seconds, then take it out and lightly touch the end – it should feel hot. The terrine should also have shrunk away from the sides of the terrine. Remove it from the roasting tin.

Take off the lid, cover the terrine with a double layer of foil and place a couple of cans of beans or some other heavy weights on top. Leave to cool, then chill in the fridge overnight. The next day, turn the terrine out on to a board and cut it into thick slices. Serve with some hot, crusty bread and butter.

FRISÉE AUX LARDONS

This classic dish has a fancy French name but it's basically a fab green salad with a tasty bacon dressing, topped with poached eggs. You'll find bacon lardons in most supermarkets – they're little chunks of diced bacon. If you don't have any, just cut up some rashers of streaky bacon. If you want to go really fancy, you could use duck eggs, but you'll need to cook them a little longer.

SERVES 4

200g smoked bacon lardons
2 shallots, finely chopped
1 garlic clove, finely chopped
4 tbsp olive oil
1–2 tbsp red wine vinegar
1 tsp Dijon mustard
pinch of sugar
1 tbsp white wine vinegar
4 very fresh eggs
1 large bag of frisée lettuce, washed and torn into pieces
1 tbsp very finely chopped parsley
a few tarragon leaves, very finely chopped.
flaked sea salt

Put the bacon lardons in a frying pan and dry fry them over a medium heat until they're crisp and brown, and much of the fat has oozed out. Add the shallot and cook for a few more minutes, then add the garlic.

Pour the olive oil into the pan, then whisk in the red wine vinegar, mustard and sugar. Remove the pan from the heat and set it aside.

Now poach the eggs. Bring a saucepan of water to the boil and add a pinch of salt and the white wine vinegar. Lower the heat to a gentle simmer. Break an egg into a cup, so it's ready to use, then create a whirlpool in the centre of the saucepan by swirling a spoon around in the water. Drop the egg into the centre of the whirlpool. The white of the egg should settle around the yolk. Cook the egg for 3 minutes, then remove it with a slotted spoon.

Trim the edges if they're looking very ragged, then drop the egg into a bowl of cold water. Repeat with the other eggs and keep the pan of water simmering.

Put the frisée into a large salad bowl. Sprinkle the herbs over the bacon vinaigrette in the pan and stir, then pour everything over the salad. Mix thoroughly, then divide the salad between 4 bowls. Put all the eggs back in the saucepan for 30 seconds to heat through, then top each bowl of salad with an egg.

Tip
It's important to use really fresh, preferably free-range, eggs for poaching and you might want to try our special tip. When the pan of water is boiling and before adding the salt and vinegar, place the eggs, still in their shells, in the boiling water for exactly 20 seconds. Remove the eggs carefully and proceed as above. We find that this helps the eggs keep their shape nicely.

JAMBON PERSILLÉ

Jellied ham with parsley doesn't sound quite as glam as the French name for this traditional terrine, but that's what it is and it's great served with toast as a starter or with salad for a summery lunch. It's made with ham hocks and we add a pig's trotter to help the juices set to jelly. If you don't like the idea of pig's trotters you can use gelatine instead – six leaves per 500ml of liquid should be about right. Another tip – when you buy your ham hocks ask if they need soaking. And if you have any leftover ham hock, try making croquetas (see page 321).

SERVES 6–8

2 ham hocks
1 pig's trotter, left whole
   (or gelatine, see method)
200ml white wine
1 onion, studded with
   4 cloves
2 bay leaves
a few parsley stems
a sprig of fresh tarragon
a sprig of fresh thyme
1 tsp black peppercorns
a strip of thinly pared
   lemon peel
1 leek, cut into chunks
1 carrot, cut into chunks
1 celery stick, cut into
   chunks
4 garlic cloves, unpeeled
2 shallots, finely chopped
a large bunch of parsley,
   finely chopped
lots of freshly ground white
   pepper

If the ham hocks need soaking, put them in a large pan, cover with plenty of cold water and leave overnight.

To cook the ham hocks, drain them (if they've been soaking), then put them in a saucepan or stockpot along with the pig's trotter. Make sure everything fits quite snugly – you don't want to dilute the flavours or the gelatine in the trotter too much.

Cover the hocks with cold water, bring to the boil and boil for 5 minutes. Drain, rinse the hocks and trotter under the tap and rinse out the saucepan too. Put the hocks and trotter back in the saucepan and cover them with fresh water.

Bring the water to the boil and keep skimming off any mushroom-coloured scum. Once any foamy scum that appears is white, add the wine, the clove-studded onion, herbs, peppercorns, lemon peel, leek, carrot, celery and garlic.

Simmer over a low heat for about 3 hours, until the ham is very tender and comes off the bone easily. Keep an eye on the pan during the cooking time and top up the water if necessary, making sure that the hocks are always just covered.

Once the hocks are cooked, strain the liquid into a clean pan, preferably through some muslin or kitchen paper, then simmer until it has reduced by about half. Skim off any fat. If using gelatine instead of a trotter, you need about 6 leaves per 500ml of liquid. Soak the leaves in cold water until soft, then add them to the strained cooking liquid. Do not reboil.

When the hocks are cool enough to handle, remove and discard all the skin, bone and large pieces of fat, then flake the meat into chunks. Mix the meat with the shallots and parsley, then season with pepper.

Line a 1kg terrine dish with clingfilm. Spread a layer of the ham mixture over the bottom, then cover with some of the reduced liquid. Put in the fridge until the liquid has almost set, then repeat another couple of times until you have filled the terrine. You will probably have meat and liquid left over, but you could use the meat in a salad and the liquid for stock.

Chill the terrine in the fridge until you are ready to eat. Lovely with cornichons, pickled onions and mustard.

PORK SUMMER ROLLS

We first came across these little lovelies in Vietnam, where they're also known as crystal spring rolls, and they've become a favourite of ours. Lots of ingredients, we know, but the rolls are easy to make and so much healthier than the deep-fried variety. Serve them as soon as they're made, or you could put everything on the table and let people assemble their own.

SERVES 4
as a starter or snack

2 tbsp fish sauce (nam pla)
1 tbsp soy sauce
1 tbsp rice vinegar
1 tsp honey
1 garlic clove, crushed
250g piece of pork
   tenderloin
12 shelled prawns, cut in
   half lengthways
50g vermicelli rice noodles
8 rice wrappers (have a few
   extra to hand in case of
   breakages)
1 little gem lettuce,
   shredded
small bunch of mint,
   leaves only
small bunch of coriander,
   leaves only
small bunch of Thai basil,
   leaves only
handful of bean sprouts
1 carrot, peeled and cut into
   matchsticks
¼ cucumber, cut into
   matchsticks
flaked sea salt
freshly ground black pepper

Dipping sauce
juice of 2 limes
2 tbsp fish sauce (nam pla)
1 tsp palm sugar (or caster
   or light soft brown)
1 shallot, thinly sliced
1 red chilli, thinly sliced

Mix together the fish sauce, soy sauce, rice vinegar, honey and garlic in a bowl big enough to hold the pork. Season with salt and pepper.

Slice the tenderloin into very thin strips, then add them to the marinade and leave to stand for a few minutes. Bring a saucepan of water to the boil. Drop in the pork, turn down the heat, and simmer for a couple of minutes until it's cooked through. Remove the pork from the saucepan with a slotted spoon and set it aside.

Add the prawns to the same boiling water and cook them for 1 minute only. Remove, drain and set aside. Leave both the pork and the prawns to cool. Cook the noodles according to the packet instructions, then rinse them under cold water and drain. Moisten them a little so they don't stick together. Make sure you have all the other ingredients ready.

Put some cold water in a wide, deep plate or bowl. Add the rice wrappers one at a time and leave them to soften. Each wrapper will take a minute or so – the trick is to get them pliable but not too sticky.

Lay a softened wrapper on a clean work surface. Place 3 prawn halves in a line down the middle, add a little pork, then small quantities of all the remaining ingredients – you'll need less than you think.

To wrap the rolls, first very gently pull each side up without putting it over the filling to make sure that the edges will overlap. If you think the rolls are in danger of gaping, remove some of the filling.

Wrap the roll by folding the left and right sides of the wrappers over the filling, followed by the bottom edge. Then turn everything over in the direction of the remaining open side and tuck it underneath. This is much easier if you keep your fingers wet, as it will stop everything from sticking. You should end up with the joins underneath and the line of prawns visible through the top of the wrapper. Continue until you have made all 8 rolls. Serve with the dipping sauce.

Dipping sauce
Put the lime juice and fish sauce in a small bowl. Add the sugar and stir until it has completely dissolved, then add the shallot and chillies. Leave to stand for a while before serving, to allow the flavours to blend.

LAMB, ASPARAGUS AND MINT SALAD

Using beautiful British ingredients, this salad is spring on a plate. You do need to marinate the lamb for an hour or so, but once that's done the rest is quick and easy to put together.

SERVES 4

2 lamb leg steaks
1 tbsp olive oil
1 tbsp cider vinegar
1 tsp dried mint
1 tsp dried oregano or
  thyme
12 small new or salad
  potatoes
bunch of asparagus
bag of pea shoots or lamb's
  lettuce
small bunch of mint,
  leaves only
flaked sea salt
freshly ground black pepper

Dressing
3 tbsp olive oil
1 tbsp lemon juice or
  cider vinegar
¼ tsp honey

Put the lamb in a glass, plastic or ceramic bowl – the acid in the marinade can react with metal. Whisk the olive oil and cider vinegar in a small bowl, then stir in the herbs and season well with salt and pepper. Pour this over the lamb, turning the meat over to make sure it is completely covered, then leave to marinate for at least an hour.

Put the potatoes in a steamer and cook them for about 15 minutes. Bend each asparagus stem until it snaps, then discard the woody ends. Put the asparagus on top of the potatoes and steam for a further 3–5 minutes. Remove from the heat and allow to cool a little.

If you don't have a steamer, just put the potatoes in a pan of cold water, bring to the boil and cook until nearly tender. Add the asparagus for the last 3–5 minutes of the cooking time.

Heat a griddle pan until it's too hot to hold your hand over – take care not to touch the pan, though. Grill the lamb steaks for 2–3 minutes on each side, until well charred but still juicy inside. Leave them to rest for at least 5 minutes, then slice thinly.

Whisk the dressing ingredients together and season with salt and some black pepper.

Arrange the pea shoots or lamb's lettuce, potatoes and asparagus on individual plates, then add some mint leaves. Top with the lamb, then drizzle over the dressing.

ROSE VEAL TONNATO

This classic Italian starter combines tender veal poached in wine and served with a tangy tuna mayonnaise. It might sound a bit weird but trust us – the flavours work brilliantly. British rose veal is fantastic and produced to much higher animal welfare standards than imported white veal, so let's eat more of it. You can also use pork fillet or boneless loin – adjust the cooking times accordingly.

SERVES 6

2 banana shallots, cut in
   half lengthways
1 carrot, cut in half
1 celery stick, cut in half
1 bay leaf
small bunch of thyme
6 peppercorns
200ml white wine
500ml chicken stock
600g rose veal fillet
flaked sea salt
freshly ground black pepper

Mayonnaise
2 large egg yolks
198g can tuna steak in
   sunflower oil, drained
1 tbsp baby capers, drained
1½ tbsp lemon juice
2 tsp Dijon mustard
½ tsp caster sugar
¼ tsp sea salt, plus extra
   to season
100ml sunflower oil
50ml olive oil

Garnish
2 tbsp baby capers, drained
roughly chopped parsley
12 caper berries
lemon wedges

Put the shallots, carrot and celery in a large saucepan with the bay leaf, thyme, peppercorns, wine and chicken stock. Add a teaspoon of salt and bring to a gentle simmer, then cover and cook the stock for 30 minutes.

Using a sharp knife, trim any fatty bits or sinew off the veal. Lower the veal into the warm stock and turn down the heat until it is barely bubbling. Poach the veal for 15 minutes, turning it 4 or 5 times, then remove it from the liquid and set it aside to cool. Reserve 100ml of the cooking liquid.

Once the veal is cool, season it all over with black pepper and wrap it tightly in clingfilm. Put it in the fridge and leave overnight to chill.

To make the mayonnaise, put the egg yolks, tuna, capers, a tablespoon of the lemon juice, the mustard and sugar in a food processor. Season with salt and black pepper. Blend until well combined, then with the motor running, very gradually add both the oils and blend until smooth and thick.

Add 2 tablespoons of the reserved cooking liquid and blend for a few seconds longer until the sauce has a soft consistency, adding a little more cooking liquid if necessary. Spoon the tuna mayonnaise into a bowl, season with more salt and pepper and the remaining lemon juice if you like. Cover the surface with clingfilm to prevent a skin forming and chill it in the fridge overnight.

When you're ready to serve, unwrap the veal and slice it very thinly. Arrange overlapping slices of the meat on a platter or on separate plates and top with spoonfuls of the chilled mayonnaise.

Garnish with baby capers, roughly chopped parsley and caper berries, then season with black pepper and a pinch of salt and serve with lemon wedges on the side. Any leftovers are great in a sandwich.

POTTED BEEF

We loved little jars of potted beef when we were kids, but this is the Rolls Royce version. It makes a wonderful starter or a great treat just to have in the fridge and dip into when you feel like a snack. Serve with some toast and it's also nice topped with apple and herb jelly (see page 346). Mace is a good old-fashioned spice, sold in small strips called blades or ground into a powder.

SERVES 6–8

500g beef shin, cut into
  chunks
2 garlic cloves, thinly sliced
2 bay leaves
large sprig of thyme
1 tsp peppercorns
1 tsp allspice berries
2 cloves
1 blade of mace
200ml white wine
pinch of cayenne pepper
25g butter, melted
flaked sea salt
freshly ground black pepper

Preheat the oven to 150°C/Fan 130°C/Gas 2.

Place the beef shin in an ovenproof dish – you want quite a snug fit here. Put the garlic, herbs and spices in a small saucepan and pour in the wine. Bring the wine to the boil, then pour it over the meat and season with salt. Add just enough water to cover the beef, then cover the dish with foil and put it in the oven for 2½ hours. Remove the dish from the oven, turn the beef over, then cover again and put it back in the oven for another 2½ hours.

Remove the dish from the oven and take out the meat, brushing off any spices or garlic. Strain the liquid into a jug.

Shred the meat with a couple of forks, then put it into a food processor and season with salt, black pepper and a good pinch of cayenne. Skim a couple of tablespoons of fat from the top of the braising liquid, and add it to the beef along with the melted butter. Blitz everything in the food processor, gradually adding some of the braising liquid if it doesn't bind together well. You should end up with a fairly smooth paste.

Spoon the potted beef into a large jar or an earthenware dish and chill. It will keep for 4–5 days in the fridge.

BEEF TARTARE

Not everyone likes the idea of raw meat, but this really is good. There are many stories about the origins of the dish – one claims that the Tartar warriors of Central Asia used to put meat under their saddles to tenderise it and then ate it raw. Don't try this on your motorbike, though – go to the butcher! Buy good steak, never mince, and use free-range eggs, since you're eating them raw.

SERVES 4

500g fillet steak
3 shallots, very finely
  chopped
3 tbsp small capers, rinsed
4 small cornichons, finely
  chopped
4 tbsp very finely chopped
  parsley
1 tbsp finely chopped dill
1 tbsp Dijon mustard
2 tsp tomato ketchup
  (optional)
a dash of Worcestershire
  sauce
a dash of Tabasco
4 free-range egg yolks
flaked sea salt
freshly ground black pepper

To make the fillet steak easier to prepare, wrap it tightly in clingfilm and put it in the freezer for an hour. This will make it firmer and much easier to slice.

Unwrap the steak and cut it into very thin slices – no more than 2–3mm thick – against the grain. Then cut into 2–3mm strips, then dice it. Put the diced meat in a bowl.

Add the shallots, capers, cornichons and herbs. Mix the mustard with the ketchup, if using, then add dashes of Worcestershire sauce and Tabasco. Season the meat mixture with a little salt and lots of black pepper, then stir in the mustard mixture. Make sure everything is very well combined.

Divide the mixture into 4 portions of 125g each and set them aside for half an hour to allow the flavours to develop.

To serve, put a chef's ring or a cookie cutter in the centre of a plate and press a portion of the mixture into it. Remove the mould and make a small indentation on the top. Repeat to make the other servings, then drop an egg yolk on to each one. Serve at once with some salad leaves and crusty bread on the side.

BRESAOLA, ORANGE AND ENDIVE SALAD

A lovely fresh simple starter, this takes minutes to put together and the combination of sweet orange and bitter Belgian endive tastes sensational. Bresaola is a kind of air-dried beef from Italy and is available in lots of supermarkets and delis.

SERVES 4

2 oranges
4 heads of Belgian endive
   (chicory)
8 slices of bresaola
a few small oregano leaves
50g skinned hazelnuts

Dressing
2 tbsp hazelnut oil
2 tsp red wine vinegar
reserved orange juice
½ tsp Dijon mustard
flaked sea salt
freshly ground black pepper

First prepare the oranges. Top and tail them with a sharp knife, then cut off the skin and outer membrane by placing the orange upright on a board and cutting down, following the contour of the orange. Cut the orange flesh into thin rounds, then slice the rounds in half, or divide the oranges into segments. Collect any juice in a bowl and squeeze the remaining membrane too. Set the juice aside.

Trim the base of the endives, then cut them into very thin wedges, lengthways.

Put the hazelnuts in a frying pan and toast them until light golden-brown, shaking the pan regularly. Remove the nuts from the pan and set them aside to cool, then crush them lightly, so they break in half.

Arrange the bresaola over the base of a serving platter, then top with the pieces of orange and endive. Sprinkle over the oregano leaves and the hazelnuts.

Whisk the dressing ingredients together and season with salt and pepper. Drizzle the dressing over the salad and serve.

SPICY MEAT ON LETTUCE (LAAB)

We love this Thai meat salad, known as laab or sometimes larb in its native land. It's a smashing little starter – dainty, easy to prepare and the flavours pack a real punch. Good tip from us – trim the ribs of the lettuce leaves slightly at the back so they sit more steadily on the plate and hold the filling.

SERVES 4

2 tbsp uncooked Jasmine rice
juice of 2 limes
1 tsp palm or caster sugar
50ml chicken stock
2 tbsp fish sauce (nam pla)
2 kaffir lime leaves, very thinly sliced
1 red chilli, finely chopped
1 lemon grass stalk, bruised
300g minced beef (or pork)
2–3 little gem lettuces
1 tbsp mint leaves, finely shredded
1 tbsp basil leaves, finely shredded
a few coriander leaves
4 spring onions, finely chopped
flaked sea salt (optional)

Put a frying pan over a medium heat. When it's hot, add the rice and dry fry until toasted and aromatic – it should smell nutty. Shake the pan constantly to make sure the rice doesn't burn. Remove the pan from the heat, tip the rice into a pestle and mortar and grind it until the grains are broken into coarse chunks.

Put the lime juice, sugar, chicken stock and fish sauce in a saucepan with the lime leaves, chilli and lemon grass. Bring to the boil, then remove the pan from the heat and leave the liquid to infuse – for at least as long as it takes to cool down.

Return the pan to the heat and add the pork or lamb. Cook over a high heat, stirring continuously, until the meat is cooked through. Remove the pan from the heat and stir in the herbs. Taste and add salt if necessary.

Separate the leaves of the little gems. To serve, pile spoonfuls of the meat mixture on to lettuce leaves, then sprinkle with the toasted rice and chopped spring onions. Serve immediately.

MEXICAN STEAK SALAD

You can use sirloin or rump steak for this salad but we like to use flank. It's cheaper and mega tasty but does need to be cooked quickly, or it will be tough. Also, make sure you slice the meat across the grain – not in the direction of the fibres. This helps to make the meat tender and is very important for the success of this dish. Don't forget to allow time to marinade the meat.

SERVES 4
*as a starter,
or 2 as a light lunch*

400g piece of flank steak,
  left whole
large bag of salad leaves
1 large avocado, peeled
  and diced
1 red onion, sliced into
  crescents
200g cherry tomatoes,
  halved
bunch of coriander

Marinade
1 tbsp olive oil
1 tbsp chipotle paste
1 tsp ground cumin
1 tsp dried oregano
1 tbsp honey or maple syrup
1 tbsp soy sauce
1 tbsp red wine vinegar
flaked sea salt
freshly ground black pepper

Dressing
2 tbsp olive oil
freshly squeezed juice
  of 2 limes
1 garlic clove, crushed
1 tsp chipotle paste

Mix the marinade ingredients together in a jug and season with salt and pepper. Put the steak in a plastic bag or a glass or china bowl – don't use a metal container as the metal can react with the vinegar in the marinade. Pour the marinade over the meat, massage it in well, then leave in the fridge to marinate for several hours, ideally overnight if you have time.

Remove the steak from the marinade and reserve the liquid. Pat the steak dry. Heat a griddle pan until it is too hot to hold your hand over – don't hold it too close!

Grill the steak for 2–3 minutes on each side, then remove it from the griddle and set it aside to rest. Once the meat has rested, slice it into strips, cutting across the grain, not in the direction of the fibres.

Whisk the dressing ingredients together and add any reserved marinade and the juices from the resting steak. Taste for seasoning and adjust if necessary, then add extra honey, lime or chipotle depending on how sweet, sour or hot you want your dressing.

Put the salad ingredients in a large serving bowl, add the steak and drizzle the dressing on top. Any leftovers go down well in a tortilla wrap.

ROAST BEEF AND BEETROOT SALAD

Can't beet this! A proper butch salad, it's a tasty way of using up leftover roast beef or you can buy ready-cooked beef at the deli counter. And the horseradish dressing is lush – it brings you the flavours of a Sunday roast in salad form. If you buy cooked beetroot, make sure it's not in vinegar, as that would disrupt the flavour of the dressing.

SERVES 4
as a starter,
or 2 as a light lunch

200g fine green beans
small bag of lamb's lettuce
  or spinach
small bag of beetroot salad
  leaves
250g cooked beetroot
  (vacuum-packed are fine),
  cut into wedges
about 300g roast beef,
  sliced into thick strips
2 shallots, thinly sliced
fronds from a bunch of dill

Horseradish dressing
2 tbsp olive oil
1 tbsp sherry vinegar
1 tbsp crème fraiche or
  soured cream
2 tbsp water
1 tbsp freshly grated
  horseradish or 1 tbsp hot
  horseradish sauce (not the
  creamed version)
pinch of sugar
flaked sea salt
freshly ground black pepper

Trim the tops off the green beans but leave their tails in place. Bring a pan of water to the boil, add the beans and cook them for 3 minutes. Drain them and refresh in a bowl of iced water.

Put the salad leaves on a large serving platter or in individual salad bowls. Arrange the other ingredients over them, then toss very gently to combine. Garnish with some fronds of dill.

Whisk together the dressing ingredients and season with salt and pepper, then drizzle over the salad and serve immediately.

Tip
If you're cooking your own beetroot, don't peel them first. Just wash them gently, place them in a pan of cold water, then bring to the boil. Cook until tender, leave to cool and then peel.

CHAPTER TWO
SOUPS AND BROTHS

CELERIAC AND APPLE SOUP WITH BACON

Eating apples bring this root vegetable soup to life. It's a perfect balance of sweet and savoury, topped off with some crispy bacon and a spoonful of crème fraiche – lush! If you prefer, use six tablespoons of soured cream instead of the crème fraiche and milk mixture.

SERVES 6

3 eating apples (about 500g)
50g butter
1 tbsp sunflower oil
2 onions, chopped
750g celeriac, cut into small
   chunks
1 large carrot, sliced
2 garlic cloves, crushed
2 medium potatoes (about
   250g), cut into small chunks
3 or 4 sprigs of fresh thyme
1 bay leaf
1.3 litres vegetable or chicken
   stock
flaked sea salt
freshly ground black pepper

Garnish

4 rashers smoked streaky
   bacon
4 tbsp crème fraiche
2 tbsp milk

Peel and slice the apples. Melt half the butter in a large saucepan and fry the apple pieces for 5 minutes or until lightly browned, turning them regularly. Using a slotted spoon, transfer the apple pieces to a plate and put the pan back on the heat.

Add the remaining butter and the oil to the pan and gently fry the onions, celeriac and carrot for 15 minutes, stirring occasionally. Add the cooked apples, then the garlic, potatoes, thyme and bay leaf and cook for 3 minutes more, stirring. Pour the stock into the pan, season with black pepper and bring it to the boil. Then reduce the heat to a simmer and cook for about 25 minutes or until the celeriac and carrots are very soft, stirring occasionally.

Remove the pan from the heat and leave the soup to cool slightly. Take out the thyme and bay leaf and blend the soup with a stick blender until very smooth. Add a little extra water if necessary until you have the consistency you like. Alternatively, let the soup cool a little longer, then blend it in a food processor until smooth and then tip it back into the pan. Check the seasoning and add salt and pepper to taste.

To make the garnish, grill the bacon rashers until crispy, then snip them into pieces with kitchen scissors. Mix the crème fraiche with the milk in a small bowl until smooth. Ladle the soup into bowls, add a tablespoon of the crème fraiche mixture and scatter with crispy bacon. Season with a little freshly ground black pepper.

HAM AND PEA SOUP

Everyone loves ham and pea soup and this is like a velvet caress for your belly. Grab a bowlful and some crusty bread and you've got an ideal meal on a cold winter day. This is a Finnish recipe – they're good at soup the Finns – but it's not that different from the version we used to eat as kids. We always soak split peas even if it says on the packet you don't have to, as otherwise they can take a long time to cook.

SERVES 4–6

300g split peas (green
   are traditional, but
   yellow are fine)
pinch of bicarbonate of soda
1 small ham hock
1 onion, stuck with 2 cloves
2 bay leaves
1 blade of mace
1 onion, diced
1 carrot, diced
1 tbsp hot mustard
100ml whipping or double
   cream (optional)
freshly ground black pepper

Soak the peas overnight in a big bowl of cold water with a pinch of bicarbonate of soda – bicarb helps to soften pulses.

Put the ham hock in a large saucepan, cover it with cold water and bring to the boil. Immediately remove the pan from the heat and drain, discarding the water. Rinse the ham hock and the saucepan to get rid of any starchy foam that may have accumulated.

Put the hock back in the pan and cover with 1.5–2 litres of water. Add the onion with cloves, the bay leaves and mace to the pan. It's a good idea to tie them all in a piece of muslin, but it's not essential. Just remember they're there and remove them before blending the soup. Bring the water to the boil and simmer for an hour.

Drain the split peas and rinse them well. Put them in a separate saucepan, cover with water and bring them to the boil, then boil hard for 10 minutes. Drain and add the split peas to the pan with the ham hock, along with the diced onion and carrot. Simmer until the peas are tender – this will take about 45 minutes to an hour. Check the water level regularly and add a little extra if necessary – the soup shouldn't be too thick.

Using tongs, fish the ham hock out of the pan and remove the onion, bay leaves and mace. Set the ham aside until it's cool enough to handle, then break it up, pulling the meat into pieces and discarding the skin and bone.

Add the mustard to the soup, check the seasoning and add some black pepper to taste – you shouldn't need any salt because of the ham. Blend to a rough purée – a quick whizz with a stick blender is all you need – then add some of the ham to the soup and warm it through. Lightly whip the cream, if using, and gently fold it into the soup, then garnish with the remaining ham and serve.

MINESTRONE

Everyone loves a good minestrone and this is nothing like the stuff you buy in cans. It looks like quite a lot of ingredients we know, but you don't have to include them all and there's nothing difficult to do. Chuck in any Parmesan rinds you have hanging about, as they add bags of flavour. We never throw them out – just store them in a bag in the freezer until needed. If you want a lighter soup, use white wine instead of red and fewer veg.

SERVES 4–6

1 tbsp olive oil
200g streaky bacon, cut into thin strips
1 onion, sliced
2 carrots, diced
200g celeriac, diced
2 celery sticks, sliced
2 garlic cloves, finely chopped
150ml red wine
1.2 litres chicken stock
1 Parmesan rind (optional)
1 ham bone (optional)
1 tsp dried oregano
1 sprig of rosemary
400g can cannellini or borlotti beans, drained and rinsed
50g spaghetti, broken into pieces
1 tomato, finely chopped
2 leeks, cut into rounds
¼ green cabbage (Savoy, green pointed) or a bunch of cavolo nero or chard, shredded
1 large courgette, sliced
4 tbsp grated Parmesan cheese, for sprinkling.
a few basil leaves, to garnish
flaked sea salt (optional)
freshly ground black pepper

Heat the olive oil in a large saucepan. Add the bacon and fry it over a medium heat until it's well browned and has given off plenty of fat, then add the onion, carrots, celeriac and celery. Turn down the heat and gently cook the veg for a few minutes, just until they take on some colour, then add the garlic and cook for a further minute.

Pour in the red wine and allow it to bubble furiously, stirring continuously to make sure you've scraped all the sticky bits off the bottom of the pan. Add the chicken stock and the Parmesan rind and ham bone, if using, then sprinkle in the herbs. Bring the liquid to the boil, then turn down the heat and cook for 5 minutes.

Add the beans, spaghetti and tomato and cook for a further 5 minutes. Taste for seasoning – the soup may be very salty from the bacon and ham bone, but add salt if necessary as well as plenty of black pepper.

Add the green vegetables and simmer gently until they and the spaghetti are tender. Remove the ham bone, rosemary sprig and Parmesan rind from the soup and serve sprinkled with grated Parmesan and some basil leaves.

Tip
A ham bone makes a great addition to this so ask at your butcher or deli counter. They'll usually let you have one for next to nothing or may even give them away.

CABBAGE AND CHORIZO SOUP (CALDO VERDE)

Caldo verde is Portugal's national dish and it's comfort in a bowl. This was the first recipe we ever cooked on our travels and we included it in our very first book – this is a much improved version! You can use spring greens, kale, chard or just plain cabbage as you fancy. We like hot spicy chorizo – labelled picante – or you can buy a much milder sweeter version called chorizo dulce. Up to you.

SERVES 4

200g cooking chorizo, sliced
2 onions, sliced
1 garlic clove, finely chopped
500g waxy potatoes
    (Charlotte are good),
    sliced into rounds
1 litre chicken stock or water
2 bay leaves
large bag of greens, such as
    spring greens, kale, cavolo
    nero or chard, shredded
flaked sea salt
freshly ground white pepper

Put the slices of chorizo in the bottom of a large saucepan and place the pan on a fairly gentle heat. Fry until the chorizo is lightly browned on both sides and some of its orange-tinted fat has oozed out. Be careful when you do this – it's all too easy to burn chorizo and you don't want the bottom of your pan to be covered in black specks.

Remove the chorizo to a plate with a slotted spoon, leaving the fat behind. See how much fat you have in the pan – you need about a tablespoon. If there's more than that, spoon some off and discard it. Add the onions to the pan and cook them quite gently until they've softened without browning. Add the garlic and cook for another minute.

Add the potatoes to the pan and stir to coat them in fat, then pour in the chicken stock or water. Tuck in the bay leaves and season with salt and white pepper. Bring the soup to the boil, then turn the heat down, cover the pan and leave to simmer until the potatoes are just cooked through – about 10 minutes.

Pile the greens into the pan, cover again and simmer until they are just tender and still a vibrant green – preferably no more than 4–5 minutes. Tip the chorizo back into the soup and serve immediately.

SMOKED BACON AND SWEETCORN CHOWDER

Chowders are generally thickened with potatoes and made with milk so have a great velvety texture. Our fine-looking soup is a lovely simple version with that all-important dash of bacon. You can buy packs of bacon lardons in supermarkets – they're handy to have in the fridge – or simply cut some smoked bacon into small chunks. We always keep some sweetcorn in the freezer but you can also use fresh or canned if you prefer.

SERVES 4–6

200g smoked bacon lardons
1 tbsp butter
2 leeks, sliced into thin rounds
2 carrots, diced
400g floury potatoes,
    cut into 1cm dice
500ml chicken or vegetable
    stock
300ml whole milk
250g sweetcorn (frozen or
    canned)
50ml single cream (optional)
1 tbsp chopped parsley
freshly ground black pepper

Put a large saucepan over a medium heat, add the bacon lardons and dry fry for several minutes until the bacon is well browned and has released plenty of fat.

Turn the heat down, add the butter, then when it's melted add the leeks. Cover the pan and leave the leeks to cook gently for several minutes until softened.

Add the carrots and potatoes, then pour the chicken stock into the pan. Season with pepper (no salt at this stage, as the bacon may be salty), then simmer for about 7 minutes until all the vegetables are tender. Stir only occasionally as you don't want the potatoes to break up too much.

Add the milk and sweetcorn, then simmer for another couple of minutes. Don't let the milk boil or it may separate. Check the seasoning and add cream if you want a slightly richer finish. Sprinkle with parsley before serving.

THAI COCONUT SOUP WITH MEATBALLS

There's something about meatballs and this fragrant Thai soup is a meal in a bowl. Make it as hot or not as you like – we love the chillies, but leave them out if you're not a fan. We've suggested poaching the meatballs in the traditional way, or you could bake or fry them instead if you want them looking nicely browned. And if you like, you could replace 100g of the minced pork with minced prawns.

SERVES 4–6

Meatballs

500g minced pork
1 shallot, finely chopped
2 tbsp coriander stems, finely chopped
1 tbsp fish sauce (nam pla)
grated zest of 1 lime
1 green chilli, finely chopped (optional)
flaked sea salt
freshly ground black pepper

Broth

2 lemon grass stems, outer leaves removed
2 kaffir lime leaves
15g galangal, peeled or 2 tsp galangal paste
2 garlic cloves
2 tbsp coriander stems
1 litre chicken stock
400ml coconut milk
1 tbsp fish sauce (nam pla)
1 tsp palm sugar (or soft light brown sugar)
50g jasmine rice, well rinsed
juice of 1 lime
4 spring onions, finely chopped
a bag of Asian greens

To serve

coriander leaves
Thai basil leaves
a few green chillies, sliced (optional)

To make the meatballs, put all the ingredients in a bowl and season with salt and pepper. Mix thoroughly, then shape the mixture into small, walnut-sized balls – about 25g each. Bring a large saucepan of water to the boil, drop in half the meatballs and simmer them for 5 minutes until they are almost, but not quite, cooked. Remove the meatballs with a slotted spoon and set them aside while you cook the remaining meatballs in the same way.

For the broth, put the lemon grass, lime leaves, galangal, garlic and coriander stems in a small food processor with a little water and blitz to a paste.

Pour the chicken stock and coconut milk into a large saucepan and add the paste, fish sauce and palm sugar. Bring to the boil, add the rice and simmer until it is just cooked through – about 15 minutes.

Add the lime juice, spring onions and greens to the pan, then the partly cooked meatballs. Simmer for a further 5 minutes until the greens are tender and the meatballs are completely cooked through.

Serve the soup sprinkled with plenty of coriander and basil and sliced chillies, if using.

PORK RAMEN

Ramen is all about the stock and wars have been fought over recipes! We like our latest tonkotsu-style version in which the bones are boiled, rather than simmered, to get as much flavour out of them as possible. Traditionally, the broth should be boiled for 10 hours but we think 3–5 hours is fine – it's still really rich and savoury. Add some marinated eggs (page 357) and pork char siu (page 145) and you have a dish fit for an emperor.

SERVES 8–10

Broth

1.5kg raw chicken carcasses
1.5kg pork bones, preferably spare ribs
1 pig's trotter
1 onion, skin included if clean enough, roughly chopped
2 carrots, roughly chopped
30g fresh root ginger, roughly chopped
1 head of garlic, cloves separated but unpeeled

Garnishes (all optional)

marinated eggs (tamago; see p.357)
bamboo shoots
bunch of spring onions, shredded
Chinese greens, such as pak choi
slices of char siu pork (see p.145)
Japanese mushrooms, such as enoki
nori (seaweed strips)
soy or tamari sauce or spoonfuls of the egg marinade
chilli oil

Put the chicken carcasses, pork bones and the pig's trotter in a stock pot that holds 8–10 litres. Cover them with cold water and bring to the boil. When a mushroom-coloured foam starts to appear, start skimming it off. Continue skimming until the foam that appears is white.

Meanwhile, heat a griddle pan over a high heat. When it's too hot to hold your hand over – don't touch the pan – add the onion, carrot and ginger. Griddle them for several minutes, turning regularly, until fairly dark char lines appear on the vegetables.

Reduce the heat under the pot slightly so the stock is bubbling, not fiercely but harder than a simmer. Add the onion, carrot, ginger and garlic, then partially cover the pan and cook the broth for at least 3 hours – up to 5 if you can. Keep an eye on the liquid level – the stock shouldn't reduce too much, but don't let it boil away in the first hour or so, and top up if necessary.

When your stock is a deep golden-brown and quite cloudy, strain it through a sieve. You can strain it again through muslin or a clean tea cloth if you like, but it isn't really necessary. As this is such a rich stock, it is a good idea to skim off some of the fat. You can either do this when it settles on top, or to make the job easier, chill the broth until the fat has set and just scrape it off.

To serve, bring the broth back to the boil and season with soy sauce or tamari. Put cooked noodles in individual bowls, along with the marinated eggs. Drop the cooked pork into the broth to heat through, then using chopsticks, divide it between the bowls and ladle over the broth. You can do the same with any of the other garnishes. Add a sprinkling of spring onions, and serve with more soy sauce, chilli oil or sauce and perhaps some pieces of nori seaweed. Fantastic!

This recipe does make a large quantity, but you can halve it if you like.

SCOTCH BROTH

Packed with veg, this is one of the most nourishing of all soups and a true classic. We both ate Scotch broth as kids and we've always made it for our own families. Never out of fashion, this soup, and we love it.

SERVES 6

75g pearl barley
about 1kg lamb shoulder,
   on the bone
2 litres lamb stock
   or water
2 onions, chopped
1 bay leaf
a few sprigs of fresh thyme
2 carrots, cut in 2.5cm pieces
2 turnips, cut in 2.5cm pieces
   (optional)
2 celery stalks, trimmed, cut
   in 2.5cm pieces
2 potatoes, cut in 2.5cm
   pieces
½ Savoy cabbage, trimmed,
   cored and finely shredded
flaked sea salt
freshly ground black pepper

Put the pearl barley in a bowl, cover it with cold water and set it aside to soak.

Meanwhile, place the lamb in a large saucepan, cover it with the lamb stock or cold water and bring to a simmer. Skim off any scum, then add the onion, bay leaf and thyme to the pan. Bring back to a gentle simmer and cook for an hour, skimming occasionally.

Add the carrots, turnips and celery to the pan and season with a heaped teaspoon of salt and some black pepper. Bring back to a very gentle simmer, cover the pan with a lid and cook for 30 minutes.

When the 30 minutes is up, drain the pearl barley and rinse it in a sieve under cold running water. Take the lid off the saucepan, turn the lamb over and add the pearl barley and potatoes. Cook gently for another 30 minutes, uncovered.

Stir in the cabbage and bring the broth back to a gentle simmer. Continue cooking, uncovered, for another 15 minutes or until the lamb is very tender and falling off the bone and the barley is softened. Remove the saucepan from the heat.

Lift the lamb out of the pan with tongs or a large fork and put it on a board. Carve off all the meat, tearing it into largish chunks and discarding any skin and bone. Season the broth with more salt and pepper to taste and ladle it into large bowls. Divide the lamb between the bowls and serve at once.

TURKISH LAMB AND CHICKPEA SOUP

Simple to make, this is a real meal in a bowl – nothing else is needed except a hunk of bread maybe and a salad to follow. The lamb, peppers and paprika give the soup a lovely sweetness and a rich satisfying flavour. It's a sultan's delight and a real belter.

SERVES 4–6

1 tbsp olive oil

2 red onions, cut into wedges

2 red peppers, deseeded and
  cut into strips

1 green pepper, deseeded
  and cut into strips

500g lamb fillet, cut into
  2cm dice

1 tsp sweet smoked paprika

½ tsp chilli flakes

2 bay leaves

1 tbsp tomato purée

1.3 litres chicken stock
  or water

4 tomatoes, skinned and
  finely chopped

1 tbsp red wine vinegar

1 tsp honey

400g can chickpeas, drained
  and rinsed

fresh parsley or mint,
  to garnish

flaked sea salt

freshly ground black pepper

Heat the olive oil in a large saucepan. Add the onions and peppers and sauté them over a high heat for a few minutes until they start to take on some colour and soften around the edges. Remove them from the pan with a slotted spoon and set them aside.

Add the diced lamb to the pan and sear it quickly on all sides. Sprinkle in the paprika and chilli flakes, then add the bay leaves and the tomato purée. Stir until the lamb is completely coated with the spices and purée, then season with salt and pepper.

Pour in the chicken stock or water and bring it to the boil, then cover the pan and simmer for 45 minutes, until the lamb is almost tender. Add the tomatoes, red wine vinegar, honey and chickpeas, and return the onions and peppers to the pan. Simmer for a further 15–20 minutes.

Serve with a sprinkling of parsley or mint leaves and a little more paprika and chilli if you like.

LAMB, LENTIL AND SPINACH SOUP

This nourishing meaty soup is inspired by our favourite curries and is a sort of 21st-century mulligatawny. The lovely spicy flavour is right up our street. Lean leg meat or neck fillet are both good cuts to use.

SERVES 4–6

1 tbsp olive oil
500g lean lamb leg or neck
  fillet, cut into 1.5cm dice
1 large onion, sliced
3 garlic cloves, finely chopped
1 tsp ground ginger
1 tsp ground cumin
1 tsp ground coriander
½ tsp turmeric
½ tsp cinnamon
¼ tsp chilli flakes
1 litre chicken stock or water
100g red lentils, rinsed
300g spinach
juice and grated zest of
  ½ lemon
flaked sea salt
freshly ground black pepper

Heat the oil in a large saucepan and add the diced lamb. Sear the lamb briefly on all sides, then remove it with a slotted spoon and set it aside, leaving as much of the oil in the pan as possible. Turn down the heat, then add the onion and sauté for several minutes until it starts to soften. Add the garlic and all the spices and stir for a couple more minutes.

Add half the stock or water, season with salt and pepper and bring it to the boil, then cover the pan and turn the heat down to a simmer. Simmer the soup for half an hour, then add the lentils with the rest of the stock or water. Simmer for another 30 minutes until the lentils have broken down and thickened the soup. Keep an eye on the liquid level and add a little more water if necessary.

Trim any thick stems off the spinach. Gradually push the spinach into the soup – as it wilts and takes up less space, you can add more.

Simmer the soup for another few minutes until the spinach has broken down. Add the lemon zest and juice and adjust the seasoning if necessary. Serve at once.

CARIBBEAN GOAT WATER

Okay, we know the name goat water might not grab you, but this is exceptionally good and well worth making. It's a traditional Caribbean soupy stew with fabulous spicing that gives a truly tropical taste. Our version uses diced goat, but others include the head and other extremities of the animal – or even a whole kid – to make 'mannish water', a dish served to bridegrooms on their wedding night. Draw your own conclusions!

SERVES 4–6

1 tbsp coconut oil
750g goat or mutton or lamb, diced into 2cm pieces
2 onions, finely chopped
1 red pepper, deseeded and finely diced
1 tsp black peppercorns
½ tsp allspice berries
2 cloves
1 blade of mace or a grating of nutmeg
2 garlic cloves, finely chopped
1 tsp dried oregano
2–3 sprigs of thyme
1 tbsp tomato purée
1 small Scotch bonnet chilli
200g pumpkin or squash, diced
1 green or semi-ripe papaya, peeled, deseeded and cubed (optional)
1 tsp pickapeppa sauce or a dash of Worcestershire sauce
1 tbsp flour
10g softened butter
flaked sea salt

To serve
squeeze of lime
1 tsp rum (optional)

Heat the coconut oil in a large saucepan, then add the meat and brown it on all sides. It's best to do this in a couple of batches so you don't overcrowd the pan. Remove each batch of meat as it's browned and set it aside.

Turn down the heat, add the onions and red pepper and sauté them until softened. Grind the spices in a pestle and mortar or spice grinder, then sprinkle them over the onions, together with the garlic, oregano and thyme. Stir for a minute or two, then return the meat to the pan and add the tomato purée. Stir everything well, then pour in a litre of water, add the Scotch bonnet and season with salt. Bring the liquid to the boil, then turn down the heat and simmer for an hour.

After an hour, add the pumpkin or squash and the papaya and simmer until they're tender – this should take about 20 minutes.

To finish, add the pickapeppa or Worcestershire sauce. Put the flour and soft butter in a small bowl and work them together to make a thick paste. Whisk this gradually into the soup to thicken it, then simmer for another 5 minutes before serving with a squeeze of lime and a tot of rum if you like.

Tip
If you can't find green papaya, a hard, semi-ripe papaya from the supermarket will be fine – it brings a slightly sweeter flavour to the dish.

FLAT-RIB BROTH

This is comfort food like no other and one of Si's favourites. It's his mum's recipe and we'd like to dedicate it to the late great Stella King. In fact, it's the only recipe we ever managed to squeeze out of her! It's cheap to make, feeds a crowd and our mouths are watering just thinking about it. A good butcher should be able to get some beef flat ribs (sometimes called short ribs) for you, but if you can't find any, brisket works well.

SERVES 4–6

125g split peas
pinch of bicarbonate
   of soda
1 tbsp vegetable oil
4 carrots, 2 finely chopped,
   2 diced
1 onion, finely chopped
1 large celery stick, finely
   chopped
1kg beef flat ribs (including
   the bone)
125g pearl barley
2 bay leaves
100g lentils
1 leek, sliced
1 small turnip, cut into
   1cm dice
2 medium potatoes, cut
   into 1cm dice
flaked sea salt
freshly ground black pepper

Soak the peas overnight in a big bowl of cold water with a pinch of bicarbonate of soda. You don't have to do this, but we think it's best, just to be on the safe side.

Heat the vegetable oil in a large saucepan over a medium heat. Add the 2 finely chopped carrots, the onion and celery and cook for 5 minutes, or until soft. Then add the flat ribs and 3 litres of boiling water to the pan.

Bring the water back to the boil and add the pearl barley, drained split peas and the bay leaves. Cover the pan, bring everything to a simmer and cook for 1½ hours.

Taste the broth and add a good pinch of salt and pepper. Add the lentils, put the lid back on the pan and cook for another 20 minutes.

Add the leek, diced carrots, turnip and potatoes and cook for another 20 minutes, or until all the veg are tender. Check the seasoning and add more salt and pepper if needed.

Remove the ribs from the pan and set them aside on a warm plate. Ladle the broth into bowls, then carve pieces of meat from the bone and serve them on top of the broth. Add some bread on the side and a smear of good English mustard and you'll be in heaven.

OXTAIL SOUP WITH PARSLEY DUMPLINGS

Oxtail fell out of favour for a while, but it's now becoming popular again and there's a good reason for that – it's super tasty and should be cheap. Oxtail soup has the most amazing flavour and texture and the addition of dumplings make this into a good substantial meal; a real winter warmer.

SERVES 6

1 whole oxtail (about 1.3kg), cut into chunky pieces
3 tbsp plain flour
3–4 tbsp vegetable oil
2 onions, halved and sliced
3 carrots, diced
2 celery sticks, trimmed and diced
2 garlic cloves, finely chopped
1 tsp dried thyme
2 bay leaves
300ml red wine
2 litres beef stock
2 tbsp tomato purée
2 tbsp cream sherry
flaked sea salt
freshly ground black pepper

Parsley dumplings
200g self-raising flour
100g shredded suet
3 tbsp finely chopped parsley
½ tsp flaked sea salt

Preheat the oven to 170°C/Fan 150°C/Gas 3–4. Wash the oxtail pieces, pat them dry with kitchen paper and trim off any excess fat. Put the flour in a strong plastic food bag and season it well with salt and black pepper. Drop half the oxtail pieces into the flour and shake them to coat, then put them on a plate. Repeat with the remaining oxtail pieces.

Heat 2 tablespoons of the oil in a large non-stick frying pan. Brown the oxtail pieces over a medium heat for about 10 minutes, or until deeply coloured, turning them every now and then. You may need to add extra oil or cook the beef in batches, depending on the size of your pan. Put the browned oxtail pieces in a large, flameproof casserole dish.

Put the frying pan back on the hob and add the onions, carrots and celery, with a little extra oil if necessary. Cook them gently for about 10 minutes, or until softened and lightly browned, stirring occasionally. Add the garlic and cook for another couple of minutes. Tip the veg into the casserole dish with the oxtail and add the thyme and bay leaves, then stir in the wine, beef stock and tomato purée. Season and bring to a gentle simmer. Put the lid on the casserole dish and cook in the centre of the oven for 3 hours, stirring and turning the oxtail pieces halfway through the cooking time. The meat should be falling off the bones.

Remove the casserole dish from the oven, take out the oxtail pieces and set them aside to cool slightly. Skim off the fat from the surface of the soup and chuck it away. When the oxtail is cool enough to handle, pull the meat off the bones and discard any gristly bits. Cut the meat into small chunks and put it back in the casserole dish. Stir in the sherry.

To make the dumplings, mix the flour, suet, parsley and salt in a large bowl. Stir in enough water to mix to a soft, spongy dough – probably 100–125ml. Roll the dough into 18 small balls.

Bring the soup to a gentle simmer, stirring occasionally. Add plenty of seasoning and drop the dumplings gently on top of the soup. Cover tightly with a lid and simmer for 15–18 minutes, or until the dumplings are well-risen and fluffy. Ladle the soup into deep bowls to serve.

BORSCHT

We've eaten many wonderful bowls of borscht on our travels around Europe, but we reckon this version is a bit special and really easy to make. We use beef stock and add some finely sliced steak before serving. Whether you're in Poland or Peterborough, you'll love this one.

SERVES 4–6

1 tbsp vegetable oil
  or 15g butter
3 medium-sized beetroot
  (about 450g unpeeled
  weight), diced
1 large carrot, diced
1 stick celery, diced
1 large waxy potato, diced
1 onion, finely chopped
2 garlic cloves, finely chopped
1.5 litres beef stock
½ green cabbage, finely
  shredded
2 tomatoes, peeled and
  chopped, or 2 tbsp canned
  tomatoes
flaked sea salt
freshly ground black pepper

To serve
300g sirloin steak
soured cream or crème
  fraiche (optional)
1 tbsp finely chopped dill

Heat the oil or butter in a large heavy-based saucepan. Add the diced beetroot, carrot, celery, potato, onion and garlic, then sauté for a couple of minutes until the veg are well combined and coated with fat. Add the stock and season with salt and black pepper. Bring the soup almost to the boil, then cover and simmer for about 15 minutes.

Add the cabbage and tomatoes. Cover the pan and leave the soup to simmer for another 20 minutes. Taste for seasoning and add more salt and pepper if necessary.

Trim the fat off the steak. Heat a griddle pan until it is smoking and cook the steak for just a couple of minutes on each side. Remove the steak and leave it to rest for 5 minutes, then slice it as thinly as you can and add any meat juices to the soup.

To serve, divide the strips of steak between the soup bowls and ladle the soup on top. Add dollops of soured cream or crème fraiche, if using, and a sprinkling of dill.

VIETNAMESE BEEF PHO

We really got a taste for this dish when we travelled to Vietnam a while back and we still love it. For us, it's all about the stock, so we make that first, then use it for the soup, but if you want a shortcut, use some decent shop-bought beef stock. Simmer it with the same aromatics as in our stock recipe – ginger, cloves, star anise and so on – for half an hour, then leave it to infuse for a while before making the soup.

SERVES 6

Beef stock
1.5kg beef shin
2kg beef bones
30g piece of fresh root
    ginger, unpeeled and
    split lengthways
1 large onion, unpeeled
1 tsp fennel seeds
1 tsp black peppercorns
3 star anise
5cm cinnamon stick
4 cloves
2 bay leaves

Soup
200g flat rice noodles
1 large carrot, finely shredded
bunch of spring onions, sliced
    into thin rounds
bag of bean sprouts
250g rump or sirloin steak,
    sliced very thinly
2–3 tbsp fish sauce (nam pla)
small bunch of fresh
    coriander, shredded
small bunch of mint, leaves
    only, shredded
handful of basil leaves,
    shredded

To serve
extra coriander, mint and basil
    leaves, left whole
2 limes, cut into wedges
a few Thai chillies, thinly
    sliced (deseeded if you like)
chilli oil or sauce
hoisin sauce (optional)

First make the stock. Preheat the oven to 220°C/Fan 200°C/Gas 7. Put the beef shin, bones, ginger and the onion, cut into quarters, in a large roasting tin and roast for an hour until the onion looks quite charred and everything is well browned.

Tip the meat, bones and onion into a large saucepan. Slice the pieces of ginger and add them too, then add water to cover – you'll probably need about 4 litres. Skim off any greyish foam that collects on top as you bring the water to the boil.

Meanwhile, put the roasting tin on the hob, add a little water and deglaze the tin, scraping up any brown bits from the bottom. When you've finished skimming the stock, add the contents of the roasting tin, along with all the spices and the bay leaves.

Simmer very slowly, partially covered, for 3–5 hours, depending on how much time you've got. You need to make sure that the meat is tender and the stock has a good depth of colour. Strain the stock, discarding all the solids. You can either use the stock immediately (in which case you will need to skim off any fat that may collect on top) or if possible, chill the stock in the fridge – the fat will then be much easier to remove.

When you are ready to make the soup, pour the stock into a saucepan and season it with salt and pepper. Bring it to the boil and leave to simmer. At the same time, cook the noodles according to the packet instructions – normally you pour boiling water over them and leave them to stand for 10–12 minutes until almost cooked through.

Add the carrot to the beef stock and simmer for 3 minutes. Add the spring onions, bean sprouts, steak and fish sauce and simmer for a further minute. Taste for seasoning and add a dash more fish sauce and/or salt if you think it needs it, then the herbs.

Drain the noodles and divide them between your bowls, then ladle the soup over them. Serve garnished with lime wedges, more herbs, chilli and sauces of your choice.

CHAPTER THREE
FAST MEAT

POTATO-CRUSTED PORK STEAKS

With its creamy honey mustard sauce, this pork dish with a rosti-style crust is a real treat – but not one for diet nights. It's inspired by a Romanian recipe and has become a firm favourite with both our families. All you need is some braised red cabbage or a nice bowl of greens alongside and you have a seriously good dinner.

SERVES 4

4 pork loin steaks
5 tsp wholegrain mustard
600g potatoes (Maris Pipers are good)
150g butter, melted, plus extra for frying
1 tbsp vegetable oil
1 banana shallot, thinly sliced
1 tsp plain flour
450ml cider
1 tsp Dijon mustard
1 tsp light brown muscovado sugar
1 tbsp clear honey
100ml double cream
flaked sea salt
freshly ground black pepper

Trim any excess fat from the pork steaks, then put each steak between 2 sheets of clingfilm and bash it with a rolling pin to flatten slightly. Season them well, then take a teaspoon of mustard for each steak and spread it over both sides.

Coarsely grate the peeled potatoes on to a clean tea towel. Gather the tea towel into a bundle, then squeeze hard to get rid of as much liquid as you can – it's important that the potato mix is as dry as possible so it sticks to the steaks well. Mix the squeezed potato with the melted butter, a pinch of salt and some pepper. Take a quarter of the potato and pack it down on top of a pork steak, then repeat with the remaining mix and steaks. Preheat the oven to 200°C/ Fan 180°C/Gas 6.

Heat a good tablespoon of butter and the oil in a large frying pan. Add 2 of the steaks to the pan, potato side up, and fry them for 2 minutes. Using a couple of spatulas to keep the potato topping in place, carefully turn the steaks over and fry them for another 2 minutes. Transfer the steaks to a baking tray, potato side up, and fry the remaining steaks in the same way. Place the baking tray in the oven and cook the steaks for 15 minutes.

Put the frying pan with all the cooking juices from the pork back on a low heat, add the shallot and fry for 2 minutes, or until soft. Sprinkle over the flour and stir well with a wooden spoon.

Gradually add the cider, stirring continuously to remove any lumps of flour. Stir in the remaining teaspoon of wholegrain mustard, the Dijon mustard, sugar and honey, then simmer for 4–5 minutes, or until the volume of liquid has almost reduced by half. Stir in the cream and cook for a further 2–3 minutes until again reduced by half and the mixture is thick enough to coat the back of a spoon.

Remove the pork steaks from the baking tray and leave them to rest on a board for about 5 minutes. Serve with the creamy mustard sauce and some veg such as our braised red cabbage (see p.354).

LEMON AND THYME PORK SCHNITZEL

Quick and easy to put together, this light crispy pork dish is a mega taste treat, with the lemon and herbs adding plenty of zing. It's our take on the classic Wiener schnitzel and we think it's worthy of a place on any Viennese table. Makes a couple of pork steaks go a long way, too.

SERVES 4

2 x 180g pork loin steaks
1 large egg
2 tbsp plain flour
75g coarse dried white breadcrumbs (Japanese panko breadcrumbs are ideal)
finely grated zest of ½ lemon
15g Parmesan cheese, finely grated
1 heaped tbsp chopped fresh thyme leaves
300ml vegetable oil
2 handfuls of watercress, to garnish
1–2 tsp extra virgin olive oil, to drizzle
flaked sea salt
freshly ground black pepper

Place a pork loin steak between 2 sheets of clingfilm and bash it with rolling pin or meat mallet until it is about 1cm thick all over. Remove the clingfilm and cut the flattened steak in half lengthways, then prepare the other steak in the same way. Season the steaks on both sides with salt and black pepper.

Beat the egg in a bowl. Sprinkle the flour on to a plate. Mix the breadcrumbs, lemon zest, Parmesan, thyme and a good pinch of salt in a shallow bowl.

Take a piece of pork and dredge it in flour, then dip it into the beaten egg, and lastly in the breadcrumb mixture until it is completely coated. Repeat with the other pieces of pork.

Heat the oil in a large frying pan until a breadcrumb sizzles and turns golden-brown when dropped into it. Take care: hot oil can be dangerous so don't leave the pan unattended.

Add 2 of the schnitzels to the pan and fry for 2–3 minutes on each side, or until the pork is cooked through and the coating is crisp and golden-brown. Remove them from the pan and set aside on a warmed plate lined with kitchen paper. Keep them warm while you cook the other 2 schnitzels.

Serve garnished with watercress and drizzled with a little olive oil. Some potato salad (see p.352) on the side is just right with these.

GAMMON STEAKS WITH PARSLEY SAUCE

Forget your pineapple rings and try this good old British classic. There's nowt better. It's a lovely comforting dish just as it is, but if you want a little more bite, stir some wholegrain mustard into the sauce. Some gammon steaks need soaking so check the packet or ask for advice at your butcher or supermarket. And take care not to overcook your gammon or you'll look like a hamateur!

SERVES 4

1 tbsp olive oil
small knob of butter
4 x 200g gammon steaks, soaked for 12 hours if necessary

Parsley sauce
500ml milk
bunch of parsley
2 bay leaves
1 small onion, sliced
a few peppercorns
30g butter
30g plain flour
flaked sea salt
freshly ground white pepper

First make the sauce. Pour the milk into a saucepan. Separate the stems of parsley from the leaves and add the stems to the milk, together with the bay leaves, onion and peppercorns. Heat the milk until it is just about to come to the boil, then take the saucepan off the heat and leave the flavours to infuse while the milk cools.

Melt the 30g of butter in a saucepan. Add the flour and stir until well combined. Continue to cook until the mixture has browned a little – the raw flavour of the flour needs to be cooked out. Strain the milk and start adding it to the butter and flour, stirring continuously until you have a creamy sauce. Season with salt and white pepper, then finely chop the parsley leaves and stir them into the sauce. Keep the sauce warm while you cook the gammon steaks.

Heat the olive oil and butter in a large frying pan. Once the butter has melted and you can feel the heat rising from the pan when you hold your hand above it – don't touch the pan – add the steaks. Cook them for 3 minutes on each side. You might need to cook them in 2 batches.

Serve the gammon steaks with some parsley sauce ladled over them and pour the rest of the sauce into a jug to bring to the table. Nice with some sauté potatoes (see p.348) and a bit of salad.

PORK CHOW MEIN

If you love noodles – like we do – you'll love chow mein. In fact, in Chinese the name chow mein just means fried noodles. We reckon the secret to success here is to have some of the noodles nice and crispy and others soft, and this is easiest to do in a wok. You could call this dish a one-wok wonder.

SERVES 4

500g pork tenderloin
1 tsp Chinese five-spice
    powder
200g dried medium egg
    noodles
4 tbsp vegetable oil
2 tbsp soft light brown sugar
2 tsp cornflour
4 tbsp dark soy sauce
2 tbsp mirin or dry sherry
1 red pepper, quartered,
    deseeded and sliced
1 large carrot, cut into thin
    strips, about 6cm long
25g fresh root ginger, peeled
    and very thinly sliced
3 garlic cloves, very thinly
    sliced
6 spring onions, sliced
50g frozen peas
225g can water chestnuts,
    drained and halved
flaked sea salt
freshly ground black pepper

Using a sharp knife, carefully trim off as much excess fat and sinew as you can from the pork. Cut the pork in half lengthways and then into thin slices. Put it in a bowl and toss it with the five-spice powder, ½ teaspoon of salt and plenty of pepper, then set it aside.

Bring a saucepan of water to the boil. Add the egg noodles and swish them around with a long wooden spoon to separate the strands. Bring the water back to the boil and cook the noodles for 3–4 minutes, or according to the packet instructions, until tender. Drain and rinse them in a sieve under running water until cold, then toss with a tablespoon of the vegetable oil and set aside.

Mix the sugar and cornflour together in a bowl and gradually stir in the soy sauce, mirin (or sherry) and 100ml water, then set aside.

Heat a tablespoon of the oil in a wok or a large non-stick frying pan. Add the pork and stir-fry over a high heat for 2 minutes or until nicely browned. Transfer it to a plate and put the pan back on the heat.

Add another tablespoon of the oil and stir-fry the pepper and carrot for 2 minutes. Add the ginger, garlic, spring onions, peas and water chestnuts and stir-fry for 2 minutes more until softened but not soggy. Tip everything on to a plate.

Pour the remaining oil into the pan and add the noodles. Stir-fry the noodles for 2–3 minutes, or until some are beginning to turn crisp and golden-brown. Tip the meat and vegetables back into the pan and stir-fry everything together, tossing all the ingredients for 1–2 minutes, or until they're evenly mixed and piping hot.

Stir the soy and mirin mixture again and pour it into the pan. Continue tossing everything together for 1–2 minutes, or until hot and glossy. Eat immediately – you'll love it, we promise.

THAI PORK STIR-FRY

When you fancy a change from Chinese stir-fries, try a Thai. This dish is aromatic and tantalisingly tasty – a true cornucopia of loveliness. Once you've done all the chopping the cooking takes no time, so you can have supper on the table in minutes. You can buy ready-prepared galangal and this is fine if you can't find fresh, or use root ginger instead.

SERVES 4

500g pork tenderloin
2 shallots, sliced
2 garlic cloves, finely chopped
1 tsp grated galangal or fresh
   root ginger
1 lemon grass stem, inner
   white part only, thinly sliced
2 tbsp finely chopped
   coriander stems
1 tbsp groundnut or
   vegetable oil
pinch of turmeric
200g green beans, topped
2 tbsp fish sauce (nam pla)
juice of 2 limes
1 tsp palm sugar or soft light
   brown sugar
flaked sea salt
freshly ground black pepper

To serve
handful of coriander leaves
handful of Thai basil
4 spring onions, shredded
2 Thai chillies, thinly sliced
   (optional; you can deseed
   for less heat)

Cut the pork tenderloin into thin strips, about 6cm long and 1cm wide. Sprinkle them with salt and set them aside.

Put the shallots, garlic, galangal or ginger, lemon grass and coriander stems in a food processor and blitz to make a coarse paste. Add a little water if necessary. Alternatively, grind everything to a paste in a pestle and mortar.

Heat the oil in a wok. When the oil is very hot and starts to shimmer, add the paste along with the pinch of turmeric. Stir-fry for a couple of minutes, then add the pork. Stir-fry for a minute to sear the meat, then add the green beans. Continue to cook for 2–3 minutes.

Mix the fish sauce, lime juice and sugar together. Pour this mixture over the contents of the wok and season with salt and pepper. Continue to stir-fry for a couple of minutes.

Garnish with the herbs, spring onions and chillies, if using, and serve with rice.

SWEET AND SOUR PORK

We've cooked sweet and sour pork in Hong Kong with the locals, and quite an experience it was. To be honest, though, we love our own version, with not a dollop of ketchup in sight. It's tasty, fresh and offers all you want from a sweet and sour. You do have to marinate the meat for half an hour, but once you've done that the dish is cooked in no time.

SERVES 4

500g lean pork, such as fillet, cut into strips
½ tsp salt
1 tbsp groundnut oil
1 large red pepper, deseeded and cut into strips
15g fresh root ginger, peeled and sliced into matchsticks
2 tsp cornflour
1 tsp sesame seeds
4 spring onions, thinly sliced or shredded

Marinade

15g fresh root ginger
1 tbsp rice wine (mirin or Shaoxing)
1 tbsp light soy sauce
1 tsp sesame oil

Sauce

250ml pineapple juice
2 tbsp dark soy sauce
1 tbsp rice wine vinegar (or cider vinegar)
2 tsp soft light brown sugar
½ tsp ground white pepper
1 tsp sesame oil

Put the pork in a bowl and season it with half a teaspoon of salt. To make the marinade, grate the ginger into a small bowl and either squeeze it or sieve it – you want the juice only. Add the ginger juice to the rice wine, soy sauce and sesame oil, then pour this mixture over the pork and set it aside to marinate for half an hour.

Whisk the sauce ingredients together and set aside. Heat the groundnut oil in a wok on a high heat until it starts to shimmer. Add the red pepper and sliced ginger, then fry them for a minute.

Drain the pork and toss the strips in the cornflour. Add them to the wok and stir-fry for a couple of minutes until the pork is well browned on all sides. Pour the sauce over the meat and cook until it has reduced to a fairly syrupy consistency.

Serve with rice and garnish with sesame seeds and spring onions.

BARNSLEY CHOPS WITH CUMBERLAND SAUCE

There's only one thing better than a lamb chop and that's a Barnsley chop, because it's a double chop cut across the loin. People say it was first cooked in a hotel or pub in Barnsley, hence the name, but whatever the history it's a big piece of meat for big appetites and a true meat feast. Cumberland sauce is a classic accompaniment; also goes well with gammon and raised pies.

SERVES 4

2 tbsp chopped fresh thyme
1 tbsp chopped fresh rosemary
4 tbsp chopped fresh mint, plus extra for garnish
4 x 375g Barnsley chops
2 tbsp vegetable oil
chopped parsley, to garnish
flaked sea salt
freshly ground black pepper

Cumberland sauce
1 orange
1 piece of stem ginger, drained and cut into very thin strips
50ml ruby port
150g redcurrant jelly
juice of ½ lemon

Mix all the herbs with a teaspoon of salt and plenty of black pepper. Take a quarter of the herb mixture and rub it into both sides of one of the chops, then coat the rest of the chops in the same way. Preheat the oven to 180°C/Fan 160°C/Gas 4.

Heat the oil in a large heavy-based frying pan. Fry the chops over a high heat for 3 minutes on each side until browned but not cooked through. Then prop up the chops on their fatty edges and cook them for 2–3 minutes more until the fat is browned and rendered slightly. Transfer the chops to a baking tray and cook them in the oven for 6 minutes for medium meat or for 8–10 minutes if you like them well done. Remove the chops and leave them to rest for 5 minutes before serving.

Serve the chops garnished with fresh parsley and some warm Cumberland sauce. A bit of buttery mash (see p.352) and some green veg are just the ticket with this.

Cumberland sauce
Using a potato peeler, pare the peel off the orange as thinly as possible. Cut this into matchstick strips and put them in a small saucepan. Add 250ml cold water and bring to the boil, then boil for 8–10 minutes. Drain the peel in a sieve and set it aside.

Juice the orange and pour the juice into the saucepan. Add the port, redcurrant jelly and lemon juice and bring to a simmer. Cook for 8–10 minutes over a low heat, or until the jelly dissolves. Stir in the orange and ginger strips and continue simmering gently for 2–3 minutes until the sauce becomes slightly darker in colour and syrupy.

Remove the pan from the heat and leave the sauce to stand at room temperature – it will thicken as it cools. Serve warm or cold, but if the sauce thickens too much, add a little more water and reheat gently before serving.

MARSALA LAMB CHOPS WITH SMOTHERED ONIONS

Lamb chops with kidneys, a melting mix of golden onions and Marsala wine, all topped with crispy sage leaves – what could be nicer? If you're not a fan of kidneys, leave them out and just cook the chops. You'll still have an excellent dish.

SERVES 4

50g butter, cut into cubes
2 large onions, halved and
  thinly sliced
1 tbsp vegetable oil
8 lamb chops
4 lamb's kidneys
1 tbsp plain flour
150ml Marsala (or Madeira
  or medium sherry)
flaked sea salt
freshly ground black pepper

Sage garnish
3 tbsp vegetable oil
24 fresh sage leaves,
  depending on size

Start by making the garnish. Pour the oil into a small frying pan and place it over a medium heat for a couple of minutes. Add the sage leaves and fry them for 20–30 seconds, but don't let them brown. Remove the leaves, drain them on kitchen paper, then set them aside until needed. They will crisp up even more as they cool.

Melt half the butter in a large non-stick frying pan and fry the onions over a low heat for 10 minutes, stirring occasionally. Turn up the heat and cook them for another 3–4 minutes, stirring continuously, until golden-brown. Tip the onions on to a plate and set them aside.

Put the pan back on the heat and add the oil. Season the lamb chops well with salt and pepper and fry them over a medium-high heat for 2½–3 minutes on each side.

While the lamb is cooking, prepare the kidneys, if using. First give them a good rinse in a colander and then cut them in half through the middle to give two equal kidney-shaped pieces. Using sharp kitchen scissors, carefully cut out the white core (see p.306 for more info on doing this).

Put the flour in a bowl and season it with salt and black pepper. Toss the kidneys in the seasoned flour until lightly coated, then shake off any excess flour before frying them.

Turn the lamb chops on to their fatty edge and leave them to sizzle for another 2–3 minutes, or until golden-brown. Add the kidneys to the pan and cook them on one side for 3 minutes.

Transfer the lamb chops to a warm plate and leave them to rest. Turn the kidneys and cook them for 3 minutes on the other side, or until they're lightly browned and cooked through. If in doubt, turn and cook for an extra minute on each side. Put the kidneys on the plate with the lamb. Drain off any excess fat from the pan and place it back on the heat.

Put the fried onions back in the pan and cook for 1–2 minutes, or until hot, stirring with a wooden spoon. Add the Marsala, then quickly stir in the remaining cubes of butter. The sauce will thicken as you stir.

Serve the lamb chops and kidneys with the onions and garnish with the fried sage leaves. Great with three-root mash (see p.352) and perhaps some green beans.

GREEK LAMB CHOPS WITH TZATZIKI

Lamb, lemon, herbs – this is simple but so good to eat and the aroma is mouthwatering. A beetroot salad on the side is nice or some beans, and we think a bowl of tzatziki is a must. You can buy this in the supermarket but it's easy to make yourself while the chops are marinating so give it a go. The chops are best cooked on a griddle pan or outdoors on a barbecue in the summer. Bet you can't stop at one chop.

SERVES 4

12–16 small lamb chops
    (3–4 per person)
3 tbsp olive oil
juice of 2 lemons
1 tbsp dried oregano
1 tsp dried thyme
1 tsp dried rosemary
1 tsp dried mint
flaked sea salt
freshly ground black pepper

Tzatziki
1 cucumber
300g full-fat Greek yoghurt
2 garlic cloves, finely chopped
1 tsp white wine vinegar
1 tsp dried mint

Put the lamb chops in a large plastic bag or in a glass or china bowl – don't use metal, as it can react with the acid in the lemon. Mix the olive oil, lemon juice and herbs together, then season liberally with salt and pepper. Pour this mixture over the lamb chops and massage it in well. Leave the chops in the fridge to marinate for several hours.

When you're ready to cook the chops, heat a griddle pan over a high heat – it needs to be so hot you can't hold your hand over it for more than a second. Don't dream of touching it, though. Remove the chops from the marinade, brushing off any excess, then place them on the hot griddle pan.

Grill the chops for 2–3 minutes on each side. They should be lightly charred on the outside but still juicy and slightly pink on the inside. If you prefer your chops cooked through, give them a further minute on each side. Leave the chops to rest for 5 minutes, then serve with tzatziki.

Tzatziki

Peel the cucumber, then cut it in half lengthways. Run a small spoon down the length to scoop out all the seeds and discard them. Grate the cucumber, then wrap it in a clean tea towel and wring out as much of the liquid as possible – cucumbers are very wet and the tzatziki will be too watery if you don't do this.

Put the yoghurt in a bowl and season with salt and pepper. Add the cucumber to the yoghurt, then stir in the garlic, white wine vinegar and dried mint and mix thoroughly.

LAMB SHASHLIK

Shashlik is a kind of kebab, popular in Eastern Europe. The meat is marinated first, then cooked on a griddle or barbecue. You can use all kinds of meat for these, but a fairly fatty cut is best, so lamb shoulder or pork shoulder work particularly well. Shashlik kebabs are usually served with some dips and sauces, such as the soured cream dip and plum sauce below, and we like some flatbread too for mopping up any juices.

SERVES 4–6

1kg lamb shoulder, cut into cubes

Marinade
1 tbsp olive or vegetable oil
100ml white wine
1 tbsp cider vinegar
1 onion, sliced
4 fat garlic cloves, thinly sliced
3 crumbled bay leaves
1 tsp paprika
4 cloves
¼ tsp cinnamon
flaked sea salt
freshly ground black pepper

Soured cream dip
200g soured cream
handful of finely chopped dill
handful of finely chopped coriander
1 tsp cider vinegar
pinch of sugar

Plum sauce
300g ripe plums, stoned and diced
1 tbsp sugar
1 tsp cider vinegar
1 red chilli, or 1 tsp ground chilli
2 tbsp finely chopped coriander
2 tbsp finely chopped dill

Mix all the marinade ingredients together in a glass or china bowl and add the cubes of meat. Make sure the meat is well covered, then leave it to marinate in the fridge for at least 2–3 hours or overnight.

If you are using wooden or bamboo skewers, soak them for half an hour before using so they don't burn when you cook the meat.

When you're ready to cook, thread the meat on to the skewers. Heat a griddle pan or a barbecue and cook the kebabs for 3–4 minutes on each side until well charred. The meat should still be very juicy and tender from the marinade. Serve with the soured cream dip and plum sauce and some salad.

If you make these with beef the cooking time is the same, but cook pork shashlik for a little longer.

Soured cream dip
Simply mix all the ingredients together and season with salt and pepper.

Plum sauce
Put the diced plums in a saucepan, cover with cold water and bring to a simmer. Continue to simmer until the plums are soft. Strain, reserving 75ml of the cooking water.

Put the plums in a food processor or a blender with the reserved cooking water, sugar, cider vinegar and chilli and purée. Pass the sauce through a sieve, season with salt and pepper, then stir in the dill and chopped coriander.

BUTTERFLIED LEG OF LAMB

Butterflied lamb is easy to carve and you get lots of nice crispy bits on the outside. Our version has some lovely warm spicing, giving it a slightly Moroccan flavour. Yes, it does take a bit longer than the others in this chapter, but it's still a super-fast way of cooking a roast. Ask your butcher to butterfly the leg, which means removing the bone and opening the meat out so it's a fairly even thickness.

SERVES 6

1 leg of lamb, butterflied
1 tbsp olive oil
1 tbsp pomegranate
  molasses
juice of ½ lemon
2 garlic cloves, crushed
1 tsp ground cumin
1 tsp ground coriander
½ tsp cayenne pepper
½ tsp black pepper
¼ tsp cinnamon
flaked sea salt

Season the lamb with salt on both sides. Whisk together the olive oil, pomegranate molasses and lemon juice with the garlic and spices. Pour this over the lamb and leave to marinate for at least an hour. You can leave it overnight in the fridge, but make sure you give it an hour out of the fridge to return to room temperature before cooking.

Preheat the oven to 220°C/Fan 200°C/Gas 7. Put the lamb in a roasting tin – reserve the marinade – and roast it in the oven for 30 minutes. Remove the lamb from the roasting tin and leave it to rest, covered with foil, for 10–15 minutes.

Put the roasting tin on a medium heat and pour in the reserved marinade. Stir the marinade into the juices in the roasting tin and allow it all to bubble. Slice the lamb into chunks and serve it with the sauce from the roasting tin.

Some couscous, garnished with lots of herbs and pomegranate seeds, is a perfect accompaniment.

VEAL SCALOPPINI

This is such a great way to eat veal – quickly cooked in butter and olive oil and served with a warm herby sauce that's cooked in the same pan. Ready in no time and flavour to savour. Use British rose veal for preference.

SERVES 4

4 x 150–200g rose veal escalopes
4 tbsp plain flour
1 tsp mustard powder
1 tsp dried oregano
1 tbsp olive oil
15g butter

Herb sauce
1 tbsp olive oil
1 small tin of anchovies, drained and finely chopped
1 garlic clove, finely chopped
50ml white wine or vermouth
1 tsp Dijon mustard
2 tbsp capers, finely chopped
small bunch of parsley, finely chopped
small bunch of basil leaves, shredded
a squeeze of lemon juice
freshly ground black pepper

Put an escalope between 2 pieces of clingfilm and beat it with a meat mallet or a rolling pin until it's very thin. Repeat with the remaining escalopes.

Mix the flour, mustard powder and oregano in a shallow bowl. Dust the escalopes with this mixture, making sure they are completely covered, then pat off any excess.

Heat the olive oil and butter in a large frying pan. When the butter is foaming, add the escalopes and fry them for a couple of minutes on each side, until golden-brown and just cooked through. You may have to do this in 2 batches, so add more oil and butter if necessary. Set the cooked escalopes aside and keep them warm while you make the sauce.

Add the olive oil to the frying pan, then the anchovies and garlic. Cook briefly, stirring until the anchovies have broken down, then whisk in the white wine or vermouth, Dijon mustard and capers. Taste for seasoning – you probably won't need salt as the anchovies provide plenty, but you might like some black pepper.

Remove the pan from the heat and stir in the herbs. Finish the sauce with a squeeze of lemon juice and serve with the escalopes.

VEAL SALTIMBOCCA

The name of this Italian classic means 'jump in the mouth' and it certainly jumps into ours. It's quick to make and full of flavour. You can make it with pork escalopes instead of veal if you prefer. As before, we recommend using British rose veal.

SERVES 4

4 x 150g rose veal escalopes
1 tbsp flour
8 fresh sage leaves
8 slices of prosciutto
1 tbsp olive oil
15g butter
fincly grated zest of 1 lemon
½ tsp dried sage
200ml Marsala (or Madeira
    or medium sherry)
100ml chicken stock
1 tbsp capers (optional)
lemon wedges, to serve
    (optional)
flaked sea salt
freshly ground black pepper

Put an escalope between 2 pieces of clingfilm and beat it with a meat mallet or a rolling pin until it's very thin. Repeat with the remaining escalopes, then cut each one in half lengthways. Season the flour with salt and pepper and dust the escalopes.

Place a sage leaf in the centre of an escalope, then wrap a slice of prosciutto around the meat and leaf.

Heat the olive oil and butter in a large frying pan and fry the escalopes for 3–4 minutes on each side until the meat is cooked through and the prosciutto is crisp. Removo the escalopes from the pan and keep them warm. You will probably need to cook the escalopes in a couple of batches, so add more oil and butter if necessary.

When all the escalopes are cooked and set aside, turn up the heat and add the lemon zest, dried sage and Marsala to the pan. Let the wine bubble fiercely for a minute or two, then add the chicken stock and simmer until well reduced and syrupy. Stir in the capers if using, then serve the escalopes with the sauce. A squeeze of lemon is nice so offer some lemon wedges if you like.

STEAK DIANE

This is quite a retro dish, but none the worse for that. We don't know who Diane was, but she must have been quite something to have such a luscious sauce named for her! This tastes amazing and is quick to make – a real treat for you and your loved one.

SERVES 2

2 tbsp whole black
  peppercorns
2 x 175g fillet steaks
25g butter
1 tsp vegetable oil
2 shallots (or 1 long banana
  shallot), thinly sliced
3 tbsp brandy
1 tsp Worcestershire sauce
1 tsp Dijon mustard
200ml beef stock
3 tbsp double cream
1 tbsp finely chopped fresh
  tarragon leaves (optional)
flaked sea salt

Crush the peppercorns in a pestle and mortar, then mix them with half a teaspoon of sea salt. Put the steaks on a board and season them well on both sides with the pepper and salt mixture until they're lightly but evenly crusted.

Melt the butter with the oil in a large non-stick frying pan and fry the steaks over a medium-high heat for 2–2½ minutes on each side for rare meat. Cook for 1–2 minutes longer on each side if you prefer your steaks medium rare and up to 3 minutes longer for medium, depending on thickness. Remove the steaks from the pan and set them aside to rest while you make the sauce.

Add the shallots to the frying pan and cook for 2–3 minutes, stirring, until they're softened and lightly browned. Pour the brandy into the pan and let it sizzle for a few seconds. With great care, light a match and carefully ignite the brandy, standing well back from the flame in the pan. (If you prefer not to do this, just cook the brandy for about 15 seconds before adding the other ingredients.)

When the flames have disappeared, add the Worcestershire sauce and mustard to the pan, stirring continuously. Pour in the stock and bring to the boil, then cook for 1–2 minutes, or until the liquid has reduced by nearly half, stirring regularly.

Stir in the double cream and bring the sauce back to a simmer, stirring. Add any juices from the resting steaks, then continue to simmer and stir until the sauce is thick enough to lightly coat the back of your spoon. Season to taste and stir in the tarragon, if using.

Serve the steaks with the sauce, some sauté potatoes (see p.348) and a green salad. What could be better?

RUMP STEAK WITH CHIMICHURRI SAUCE

Liven up your steak and chips with some chimichurri. It's an amazing Argentinian sauce that we found in every restaurant on our trip there, and we've been addicted to it ever since. There are lots of different versions, so feel free to play around and make your sauce as spicy or not as you like. We like coriander in ours, but if you're not a fan use more parsley instead.

SERVES 4

4 x 200g rump steaks
    (about 2cm thick)
pinch of cayenne pepper
flaked sea salt

Chimichurri sauce
large bunch of parsley,
    roughly chopped
small bunch of coriander,
    roughly chopped
2 tbsp fresh oregano leaves,
    or 1 tsp dried oregano
4 garlic cloves, chopped
1 shallot, chopped
½ tsp chilli flakes
juice of ½ lemon
1 tbsp red wine vinegar
50ml olive oil
flaked sea salt
freshly ground black pepper

Take the steaks out of the fridge at least an hour before cooking, so they can come up to room temperature – they will cook much better that way. Pat them dry with kitchen paper.

To make the sauce, put all the ingredients except the olive oil into a food processor, then season with salt and freshly ground black pepper. Blitz to a rough paste, then drizzle in the olive oil while the motor is still running until you have a piquant, herb-flecked sauce. If you prefer, simply chop everything finely by hand, then whisk in the lemon juice, red wine vinegar and olive oil.

To cook the steaks, heat a griddle pan for several minutes over a high heat until it is too hot to hold your hand over. Season the steak with plenty of salt, but not pepper, as the pepper will just burn. Add the steaks, making sure you don't overcrowd the pan.

For blue (very rare) steak, cook for 1 minute on each side. For rare, cook for 1½ minutes on the first side, then 1 minute on the second. For medium rare, cook for 2 minutes on the first side, then 1½ on the second. For medium, cook for 2 minutes on each side.

Transfer the steaks to a board, season with black pepper and a pinch of cayenne, then leave them to rest for 5–10 minutes. Serve with the chimichurri sauce.

Tip
The timings above – and for the steak recipes on the following pages – depend on three things: first, the meat being at room temperature before you start cooking; second, having a really hot pan; and third, allowing the meat to rest.

SIRLOIN OR RIB-EYE STEAK WITH BÉARNAISE SAUCE

Sirloin and rib-eye are both mega tasty – they're not quite as tender as fillet but have such awesome flavour. And to make your steak into a real feast, try making a béarnaise, one of the most luxurious of all sauces. It's not that difficult – honest – and it's best to make it first, as the steaks cook very quickly.

SERVES 2

2 x 200g sirloin or rib-eye
  steaks, about 2cm thick
flaked sea salt
freshly ground black pepper

Béarnaise sauce
50ml white wine vinegar
½ tsp black peppercorns
1 small shallot, finely chopped
large sprig of tarragon,
  bruised
3 egg yolks
200g unsalted butter, diced
  and softened
squeeze of lemon juice
3 tbsp tarragon leaves,
  finely chopped
flaked sea salt
freshly ground white pepper

Take the steaks out of the fridge at least an hour before cooking, so they can come up to room temperature – they will cook much better that way. Pat them dry with kitchen paper.

Heat a griddle pan for several minutes over a high heat until it is too hot to hold your hand over – don't ever touch the pan. Season the steak with plenty of salt, but not pepper, as the pepper will just burn. Add the steaks, making sure you don't overcrowd the pan.

For blue (very rare) steak, cook for 1 minute on each side. For rare, cook for 1½ minutes on the first side, then 1 minute on the second. For medium rare, cook for 2 minutes on the first side, then 1½ on the second. For medium, cook for 2 minutes on each side.

Remove the steaks from the griddle and set them aside to rest for 5–10 minutes so the meat can relax and hold on to more of its juices. At this point season them with black pepper. Serve with the sauce, salad, chips – whatever takes your fancy.

Béarnaise sauce
Put the vinegar, peppercorns, shallot and tarragon into a small saucepan, add 50ml of water and bring to the boil. Simmer until the liquid has reduced to about 2 tablespoons. Strain, reserving the liquid.

Place a heatproof bowl over a saucepan of just simmering water. Make sure the bottom of the bowl isn't touching the water.

Put the egg yolks, a cube of butter and a pinch of salt into the bowl. Whisk them together, then add half the reserved liquid. Whisk until the mixture emulsifies and starts to thicken, then gradually add all the butter, a cube at a time. Make sure that the mixture is emulsifying and not separating before adding more butter. If it starts to get too thick, add teaspoons of warm water.

When you have added all the butter, remove the bowl from the pan. Add a squeeze of lemon and stir in the tarragon leaves. Taste for seasoning and acidity and add salt, pepper and perhaps more of the reduced liquid if necessary. The sauce will keep warm for up to 30 minutes. Leave it in the heatproof bowl, but off the heat, and stir it regularly.

ONGLET WITH FLAVOURED BUTTERS

Onglet, sometimes known as poor man's fillet, probably has the strongest flavour of any steak, so these gutsy butters are just right with it. When you buy onglet you'll see it has a central line of gristle running through it. The butcher can remove this, leaving the steak whole or cutting it into two long pieces. Don't cook onglet for long – no more than medium rare – or it will be tough. It really needs to rest too, so don't skimp on that.

SERVES 2

1 onglet steak
flaked sea salt

Garlic and parsley butter
150g butter, softened
2 garlic cloves
3 tbsp finely chopped parsley
flaked sea salt
freshly ground black pepper

Blue cheese butter
150g butter, softened
75g blue cheese (Roquefort or Stilton both good)
½ tsp Dijon mustard
1 small shallot, finely chopped
1 tbsp finely chopped chives

Chilli and coriander butter
150g butter, softened
3 tbsp finely chopped fresh coriander
1 garlic clove, finely chopped
zest and juice of 1 lime
1 hot chilli, deseeded and finely chopped.

Make your flavoured butter in advance so it has a chance to chill.

Take the steak out of the fridge at least an hour before cooking, so it can come up to room temperature – it will cook much better that way. Pat it dry with kitchen paper.

Heat a griddle pan for several minutes over a high heat until it is too hot to hold your hand over – don't ever touch the pan. Season the steak with plenty of salt, but not pepper, as the pepper will just burn. Add the steak to the pan and cook to taste.

For blue (very rare) steak, cook for 1 minute on each side. For rare, cook for 1½ minutes on the first side, then 1 minute on the second. For medium-rare steak, cook for 2 minutes on the first side, then 1½ on the second.

Transfer the steak to a board and leave it to rest for 10 minutes, then drain off any liquid that's been released and reserve it. Cut the steak diagonally into slices across the grain. Pour over the reserved juices and serve with one of the following flavoured butters and perhaps some amazing triple-cooked chips (see p.351).

Flavoured butters
For each butter, put the butter in a small bowl and season well with salt and pepper. Add the extra ingredients and mix thoroughly, making sure everything is evenly distributed. With the blue cheese butter, make sure the cheese is well crumbled and that you really mash it into the butter.

Wet your hands and form the butter into a rough sausage. Wrap this tightly in clingfilm, twisting the ends together, and chill in the fridge until needed. To serve, cut the butter into slices and melt on top of steak.

The butters will keep for several days or longer in the fridge, but if you don't think you will use them immediately, chill them well, cut into slices and freeze.

BEEF STROGANOFF

This is a fast version of stroganoff, using beef fillet and seasoned with mustard and brandy instead of paprika. It takes no time to cook and it's wonderfully tender and delicious – makes an expensive cut of meat go a long way too. Serve with noodles if you like, or some chips go down a treat. If you prefer, you could use some well-trimmed sirloin instead of fillet.

SERVES 4

600g beef fillet
25g butter
1 onion, thinly sliced
250g button mushrooms,
    thinly sliced
1 tbsp Dijon mustard
400ml beef stock
1 tbsp vegetable oil
2 heaped tbsp soured
    cream or crème fraiche
1 tbsp (or more) brandy
    (optional)
squeeze of lemon
    (optional)
finely chopped parsley,
    to serve
flaked sea salt
freshly ground black
    pepper

First prepare the beef fillet. Cut it into slices ½–1 cm thick, then slice these into strips about 1cm wide. Season the meat with salt and pepper and set it aside for a few minutes.

Heat the butter in a large frying pan. Add the onion and sauté for 2 minutes, then add the mushrooms and continue to cook until both are soft. Stir the mustard into the pan, coating the onion and mushrooms thoroughly – we find it easier to add the mustard at this stage than to mix it into the stock. Pour the stock into the pan, then leave it to simmer until the liquid has reduced by about half. Stir in the crème fraiche and set the pan aside for a few minutes.

In another large frying pan, heat the vegetable oil. When it's smoking hot, add the strips of beef. Fry, stirring continuously, until the meat is browned on all sides. This should take about a minute at the most.

If you want to flambé the beef, put the brandy in a ladle and carefully heat it over a flame. When the alcohol starts to burn off (you will see the fumes), tip it very gently towards the flame and it will ignite. Immediately pour this over the beef and give it a quick stir. Stand well back when doing this and be very careful.

Reheat the onion and mushroom sauce, then add the beef. Check the seasoning and add more salt and pepper to taste. If you find the sauce too rich, add a squeeze of lemon. Sprinkle with parsley before serving.

FAJITAS

This Mexican favourite makes a great dish to share with friends. Just put the steak and all the accompaniments on the table and let everyone dive in and help themselves. Flank is cheaper than some other cuts and works well, but you can use sirloin if you prefer. And if you ask your butchers nicely they'll prepare the flank for you. If you want extra heat, add some chilli to the marinade.

SERVES 6

750g flank steak, butterflied
  (see method) in 1 piece
3 peppers (red, yellow
  and orange), sliced
red onion, thinly sliced

Marinade
juice of 2 large limes (about
  60ml)
1 tbsp tomato purée
a dash of Worcestershire
  sauce
2 garlic cloves, crushed
pinch of ground cumin
pinch of ground coriander
2 tbsp coriander stems,
  finely chopped
flaked sea salt
freshly ground black pepper

Fajitas salsa
6 medium, ripe tomatoes,
  cored and finely diced
1 small red onion, finely
  chopped
2 tbsp finely chopped fresh
  coriander (stem and leaf)
1 jalapeño chilli, finely
  chopped or ½ tsp chilli
  powder (optional)
2 tsp red wine vinegar
juice of half a lime
1 red chilli (or ½ tsp chilli
  powder)

First, butterfly the steak. Put the steak on a work surface so the grain is running vertically. Put your hand flat on the meat, cut horizontally into the centre of the side nearest to you and continue to cut within 1cm of the far side. You should then be able to open out the steak like a book into one complete, much thinner piece. Flatten the central join with the heel of your hand. You can cut the meat into 2–3 pieces if you like, to make it more manageable for cooking.

Mix together all the marinade ingredients, then season with salt and pepper. Put the meat in a glass or china bowl – metal can react with the lime juice – and pour over the marinade. Leave to marinate in the fridge for at least 2 hours or overnight if you like.

When you are ready to cook the fajitas, heat a griddle until it is too hot to hold your hand over. Don't ever touch the pan, though. Remove the meat, reserving the marinade, and pat it dry. Griddle for 2–4 minutes on each side, depending on how well done you like your steak, then leave it to rest.

Meanwhile, heat the olive oil in a large frying pan or wok. Add the peppers and onion, and sauté on a medium heat for 5 minutes. Pour over the reserved marinade and simmer until the peppers and onions are almost tender.

Pour any juices from the resting meat into the pan with the peppers. Slice the steak thinly across the grain, add it to the peppers and onions, then remove the pan from the heat. Serve immediately with the salsa below. You might also like to serve warmed tortillas, guacamole (see p.345), soured cream, lime wedges and hot sauce.

Fajitas salsa
Put the tomatoes, onion, coriander and chilli, if using, in a bowl. Pour over the red wine vinegar and lime juice, then season well with salt and pepper. Stir thoroughly, then leave to stand at room temperature for a while to let the flavours develop.

BEEF FONDUE

Most people think of cheese when it comes to fondue, but beef works really well and is a good excuse to use that fondue set you'd forgotten about and has been gathering dust in your cupboard. Fondue makes a dead easy and fun meal and the nice thing is that everyone can cook their steak exactly how they like it.

SERVES 4

500g rump steak
250ml red wine
2 bay leaves
4 garlic cloves, thinly sliced
a few pieces of thinly pared
 orange peel
½ tsp black peppercorns
250ml groundnut or
 sunflower oil
flaked sea salt

Mustard and dill dip
200g crème fraiche or
 soured cream
1 tbsp Dijon mustard
¼ tsp honey
a dash of Tabasco
squeeze of lime juice
1 dill pickle or 4 small
 cornichons, finely chopped
small bunch dill, fronds only,
 finely chopped
flaked sea salt
freshly ground black pepper

Season the steak with salt, then put it in a glass or ceramic container – metal can react with the acid in the marinade. Cover the steak with the red wine, then crumble the bay leaves and add them to the beef along with the garlic, orange peel and peppercorns.

Leave the beef to marinate for at least an hour at room temperature or overnight in the fridge. If chilling the beef, remove it from the fridge and allow it to come to room temperature before cooking it.

Drain the steak and pat it dry, scraping off any marinade ingredients. Cut the steak into thin slices or into cubes.

Heat the oil in your fondue pot until it's hot. Check it with a probe thermometer if you have one – it should be 190°C. Otherwise drop a cube of meat into the oil. If it cooks in about a minute the oil is ready.

Arrange plates and fondue forks around the fondue and give everyone a pile of meat. They can then spear cubes of meat and lower them into the hot oil. Cook for a minute, or longer according to taste. Remove and let the meat rest on the plates before eating -- it will be very hot. Serve with dips, such as the mustard and dill one below, and some salad.

Mustard and dill dip
Put the crème fraiche or soured cream in a bowl. Whisk in the mustard and honey, then add dashes of Tabasco and lime juice and season with salt and pepper. Stir in the pickles and dill, then taste. Adjust the seasoning and add more Tabasco, lime juice or honey if necessary.

CHAPTER FOUR
ROASTS AND POT ROASTS

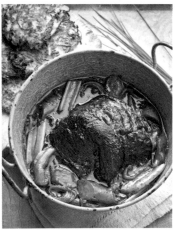

STUFFED PORK TENDERLOIN

Pork tenderloin can be dry if overcooked, but the stuffing and bacon wrapping in this recipe keeps the meat lovely and moist so satisfaction is guaranteed. We know there are lot of ingredients listed, but each one is there for a reason and by heck, this is worth the effort. Great hot with some creamy mash (see page 352) and green veg, or cold with salad.

SERVES 6

2 x 500g pork tenderloin fillets
16 smoked streaky bacon rashers
vegetable oil, for greasing

Stuffing
knob of butter
1 tbsp vegetable oil
1 large banana shallot, finely chopped
2 garlic cloves, crushed
1 eating apple, chopped
75g ready-to-eat dried apricots, quartered
50g sultanas
3 balls of stem ginger in syrup, drained, roughly chopped
75g fresh white breadcrumbs
1 tsp ground ginger
finely grated zest and juice of 1 lemon
3 tbsp finely chopped parsley leaves
1 tbsp finely chopped thyme leaves
1 tbsp stem ginger syrup (from the jar)
flaked sea salt
freshly ground black pepper

Sauce
100ml ginger wine
100ml double cream
1 tsp cornflour

First make the stuffing. Melt the butter with the oil in a large non-stick frying pan and gently fry the shallot and garlic for 5 minutes until softened but not coloured, stirring regularly. Remove the pan from the heat and stir in the apple, apricots, sultanas, stem ginger, breadcrumbs, ground ginger, lemon zest and juice and the herbs. Season with salt and pepper and mix together well. Add the tablespoon of stem ginger syrup and mix again until the stuffing comes together. Leave it to cool.

Put the tenderloins on a board and trim off as much excess fat and sinew as possible. Place each tenderloin between 2 sheets of clingfilm and bash them with a rolling pin until they're about 1cm thick.

Place a large clean sheet of clingfilm on the board and arrange the bacon in slightly overlapping lengths on top to make a rectangle of bacon. This should measure roughly 32 x 28cm and be slightly longer and just over 3 times as wide as the flattened pork. If some of the rashers are a little short, stretch them with the back of a knife.

Place one tenderloin in the centre of the bacon, spread the stuffing on top and cover it with the other tenderloin to sandwich the stuffing. Bring the bacon rashers over the pork to enclose it completely, using the clingfilm to help you. Wrap the pork tightly in more clingfilm to help hold the shape and put the parcel in the fridge for an hour.

Preheat the oven to 200°C/Fan 180°C/Gas 6. Carefully remove the clingfilm from the pork and place it on a lightly greased baking tray, with the ends of the bacon tucked underneath. Roast for about 50 minutes, or until the bacon is crisp and the pork is piping hot throughout. Remove the tray from the oven and put the pork on a board, then cover it with foil and leave it to rest. (If serving the meat cold, leave it to cool and then wrap it in foil and keep in the fridge until needed.)

To make the sauce, put the baking tray on the hob and add 200ml water. Bring to a simmer over a medium heat and cook for 2 minutes, stirring and lifting the sticky juices from the bottom of the tin. Strain the liquid through a sieve into a pan, adding any juices from the pork. Pour the wine and cream into the pan and bring the sauce to a simmer, stirring.

Mix the cornflour with a teaspoon of cold water in a bowl until smooth. Pour this into the sauce and bubble for a couple of minutes until thickened, stirring. Remove from the heat, season and add a dash more ginger wine if you like. Slice the pork and serve with the sauce.

PORK BELLY
WITH APPLES
AND SAGE

Pork belly is so popular these days that it's not as cheap as it once was, but it still costs less than most cuts for roasting – and it's dead good. What you're looking for here is crisp crunchy crackling and melt-in-the-mouth tender meat underneath. The better the meat, the better the result will be. You'll love our special cider gravy too.

SERVES 4–5

1.5kg pork belly, skin scored
2 tbsp finely chopped fresh
    thyme leaves
2 tsp flaked sea salt
1 tsp coarsely ground black
    pepper,
3 apples, cut into thick slices
2 medium onions, sliced
large handful of fresh
    sage leaves
2 tsp plain flour
200ml cider

Preheat the oven to 240°C/Fan 220°C/Gas 9.

Dry the pork belly skin with kitchen paper. Mix the thyme, sea salt and black pepper together and rub this mixture all over the skin, then turn the belly over and rub it on the underside.

Place the pork in a roasting tin and roast for 25–30 minutes, or until the skin is crisp. Turn the oven down to 180°C/Fan 160°C/Gas 4 and roast the pork for another hour.

Mix the apples with the onions, sage and a little freshly ground black pepper and place them in the middle of a small roasting tin.

Remove the pork from the oven and place it on top of the apples and onions, making sure the apple and onion pieces are underneath the meat so they don't burn. Set the first roasting tin aside with all the cooking juices. Put the pork back in the oven and cook for a further hour, or until the meat is really tender.

Skim any fat from the cooking juices in the reserved roasting tin and place the tin over a medium heat. Stir in the flour and cook for a minute or so, stirring continuously. Gradually stir in the cider and 100ml of water and bring to a simmer, then cook for 3–4 minutes, stirring continuously. Strain the gravy through a sieve into a small pan and season to taste.

When the pork is ready, carve the meat and crackling into thick slices. Spoon the apple and onion into a bowl to serve alongside and reheat the cider gravy until bubbling. Serve with some roasties (see p.348) and you've got a real feast.

SLOW-ROAST PORK WITH ROOT VEGETABLES

British pork is a national treasure and we think we breed some of the best pigs in the world in this country. Pork shoulder is ideal for slow-roasting, as the fat content keeps the meat moist. We cook it until the meat is falling off the bone – no need to carve this joint! One of the nicest of all Sunday dinners.

SERVES 4

2kg pork shoulder (bone in), with scored skin
1 tbsp vegetable oil
2 red onions, cut into wedges
3 carrots, cut in half lengthways
3 parsnips, cut into thick batons
2 celery sticks, cut into lengths
½ head of garlic, cloves left unpeeled
a few sprigs of thyme
1 tbsp plain flour
200ml white wine or vermouth
400ml chicken stock
flaked sea salt
freshly ground black pepper

Preheat the oven to 220°C/Fan 200°C/Gas 7. Rub the pork with the vegetable oil and sprinkle it with salt. Place it in a large roasting tin and roast in the preheated oven for half an hour. Turn the oven down to 160°C/Fan 140°C/Gas 3, cover the tin and the pork with foil, then roast for another 4½ hours.

Take the tin out of the oven and set the pork aside on a board. Drain off most of the fat in the bottom of the roasting tin, leaving about 2–3 tablespoons. Add all the vegetables, then stir to coat them with the juices in the pan. Make sure the celery and onion are placed quite centrally as these are best cooked under the pork. Tuck in the garlic and thyme, then put the pork back on top. Put the pork back in the oven for another hour, this time uncovered. By this time the vegetables should be lovely and tender.

Take the tin out of the oven and transfer the pork and the vegetables to serving platters. Cover the pork with foil and leave it to rest. Keep the vegetables warm.

Put the roasting tin over a low heat. Sprinkle over the flour, then stir well to scrape up any caramelised bits on the bottom of the tin. Pour in the white wine or vermouth, stirring continuously, and allow it to reduce, then add the chicken stock. Simmer until you have a fairly thin but rich gravy, then taste for seasoning and add salt and pepper if needed. Pour the gravy into a warm jug and serve it with the pork and vegetables.

LOIN OF PORK, ITALIAN STYLE

In this Italian classic, the pork is cooked in milk which makes it beautifully tender and delicious. Meat and milk sounds an unlikely combo but trust us – it works. Serve the pork hot or at room temperature, not fridge cold. You could also add some waxy potatoes to make this into a one-pot supper, served with some greens.

SERVES 4–6

1 tsp coriander seeds
½ tsp white peppercorns
1 tsp dried thyme
1 loin of pork (about 1.2–1.5kg), boned and skinned
2 tbsp olive oil
1 onion, finely chopped
50g smoked back bacon or smoked ham, finely chopped
about 1 litre whole milk
3 garlic cloves, sliced
3 wide pieces of thinly pared lemon peel
2 bay leaves
flaked sea salt

Crush the coriander seeds and peppercorns. You don't need to make a powder, so using a pestle and mortar will probably work best. Mix the spices with the thyme and half a teaspoon of sea salt, then sprinkle this all over the pork, pressing it in where necessary.

Heat the olive oil in a flameproof casserole dish. Brown the pork on all sides, then remove it. Spoon off any black bits left in the casserole dish, then add the onion and bacon. Sauté until the bacon has browned and the onion has softened. Preheat the oven to 160°C/Fan 140°C/Gas 3.

Put the pork back in the casserole dish. Pour over enough milk to cover it – probably about a litre – then add the garlic cloves, lemon peel and bay leaves. Leave the casserole dish on a low heat until the milk is close to boiling, then transfer it, uncovered, to the oven.

Cook for 45 minutes, then remove the casserole, turn the meat over and give the sauce a stir, scraping it down from the sides. Put the dish back in the oven and cook for a further 45 minutes – a lovely golden crust will form on top of the sauce. Remove, transfer the pork to a platter and cover it loosely with foil. Leave it to rest.

Skim some of the fat from the sauce in the casserole, then simmer it on a fairly high heat until the liquid has reduced by at least half. Check for seasoning and fish out the bay leaves and lemon peel. Serve the pork thinly sliced, with the sauce spooned over the top.

ROAST LEG OF LAMB WITH ROSEMARY AND GARLIC

Everyone loves roast lamb – it's a real crowd pleaser. A leg of lamb isn't cheap these days, but is well worth cooking every now and then for a treat. We like to stud the meat with little bits of garlic and rosemary, both of which complement the meat's sweet flavour, and roast it on a base of red onions and dried apricots. Lamb and apricots make perfect partners.

SERVES 6–8

1 leg of lamb, around 2.5kg
3 garlic cloves, thinly sliced
a few stems of rosemary, leaves only
1 tbsp olive oil
2 red onions, thinly sliced
100g dried apricots
200ml white wine
flaked sea salt

Remove the lamb from the fridge well before you want to start roasting it so it can come up to room temperature. Make sure you know how much it weighs. Preheat the oven to its highest setting.

Cut deep slits at regular intervals all over the lamb, then stuff the slits with slivers of garlic and rosemary leaves. Rub the leg with olive oil, then season with salt.

Spread the onions and apricots over the base of a roasting tin and place the leg of lamb on top. Pour the wine into the tin, plus the same amount of water.

Roast the lamb for 20 minutes, then reduce the oven temperature to 180°C/Fan 160°C/Gas 4. Roast for 10 minutes per 500g for rare meat, 12 minutes per 500g for medium rare, 15 minutes per 500g for medium or 18 minutes per 500g for well done. The narrower part of the leg will be more well done than the thicker part whatever your timing.

When the meat is cooked to your liking, remove it from the oven and put it on a platter or board. Cover it loosely with foil and leave it to rest for at least 20 minutes. Strain off most of the fat from the roasting tin and serve the lamb with the reheated roasting juices, red onions and apricots. And you'll need some roast potatoes (see p.348) of course.

Any leftovers can be used in a shepherd's pie (see p.331).

RACK OF LAMB WITH A HERB CRUST

The rack is one of the most expensive cuts of lamb, but the meat is so tender and delicious it's worth splashing out once in a while. This looks really impressive too, although it's not difficult to cook. Racks are usually sold French-trimmed, which means that the fat is neatly trimmed off the bones, making the dish look pleasingly cheffy. The meat is best served pink and the crunchy herby crust is a perfect partner.

SERVES 4–5

2 x racks of lamb, French-trimmed
40g fresh white breadcrumbs
3 tbsp chopped fresh parsley
3 tbsp chopped fresh mint leaves
1 tsp chopped fresh rosemary
2 garlic cloves, crushed
1 tbsp Dijon mustard
flaked sea salt
freshly ground black pepper

Preheat the oven to 200°C/Fan 180°C/Gas 6. Heat a large heavy-based frying pan and brown the meat, skin side down, for 5 minutes. Brown the remaining sides, then remove the racks from the pan. Place them in a roasting tin, facing each other, with the bones crossing at their tips.

Mix the breadcrumbs with the herbs and crushed garlic, then stir in a pinch of salt and some black pepper. Brush the skin side of each rack with the mustard and then cover with the breadcrumb mixture, pressing it carefully so it sticks.

Roast the lamb racks in the oven for 25–30 minutes for medium-rare meat. Remove the racks from the oven, cover them loosely with foil and leave to stand for 8–10 minutes. Carve each rack into individual ribs and serve with a red wine gravy (see p.134). Dauphinoise potatoes (see p.349) are just right with this and make for a really fine feast.

SLOW-ROAST SHOULDER OF LAMB

This is a perfect family roast and one that we both love – the meat is cooked for hours until it is melting and the texture and taste is so good. Shoulder is quite a bit cheaper than leg too. Good with roast potatoes – try parboiling them with a pinch of turmeric and adding a sprinkling of nigella seeds when you put them in the roasting tin. This lamb is also great with rice or stuffed into some flatbreads.

SERVES 6–8

1 shoulder of lamb, on
  the bone
1 tbsp olive oil
200ml yoghurt
3 garlic cloves, finely chopped
20g fresh root ginger, grated
2 tbsp mild curry powder
  or garam masala
2 onions, sliced
250ml white wine
250ml chicken stock
small bunch of coriander,
  chopped
squeeze of lemon juice
  (optional)
flaked sea salt

Cut small slits all over the lamb shoulder and put it in a glass or ceramic container, which fits comfortably in the fridge.

Mix the olive oil, yoghurt, garlic, ginger and curry powder or garam masala in a bowl, stir thoroughly and season with salt. Pour the mixture over the lamb, then massage it into the skin and the exposed flesh, pushing it into the slits where possible. Cover the lamb with clingfilm and leave it in the fridge to marinate for at least 2–3 hours, but preferably overnight. If you don't have a container that's the right size, put the meat in a strong plastic bag, add all the marinade ingredients and massage them in well.

Remove the lamb from the fridge and leave it for an hour to come to room temperature. Scrape off any excess marinade, but leave anything that has dried on the joint. Preheat the oven to 220°C/Fan 200°C/Gas 7.

Arrange the onions over the base of a large roasting tin and place the lamb on top. Add the wine and stock. Put the lamb in the preheated oven for 30 minutes until the crust has browned, then reduce the temperature to 150°C/Fan 130°C/Gas 2. Roast for up to 4 hours, checking after 3 to see if the meat is ready – it should be tender and close to falling off the bone.

Remove the lamb from the roasting tin, place it on a board and cover it with foil. Leave it to rest for at least 20 minutes. Put the roasting tin over a low heat and stir, making sure any caramelised bits of meat or onion are well mixed with the cooking liquid. Pour any juices from the resting lamb into the roasting tin too. Taste for seasoning, then add the coriander and a squeeze of lemon juice if you like.

Serve the lamb with the onions and gravy from the roasting tin, with more coriander sprinkled over if you like.

ROAST BREAST OF LAMB WITH CAPER SAUCE

Lamb and capers are brilliant partners and the sauce makes this cheap cut of meat into something delicious. It doesn't look like a lot of meat, but breast of lamb is quite rich so this amount should serve four nicely. A whole breast is very long and hard to fit into a roasting tin. You can cook the meat on the bone, but it's easier to cut and serve if boned. Must be eaten hot.

SERVES 4

2 red onions, sliced into
   thin wedges
large sprig of thyme,
   leaves only
750g boned breast of lamb,
   (or about 1kg with bone)
1 tsp olive oil
flaked sea salt
freshly ground black pepper

Caper sauce
25g butter
25g flour
100ml white wine
300ml chicken or lamb stock
3 tbsp capers, rinsed and
   roughly chopped
squeeze of lemon or a few
   drops of red wine vinegar
   (optional)
freshly ground white pepper

Preheat the oven to 150°C/Fan 130°C/Gas 2. Put the onions in a roasting tin and season them with salt and pepper. Sprinkle over most of the thyme leaves. Rub the breast of lamb with the olive oil and season it with salt and pepper, then put it in the tin on top of the onions.

Roast the lamb for about 1½ hours, until the skin is well browned and much of the fat is rendered. Remove the meat and place it on a board, then cover it with foil and leave it to rest for 10 minutes. Scoop out the onions with a slotted spoon and set them aside, then drain off any liquid and fat from the tin into a jug. Leave it to cool, then strain it and set it aside.

To make the sauce, melt the butter in a saucepan, then add the flour. Stir to make a paste, then continue to cook for a few minutes so the flour loses its raw flavour. Pour in the wine and stir vigorously, then gradually add the stock and the strained cooking liquid, stirring with each addition, until you have a sauce with the consistency of single cream.

Stir in the capers and taste before you season, as capers can be very salty. Add salt if necessary, and lots of white pepper. Add a squeeze of lemon or some red wine vinegar if you think the sauce needs added piquancy. Cut the lamb into strips and serve hot with the onions and sauce and some veg on the side.

POT-ROAST BRISKET

The beauty of a pot-roast is that it's packed with flavour and it's a good way of making a special meal from a cheap cut. This method of cooking always gives you really tender meat and sensational gravy. Choose a well-marbled piece of brisket if you can, as it will be far more succulent than a very lean cut, or you could use silverside. Makes great sandwiches if you have any leftovers.

SERVES 5–6

1.2kg well-marbled beef
   brisket, rolled and tied
4–5 tbsp vegetable oil
4 onions
3 bushy sprigs of thyme
1 large bay leaf
2 tbsp tomato purée
500ml hot beef stock
200ml red wine
4 large carrots, cut into
   3cm chunks
6 celery sticks, cut into
   4cm lengths
flaked sea salt
freshly ground black pepper

Season the beef all over with a teaspoon of salt and lots of black pepper. Heat 2 tablespoons of the oil in a large flameproof casserole dish and brown the beef over a fairly high heat for 8–10 minutes, turning every couple of minutes. Preheat the oven to 160°C/Fan 140°C/Gas 3.

While the beef is frying, thinly slice 2 of the onions. Remove the beef from the casserole dish and set it aside. Add the onions to the dish and fry them for 5 minutes or until nicely browned, stirring regularly. Add a little more oil if the onions begin to stick.

Stir in the thyme and bay leaf and cook for 20–30 seconds more, stirring, then put the beef back in the casserole dish. Stir the tomato purée into the hot beef stock and pour it around the beef. Add the wine and bring it to a gentle simmer on the hob, then cover the dish with a lid and place it in the oven. Cook for 3 hours. After about 1½ hours, take the dish out of the oven and turn the beef. If you press it with a fork, the meat will feel very firm.

While the beef is cooking, cut the remaining onions in half from root to tip and then cut each half into 4 wedges. Heat another tablespoon of oil in a large non-stick frying pan. Fry the onions for 5 minutes, stirring occasionally, then add the carrots and celery and cook for another 5 minutes over a medium heat until the onions are softened and all the vegetables are lightly browned, stirring regularly.

Remove the beef from the oven and take the lid off the casserole. Press the beef with a fork. You should be able to feel that it has become much softer, but if not, put it back in the oven for a further 30 minutes before adding the vegetables.

Turn the beef over and nestle the browned vegetables around it. Cover with the lid again and put the casserole dish back in the oven for another 1–2 hours, or until the beef is very tender and yields completely to the pressure of a spoon.

When the beef is ready, cut off the string and carve the meat into slices. Serve with the poached vegetables and the rich cooking liquor for gravy. Some potato latkes (see p.350) will soak up the juices beautifully. And English mustard is a must with this.

ROAST RIB OF BEEF

Nothing beats roast beef and this is the emperor of roasts. Not cheap, but a real celebration dish. You can anoint it with mustard and this, that and the other, but we think it's best with just a bit of salt. Let the meat speak for itself. Serve with Yorkshire pud (see page 357), some horseradish sauce (see page 344), roast potatoes (see page 348) and lots of good gravy.

SERVES 6–8

1 rib of beef on the bone,
   about 2.5kg (2–3 ribs)
flaked sea salt

Rich red wine gravy
15g butter
2 shallots, finely chopped
a large sprig of thyme
400ml red wine
1 tbsp flour
juices from the roast
up to 400ml additional
   beef stock
1 tsp redcurrant or apple jelly
flaked sea salt
freshly ground black pepper

Remove the rib of beef from the fridge well before you want to start roasting it, so it can come to room temperature. Make sure you know how much the beef weighs. Preheat your oven to its highest setting.

Season the beef with salt, then place it in a large roasting tin. Roast for 20 minutes, then reduce the oven temperature to 180°C/Fan 160°/Gas 4. Roast the beef for a further 13 minutes per 500g for rare meat, 16 minutes per 500g for medium rare, 18 minutes per 500g for medium, and 20 minutes for well done.

Remove the meat from the oven. Put it on a platter or carving board, cover loosely with foil and leave it to rest for 20 minutes. Use the roasting pan juices and any juices from the resting meat to make gravy (see below). Serve with all the trimmings.

Rich red wine gravy
Heat the butter in a small saucepan and add the shallots. Sauté them on a medium heat until golden-brown, then add the thyme and red wine. Bring to the boil and cook until the wine has reduced by half. Leave to infuse with the onion and herbs until you are ready to make the gravy, then strain.

Strain off any liquid from the meat roasting tin and reserve it. Sprinkle over the flour, and stir, scraping up any bits from the bottom of the tin. Pour in the strained wine mixture and stir until smooth, then gradually add the juices from the roast, a drop more wine if needed and the additional stock.

Stir until the tin is clean, then transfer the gravy to a saucepan. Whisk in the redcurrant or apple jelly, then taste for seasoning. Leave to simmer gently until you are ready to serve. This gravy can be used for any roast and you can vary the herbs and other flavourings – for example, use rosemary with lamb.

ROAST BEEF TOPSIDE

Topside makes a lovely roast and is a lot cheaper than rib or sirloin. The larger the piece of topside you want, the harder it is to get one which is the same thickness throughout, but as there's usually someone who wants their meat slightly more done than everyone else, this shouldn't be too much of a problem.

SERVES 6–8

1.5kg piece of topside, tied
2 tsp ground black peppercorns
1 tbsp English mustard powder
1 tsp onion or garlic powder (optional)
1 tsp dried thyme

Gravy
1 tbsp flour
100ml red or white wine
400ml well-flavoured beef stock
1 tsp redcurrant jelly (optional)
flaked sea salt
freshly ground black pepper

Be sure to take the meat out of the fridge at least 45 minutes to an hour before you want to roast it, so it can come up to room temperature. Preheat the oven to its highest setting and note the weight of the meat so you can work out the roasting time.

Mix the peppercorns, mustard powder, onion or garlic powder, if using, and the dried thyme in a small bowl. Sprinkle this mixture over the joint, pressing it in as you go, until the meat is completely covered. Put the beef in a roasting tin, place it in the preheated oven and roast for 15 minutes.

Reduce the oven temperature to 200°C/Fan 180°C/Gas 6. Roast the beef for a further 12 minutes per 500g if you want it rare, 15 minutes per 500g for medium rare, 17 minutes per 500g for medium, and 20 minutes per 500g for well-done meat.

When the beef is cooked to your liking, remove it from the oven. Put the meat on a platter or carving board, cover it with foil and leave it to rest for 20 minutes.

Meanwhile, make the gravy. Strain the contents of the roasting tin into a jug and set it aside for a few minutes – the fat will rise to the top. Put the roasting tin over a low heat. Take a tablespoon of fat from the jug and add it to the roasting tin, then sprinkle in the flour. Stir thoroughly, making sure you scrape up all the sticky bits from the bottom of the tin, as they add flavour.

Pour the wine into the pan and stir continuously. Gradually add the beef stock and the separated pan juices, stirring until you have a nice gravy. Pour the gravy into a small saucepan; the bottom of the roasting tin should look clean.

Leave the gravy on a fairly low heat and add any juices from the resting meat. Season with salt and pepper and if you would like a little sweetness, add a teaspoon of redcurrant jelly.

Carve the beef and serve with veg, Yorkshire pudding (see p.357) and the piping hot gravy.

ROAST HAUNCH OF VENISON WITH QUINCE

Venison is healthy and delicious, and it goes really well with quinces. But you can't always get quinces so we use quince cheese (membrillo), which is available in delis and supermarkets. If you can get fresh quinces as well, even better. Your butcher will bone and roll the meat for you, so it's nice and easy to carve, and just in case you were wondering, haunch just means the back leg.

SERVES AT LEAST 8

2 quinces, peeled and sliced
    into wedges (optional)
juice of ½ lemon
1 tbsp honey
1 tsp juniper berries
1 tsp black peppercorns
2kg venison haunch, boned
    and rolled
6 thick slices of streaky
    unsmoked bacon, stretched
1 tbsp flour
100ml white wine
200ml beef or chicken stock
15g quince cheese
    (membrillo)
15g butter
a few sage leaves
flaked sea salt
freshly ground black pepper

If you're using quinces, put the wedges in a small saucepan with the lemon juice and honey. Cover them with water, then simmer for 25–30 minutes, until they're tender. Strain, reserving the liquid, and set both the quinces and liquid aside.

Preheat the oven to 220°C/Fan 200°C/Gas 7. Crush the juniper berries and black peppercorns and mix them with ½ teaspoon of salt. Rub this mixture over the venison.

Cover the top of the venison with the bacon slices, then put the meat in a roasting tin and roast it in the preheated oven for 20 minutes. Lower the heat to 160°C/Fan 140°C/Gas 3, then cook according to how you like your meat. For rare meat, roast for another 10 minutes per 500g; for medium rare, 12 minutes per 500g; for medium, 15 minutes per 500g.

When the venison is cooked to your liking, take it out of the oven. Remove the meat from the tin, cover it with foil and leave it to rest while you make the gravy and fry the quinces.

Pour off any juices from the roasting tin and set them aside. Place the tin over a medium heat, sprinkle in the flour and stir, scraping up any brown bits on the bottom of the tin.

Pour in the wine, allow it to bubble until it has reduced by half, then pour everything into a small saucepan. Add any reserved juices from the roasting tin, together with any juices from the resting venison, then pour in the stock and a ladle of the reserved quince syrup. Simmer until the gravy is well reduced and starting to turn syrupy, then stir in the quince cheese. Season with salt and pepper.

Melt the butter in a frying pan. Add the quince wedges, season them with pepper and sprinkle with the sage. Fry until both sides are golden-brown and the edges have crisped up a little. Carve the venison and serve with the wedges of quince and the sweet gravy.

CHAPTER FIVE
SLOW COOKING

ROLLED BACON JOINT AND PEASE PUDDING

This is a good old British dish and real comfort food. Split peas and bacon are made for each other and the mustard sauce adds a bit of punch. You'll need a piece of muslin for the pease pud and you can buy this from most kitchen supply shops or online sites. Don't forget to soak the peas overnight before you make this. It's also good made with a piece of gammon.

SERVES 6

1kg smoked or unsmoked
   bacon joint, tied
1 medium onion
4 cloves
1 large carrot, roughly
   chopped
2 celery sticks, roughly
   chopped
2 bay leaves
10 black peppercorns

Pease pudding
50g butter
1 onion, roughly chopped
½ tsp dried thyme
1 bay leaf
300g dried yellow split peas,
   soaked overnight
1 tsp sea salt
½ tsp finely grated nutmeg
1 egg, beaten
freshly ground black pepper

Mustard sauce
25g butter
25g plain flour
300ml stock (from cooking
   the bacon)
1 tsp English mustard
1 tsp wholegrain mustard
5 tbsp single cream

First make the pease pudding. Heat half the butter in a heavy-based frying pan and cook the onion, thyme and bay leaf very gently for 15 minutes, or until softened and only just beginning to colour. Stir regularly. Drain the soaked peas and add them to the pan. Pour in 1 litre of water and bring it to the boil, then reduce the heat slightly and simmer for 30–40 minutes, or until the peas soften and start falling apart. The liquid should be well reduced by this time.

Take the peas off the heat, remove the bay leaf and blitz them to a thick purée with a stick blender or in a food processor. Beat in the remaining butter, then add the nutmeg and the egg. Season with salt and pepper.

Meanwhile, put the bacon joint in a large lidded saucepan and cover it with cold water. Bring the water to the boil then discard it. Cut the onion in half and stud each piece with cloves.

Spoon the pea mixture into the centre of a piece of muslin. Tie the ends tightly with kitchen string just above the peas, allowing a little room for expansion.

Tuck the pease pudding and onion into the pan beside the bacon joint and add the carrot, celery, bay leaves and peppercorns. Add enough cold water to cover the bacon and put the pan back on the hob. Bring to a simmer, cover loosely with a lid and cook for 1–1¼ hours.

Remove the bacon, place it on a board and cover it with foil and a couple of tea towels. Leave it to stand for 10 minutes before carving. Ladle 300ml of the stock into a heatproof jug.

For the mustard sauce, melt the butter in a heavy-based saucepan over a medium heat. Stir in the flour and cook for a few seconds before slowly adding the reserved stock, stirring well between each addition. Bring the sauce to a simmer, stir in the mustard and then the cream. Season to taste.

Carve the bacon into thick slices. Unwrap the pease pudding and serve it with the bacon and the mustard sauce.

TWICE-COOKED PORK (CHAR SIU)

There are countless versions of this popular Chinese dish, but this is a simple way of making it. The pork is simmered first, then fried and served with rice and greens or used in ramen (see page 55). Any leftovers make a tasty base for a stir-fry or a sensational egg-fried rice. Pricking the pork all over allows the sauce to penetrate well and also tenderises the meat nicely.

SERVES 4–6

750g piece of pork loin, skinned, trimmed of fat, and rolled and tied
250ml soy sauce
100ml sake
100ml mirin
50ml hoisin sauce
3 garlic cloves, sliced
30g fresh root ginger, sliced
2 star anise
vegetable oil, for frying
freshly ground black pepper

Prick the pork loin all over with a sharp skewer or needle, then put it in a saucepan. The pork should fit quite snugly, so don't use a pan that's bigger than necessary. Add all the ingredients, except the vegetable oil, and season with black pepper. Pour in water until the pork is just covered – ideally no more than about 500ml. Bring the water to the boil, then turn down the heat and cover the pan. Leave to simmer very gently for a couple of hours, until the pork is tender.

If possible, leave the pork to cool in the liquid, preferably overnight, then remove it, reserving the cooking liquid. Pat the meat dry and wrap it tightly in clingfilm and chill – the wrapping and chilling will help to firm up the meat and make it easier to slice thinly.

To serve, cut the meat into very thin slices. Heat some vegetable oil in a frying pan and fry the slices of pork, ladling in small amounts of the cooking liquid, so it reduces and clings to the slices in a sticky sauce. Serve with greens and steamed rice or noodles. Alternatively, drop the slices – fried or not as you prefer – into ramen broth (see p.55).

PULLED PORK

Pulled pork is eaten in huge quantities all over the southern USA. This is a recipe we perfected while on a visit to Nashville and you can make it without a barbecue. You apply a rub to the meat in the usual way, then slow cook it, but instead of finishing it on the grill you serve it with the reduced cooking liquid. All very easy to do and just as delicious.

SERVES 6–8

1.5–2kg pork shoulder, in 1 or 2 pieces, skinned, but with a reasonable layer of fat
250ml light ale or lager
50g maple syrup
200g tomatoes, roughly chopped
flaked sea salt
freshly ground black pepper

Dry rub

1 tbsp sweet smoked paprika
1 tbsp mustard powder
1 tbsp garlic powder
1 tbsp dried thyme
1 tbsp fennel seeds, roughly crushed
1 tbsp ground black pepper, roughly crushed
2 tbsp salt
2 tbsp soft light brown sugar

To serve

1 tsp vegetable oil
soft white burger buns
coleslaw (see p.355)
hot sauce (optional)

Mix together the rub ingredients, then press this mixture into the pork shoulder until it is completely covered. Leave the meat to stand for an hour or so.

Preheat the oven to 150°C/Fan 130°C/Gas 2. Put the pork in a roasting tin. Mix the beer with the maple syrup and tomatoes, then season with salt and pepper and pour the mixture into the tin around the pork. Cover with foil, put the pork in the oven and cook for about 5 hours. The pork should be very tender by this point, and you should have a well-flavoured gravy in the roasting tin. Remove the tin from the oven and leave the meat to rest for 20 minutes.

Pull the pork apart with 2 forks. You can serve this as it is, but it's also very good lightly fried, with some of the cooking liquid added. To do this, simply heat the vegetable oil in a large frying pan, add a thick layer of the pulled pork and season with salt and pepper.

Gently fry for a few minutes, then ladle over some of the cooking liquid. You will only need a few tablespoons – the idea is to keep the pork moist while the sauce reduces down and helps to caramelise the pork around the edges.

Pile the pork into the buns and serve with coleslaw and some hot sauce if you want to add some heat.

PIG'S CHEEK CASSEROLE

You'll find ready-trimmed pig's cheeks at some supermarkets or at the butcher's (or they can order them in for you) and they're tasty little morsels. They need a good long cook, but they're full of flavour so just right for a casserole like this. We love a bit of cream in a cider sauce once in a while, but if that's too rich for you, leave it out – the sauce will still be good.

SERVES 4

1 tbsp olive oil
15g butter
2 leeks, sliced into rounds
250g chestnut mushrooms, halved
1 tbsp plain flour
1kg pig's cheeks (trimmed weight)
2 bay leaves
a large sprig of thyme
500ml cider
50ml single cream (optional)
flaked sea salt
freshly ground black pepper

Heat the olive oil and butter in a large flameproof casserole dish. Add the leeks and mushrooms, then sauté them on a medium heat until they've taken on a little colour. Be sure not to do this on a lower heat, as you don't want the mushrooms to give out liquid and stew. Remove the leeks and mushrooms from the casserole dish and set them aside.

Turn up the heat. Season the flour with salt and pepper and dust the pig's cheeks, then add them to the casserole and sear on both sides. Tuck in the herbs and pour over the cider. Bring the liquid to the boil, then turn the heat down to a low simmer and cover the casserole. Cook for an hour, then put the mushrooms and leeks back in the casserole and simmer for another 30 minutes.

Add the cream, if using, and simmer, uncovered, for a few more minutes until the sauce has reduced and thickened. Serve with a pile of spring greens and mash (see p.352) to soak up the juices.

PORK CHOPS WITH FENNEL AND LEMON

Fennel goes well with pork and the lemon tops the whole thing off beautifully and makes an awesome sauce. And by the time the lemon slices have been cooked for a long time they taste nice and mellow so are good to eat if you want.

SERVES 4

2 fennel bulbs, trimmed and
   cut into thin wedges
1 tbsp olive oil
150ml white wine
1 tbsp ouzo (optional)
1 lemon, topped, tailed and
   thinly sliced into rounds
4 pork chops, each about
   150–200g
a few fresh thyme or
   oregano leaves, to serve
flaked sea salt
freshly ground black pepper

Preheat the oven to 200°C/Fan 180°C/Gas 6.

Put the wedges of fennel in a roasting tin and drizzle them with the olive oil. Pour over the white wine and ouzo if using, then arrange the lemon slices on top. Season with salt and pepper, then sprinkle over the thyme leaves and cover the tin with foil.

Bake in the preheated oven for 45 minutes. By this point the fennel and lemon should be very tender and there should be a well-flavoured sauce in the tin.

Turn the oven up to 220°C/Fan 200°C/Gas 7. Put the pork chops on top of the fennel and lemon, then season with salt and pepper. Put the tin back in the oven, uncovered, and bake for 20 minutes, until the chops are browned. Check with a probe thermometer if you have one – the interior temperature should read 62°C, but if it's just under you can remove the tin from the oven as the pork will continue to cook while it is resting. If you don't have a probe thermometer, insert a skewer into the centre. Hold it for 10 seconds, then take it out and lightly touch the end – it should feel hot.

Put the chops on a board or a warm plate, cover with foil and leave them to rest for 10 minutes. Serve the chops with the fennel and lemon and any juices from the roasting tin and scatter with thyme or oregano leaves. Some new potatoes are a great finishing touch.

PORK OSSO BUCO

Osso buco is so Italian that serving it is like having Pavarotti round to dinner. The classic version is made with veal shin bones – the name literally means hollow bones, or something along those lines. But we think it's just as good with pork shin and this is a lot cheaper than veal. Some supermarkets sell pork osso buco or you can order it from your butcher. Gremolata is a tasty Italian garnish, made from lemon zest, parsley and garlic.

SERVES 4

4 pieces of pork osso buco
    (pork shin), about 1kg
flour, for sprinkling
4 tbsp olive oil
1 onion, finely chopped
2 carrots, finely chopped
2 celery sticks, finely
    chopped
2 garlic cloves, finely
    chopped
grated zest of 1 lemon
a sprig of rosemary
250ml white wine
150ml veal or chicken stock
flaked sea salt
freshly ground black pepper

Gremolata
grated zest of 1 lemon
2 tbsp finely chopped
    parsley
1 garlic clove, finely chopped

Season the pieces of osso buco with salt and pepper, then dust them with flour, making sure you pat off any excess.

Heat 2 tablespoons of the olive oil in a frying pan large enough to hold the meat in a single layer. When the oil is hot (the first piece of meat should sizzle when you add it), sear the meat on all sides, then set it aside on a plate.

Heat the remaining olive oil in a large flameproof casserole dish, preferably one large enough to hold the meat in a single layer. Add the onion, carrots and celery, then sauté the vegetables until they've taken on some colour and started to soften – about 6–7 minutes. Add the garlic, lemon zest and rosemary and cook for a further minute, then place the pieces of meat on top.

Deglaze the frying pan with the wine, allowing it to bubble furiously and scraping up any sticky bits, then pour the wine over the contents of the casserole. Add the stock. Bring to the boil, then turn the heat down and simmer gently for 1½–2 hours, until the meat is tender and has started to come away from the bone. Keep an eye on the liquid during the cooking time and add a little extra if necessary.

To make the gremolata, mix together the lemon zest, parsley and garlic and sprinkle it over the osso buco when serving. Risotto alla Milanese (see p.356) is the ideal – and traditional – accompaniment.

BIGOS

The national dish of Poland, bigos is a beautifully rich casserole that can be made with any kind of meat, but always contains some spicy Polish sausage. In Poland, everyone has their own favourite recipe for bigos and many say it's best made in advance and reheated when serving. We think it tastes pretty good the first day, but if you want a good 'prepare ahead' dish, this is it.

SERVES 4–6

50g butter
1 onion, sliced
1 tsp juniper berries, crushed
½ tsp caraway seeds
300g pork belly or 500g pork ribs, cut into pieces
1 tbsp brown sugar
500g sauerkraut
200g fresh or canned tomatoes, chopped
½ white cabbage, shredded
500ml chicken or beef stock
10g dried mushrooms
300g smoked Polish sausage, such as kabanos
1 eating apple, grated
flaked sea salt
freshly ground black pepper

Melt the butter in a large flameproof casserole dish. Add the onion and fry it gently over a medium heat until it's softened and translucent. Sprinkle over the juniper berries and caraway seeds, then add the pork. Turn the meat to coat it with the spices, then sprinkle over the brown sugar. Increase the heat for a couple of minutes to brown the meat, turning it to colour on all sides.

Drain the sauerkraut well and give it a rinse if you want to lessen the vinegary flavour. Squeeze it with your hands to get rid of any excess liquid. Add the sauerkraut to the onion and meat, along with the white cabbage and the tomatoes, then pour over the stock. Simmer for about 30 minutes.

Soak the dried mushrooms in some warm water. When they have softened, drain them and add their soaking liquor to the casserole. Chop the mushrooms finely and add them too, together with the sausage and the grated apple. Simmer for a further 1½ hours. Check the seasoning and add salt and pepper to taste.

If preparing the bigos ahead, allow it cool, then refrigerate overnight. Reheat it for an hour the following day and again the day after that. Then eat! Baked potatoes or mash are good accompaniments.

BBQ SPARE RIBS

Everyone's favourite barbecue dish, spare ribs can be cooked in the oven if that's easier for you and they still taste epic. The meat gets really sticky and gorgeous and falls off the bone into your mouth. Bring it on.

SERVES 4

2kg rindless, well-trimmed pork spare ribs

Rub
25g soft light brown sugar
2 tbsp paprika
1 tbsp sea salt
2 tsp cayenne pepper
2 tsp mustard powder
2 tsp black pepper
2 tsp oregano

Barbecue sauce
200ml ketchup
75ml cider vinegar
100g soft light brown sugar
2 tbsp clear honey
2 tbsp Worcestershire sauce
3 garlic cloves, crushed

To make the rub, mix all the ingredients in a bowl. Take 3 tablespoons of the mixture and put them in a medium saucepan to use in the barbecue sauce later.

Put the pork on a board and rub both sides with the remaining dry rub, massaging it into the meat. Place the pork on a low metal rack in a large roasting tin and leave it to stand for 1 hour, or overnight if you have time.

Preheat the oven to 160°C/Fan 140°C/Gas 3. Add 100ml cold water to the roasting tin and cook the pork in the oven for 3 hours or until it's very soft and tender – the meat should be almost falling off the bones. Turn the ribs every hour and add a little extra water if the base of the pan becomes dry to prevent the pork sticking and burning. Cover the ribs with a piece of foil if they begin to dry out.

Meanwhile, make the barbecue sauce. Add all the ingredients to the pan containing the reserved dry rub and stir in 100ml of water. Place the pan over a medium heat and bring the mixture to the boil, stirring. Reduce the heat slightly and simmer for 5 minutes or until the sauce has thickened, stirring regularly. Remove the pan from the heat and pass the sauce through a sieve into a bowl to get rid of the garlic that might otherwise burn. Pour about half the sauce into a serving dish and set it aside. Leave the rest in the bowl.

Take the pork out of the oven and use a pastry brush to brush it liberally on both sides with the barbecue sauce. Put the ribs back in the oven and continue to cook for 45 minutes. The idea is to get a thick, sweet, smoky coating on the pork. Leave the ribs to rest for 10 minutes, then carve and serve with the reserved barbecue sauce for dipping or drizzling.

To cook on a barbecue
Cook the pork for 3 hours in the oven as above, then about 45 minutes before it's due to be ready, prepare the barbecue. Brush the pork with sauce, place it on the grill and cook over a low heat for 20–30 minutes, turning and brushing with more of the barbecue sauce every 5–8 minutes as it cooks.

Don't leave the pork for a minute or the marinade could burn, and be prepared to move the rack up if the coating starts catching.

LAMB WITH SPRING VEGETABLES

Cooked more briefly than many of the recipes in this chapter, this braised lamb dish has a lovely golden broth and is packed with vegetables, which should stay fresh and green. It will put a spring in your step. We've suggested lamb neck fillet, but some diced lamb shoulder would work very well too.

SERVES 4

1 tbsp olive oil
750g lamb neck fillet, cut diagonally into 2cm thick slices
10g butter
1 onion, finely chopped
250ml white wine
250ml lamb or chicken stock
a sprig each of rosemary, mint and parsley
8 baby or chantenay carrots
1 large fennel bulb
4 baby turnips, halved lengthways
1 large courgette
2 leeks
200g sprouting broccoli, trimmed
100g broad beans or peas, fresh or frozen
chopped parsley leaves, to garnish
shredded mint leaves, to garnish
flaked sea salt
freshly ground black pepper

Heat the olive oil in a large flameproof casserole dish. Add the lamb and sear it on all sides, then remove it with a slotted spoon and set it aside.

Turn down the heat and add the butter to the casserole. When it has melted, add the onion and cook for a few minutes until it has softened without taking on any colour. Put the lamb back in the casserole dish and season it with salt and pepper.

Turn the heat up a little, then pour in the wine and the stock. Allow the liquid to bubble, then add the herbs. Bring to the boil, then cover the casserole, turn the heat down to a low simmer and cook for 45 minutes.

Meanwhile prepare the vegetables. Peel the carrots and cut them in half lengthways. Trim the fennel bulb and cut it into wedges. Cut the baby turnips in half and cut the courgette and leeks into diagonal slices.

Once the lamb has simmered for 45 minutes, add the carrots, fennel and turnips and simmer for another 10 minutes. Add the leeks, then 5 minutes later add the courgette, sprouting broccoli and broad beans or peas. Continue to simmer until the meat and all the vegetables are tender – at least another 5 minutes.

Serve garnished with parsley and mint leaves.

LANCASHIRE SAUSAGE HOTPOT

We've already given you our classic lamb hotpot in *Perfect Pies*, so we've been racking our brains as to what to do here – we knew our meat book wouldn't be complete without a hotpot. Dave would be drummed out of Lancashire. Then we came up with this idea and it really works. You're going to love it, we promise, and it'll become part of your family repertoire.

SERVES 4–6

1 tbsp vegetable oil
600g sausages
2 onions, thinly sliced
1 tbsp flour
750ml beef or chicken stock
1 bay leaf
2 sprigs thyme or
  1 tsp rubbed sage
a good dash of
  Worcestershire sauce
butter, for greasing
  and dotting
1kg floury potatoes,
  thinly sliced
250g black pudding, peeled
  and cut into slices
flaked sea salt
freshly ground black pepper

Preheat the oven to 180°C/Fan 160°C/Gas 4. Heat the oil in a large frying pan. Skin the sausages, break each one into a couple of pieces and flatten them slightly into little patties. Fry the sausage patties for a couple of minutes on each side until seared, then remove them and set them aside on a plate.

Add the onions to the frying pan with a pinch of salt and a splash of water. Fry them until they're starting to soften – a few minutes – then sprinkle over the flour. Stir until the onions are completely coated with the flour. Add the stock, together with the herbs and Worcestershire sauce, and simmer until the liquid has thickened.

Grease a large casserole dish with some butter. Divide the potatoes into 3 batches and arrange the first batch in the base of the casserole. Season them with salt and pepper, then add half the sausages and half the black pudding. Pour over half the gravy.

Arrange a second layer of potatoes over the sausages and black pudding, season again, then add the remaining sausage, black pudding and stock. Top with a last layer of potatoes, then dot with butter. Press down each layer to get rid of any gaps.

Put the lid on the casserole dish and cook the hotpot in the preheated oven for an hour. Remove the lid and cook for a further 30 minutes until the potatoes on the top are crisp and golden. Good served with some spring greens.

LAMB SHANKS WITH FLAGEOLET BEANS

We love a lamb shank and they love flageolets – small pale green dried beans that have a fine flavour. Put them together with herbs, spices, veg and stock and you have a supper to relish – everyone has their own mini-joint. This does need a long cooking time, but it's not much trouble to prepare and it's well worth it. The shanks are done when the meat has shrunk well back from the bone.

SERVES 4

300g dried flageolet beans,
 soaked in water overnight
2 tbsp olive oil
4 lamb shanks
1 large onion, finely chopped
2 carrots, finely chopped
1 fennel bulb, finely chopped
4 garlic cloves, finely
 chopped
a few sprigs of thyme
1 red chilli, finely chopped
1 tsp sweet smoked paprika
1 bay leaf
1 tbsp tomato purée
1 small tin of anchovies,
 drained and diced
250ml white wine
1 litre lamb or chicken stock
 or water
250ml white wine
4 ripe tomatoes, peeled
 and deseeded
finely chopped parsley,
 to garnish
flaked sea salt
freshly ground black pepper

Put the soaked flageolet beans in a large saucepan and cover them with fresh water. Bring to the boil and cook for 10 minutes. Remove the pan from heat and leave the beans in the water until needed.

Heat the oil in a large flameproof casserole dish, brown the lamb shanks on all sides, then remove them from the pan and set them aside. Add the onion, carrots and fennel to the dish and cook them over a medium heat for about 10 minutes until they're browning round the edges.

Add the garlic, thyme, chilli, smoked paprika and bay leaf and stir, then add the tomato purée and anchovies. Stir again, then pour in the white wine. Bring to the boil, then reduce by half.

Return the lamb shanks to the casserole. Drain the flageolet beans and add them too, then pour over the stock or water. Bring the liquid to the boil, then put a lid on the casserole dish and place it in the oven. Cook for 1½ hours, then add the tomatoes and season with salt and pepper. Cook for another 1–1½ hours until the beans and lamb are very tender.

The sauce should be quite well reduced, as the beans will soak up liquid and release starch. If you want to reduce the sauce further, boil it on the hob for a few minutes. This is a complete meal in itself, but a salad to follow is nice.

Tip
If you forget to soak your beans, try boiling them unsoaked for 5 minutes, then leave them to stand for an hour. That should give the same effect.

LAMB TAGINE

A tagine is a North African stew, usually containing some dried fruit and lots of spices. If you like yours hot, hot, hot you could add a teaspoon of cayenne or hot chilli or a spoonful of harissa paste with the other spices. Be careful with the rose water, as it varies a lot in strength. It's best to add a little at a time until you get the flavour you like.

SERVES 4–6

2 tbsp olive oil
1kg lamb neck fillet or boned shoulder of lamb, cut into thick 5cm chunks
2 onions, cut into thin wedges
2 garlic cloves, finely chopped
2 tsp ground cumin
1 tbsp ground coriander
½ tsp cinnamon
½ tsp ground allspice
½ tsp ground cardamom
½ tsp turmeric
½ tsp ground ginger
600ml chicken stock or water
large pinch of saffron, soaked in a little warm water
100g apricots or prunes
1 tbsp pomegranate molasses
½–1 tsp rose water
small bunches of parsley and mint, finely chopped (optional)
flaked sea salt
freshly ground black pepper

Heat the olive oil in a large flameproof casserole dish or a tagine dish. When the oil is hot, add the lamb pieces – they should start sizzling as soon as they hit the oil – and quickly sear them on all sides. It's probably best to do this in batches so you don't overcrowd the pan. Remove the lamb from the casserole as it's browned and set it aside.

Add the onions and fry them on a medium heat until they are starting to brown, then add the garlic and all the spices. Stir to coat the onion wedges in spice, then pour in the stock or water, and add the saffron, apricots and pomegranate molasses. Season with salt and pepper.

Put the lamb back into the dish. Bring the liquid to the boil, then turn down the heat to a simmer and cover. Cook the tagine on the hob for about 1½ hours, turning the lamb every so often, until the meat is really tender. Remove the lamb and keep it warm.

Reduce the remaining liquid until it thickens slightly, then add the rose water a few drops at a time, until the flavour is to your liking. Garnish with parsley and mint if using.

This is traditionally served with bread, but we like some couscous with lots of herbs and pomegranate seeds.

TURKISH LAMB PILAF

Rice, spice and lamb – what more could you want? You've got to love a good pilaf. This makes a beautiful one-pot meal with the yoghurt dip on the side and perhaps a green salad. Sumac is a lemony-flavoured spice popular in Middle Eastern cooking and it's available in supermarkets now. Use large golden sultanas if you can find them.

SERVES 6–8

1 tbsp olive oil
600g lean lamb (leg is good), diced into 2cm pieces
½ tsp black peppercorns
½ tsp allspice berries
4 cloves
½ cinnamon stick
a large pinch saffron, soaked in a little warm water
500ml chicken stock or water
15g butter
1 large onion, sliced vertically into thin strips
500g long-grain rice, rinsed and soaked for 30 minutes in warm water
100g sultanas, soaked with the rice
50g pine nuts
a small bunch of fresh mint or dill leaves
flaked sea salt

Yoghurt dip (cacik)
300ml Greek yoghurt
½ cucumber, peeled and deseeded
1 tsp dried mint
pinch of sumac

Heat the olive oil in a large flameproof casserole dish, then add the lamb and sear it on all sides.

Lightly crush the peppercorns, allspice berries and cloves in a pestle and mortar and sprinkle them over the lamb. Stir for a minute or two, then add the cinnamon stick and the saffron with its soaking water. Pour over the stock or water and season with salt. Bring to the boil, then turn the heat down to a simmer. Put a lid on the casserole dish and cook for about an hour, until the lamb is tender.

Remove the lamb from the casserole with a slotted spoon and set it aside, then drain off the cooking liquid into a measuring jug. Top this liquid up to 1 litre with water (or more chicken stock if you prefer) and set it aside. Wipe out the casserole, then add the butter and melt it over a medium heat. Add the onion, and cook it for about 10 minutes until golden-brown. Stir regularly so the strips of onion colour evenly.

Put the lamb back in the dish, shredding it into pieces if you like. Drain the rice and sultanas and add them too. Stir to coat the rice in the juices from the onions and pour in the topped-up cooking liquid.

Bring to the boil, then turn down the heat and put the lid on the dish. Simmer for 20 minutes, until the rice is cooked and has absorbed all the liquid, then remove the casserole dish from the heat. Take off the lid, put a folded tea towel over the casserole, then replace the lid. Leave the pilaf to stand for another 15 minutes, during which time the rice will become fluffier.

Meanwhile, toast the pine nuts in a dry frying pan for a couple of minutes, until light golden-brown.

To serve, pile the pilaf on to a warm platter. If a crust has formed on the bottom of the casserole, try to peel this off in one piece and serve it on the side – this is the 'tahdig', considered a special treat and usually served to honoured guests. Sprinkle the pilaf with the pine nuts and freshly chopped mint and serve with a refreshing bowl of yoghurt dip.

Yoghurt dip (cacik)
Put the yoghurt in a bowl. Coarsely grate the cucumber and strain it through a sieve, or wring it out in a clean tea towel to remove as much water as possible. Stir the cucumber and dried mint into the yoghurt, then season with salt and pepper and a pinch of sumac.

RABBIT WITH PRUNES AND MUSTARD

Rabbit is readily available now in butchers and supermarkets and it's a good healthy meat. We love this hearty dish that teams rabbit with prunes and tangy mustard. You can buy the rabbit skinned and jointed if the thought of cooking bunny worries you.

SERVES 4–6

200g ready-to-eat
  pitted prunes
6 tbsp brandy
50g butter
1 tbsp vegetable oil
2 rabbits, each jointed
  into 6 portions
8 rashers streaky bacon,
  cut into 2cm pieces
2 large long shallots, sliced
  lengthways
2 tbsp plain flour
200ml white wine or cider
500ml chicken stock
1 tbsp Dijon mustard
2 tsp wholegrain mustard
1 bay leaf
1 small bunch fresh thyme
100ml double cream
flaked sea salt
freshly ground black pepper

Put the prunes in a small saucepan and pour the brandy over them. Bring the brandy to a simmer over a medium heat, turning the prunes regularly, then set them aside to cool. Preheat the oven to 180°C/Fan 160°C/Gas 4.

Melt half the butter with the oil in a large non-stick frying pan. Season the rabbit portions on all sides with salt and black pepper, then fry them until golden-brown, turning occasionally. It's best to do this in 2 or 3 batches so you don't overcrowd the pan. Transfer the browned rabbit portions to a large flameproof casserole dish.

Fry the bacon pieces in the same frying pan for 4–5 minutes or until the fat is crisp, adding a little extra oil if necessary, then scatter them over the rabbit. Melt the remaining butter in the pan and gently fry the shallots for 5–6 minutes or until softened, stirring regularly.

Stir the flour into the pan with the shallots and cook for a few seconds before slowly adding the wine and half the stock, stirring continuously until the sauce thickens. Add the mustard, bay leaf and thyme. Bring to a gentle simmer and season with a little salt and plenty of ground black pepper. Pour all this over the rabbit and bacon in the casserole dish, then stir in the remaining stock and bring everything to a simmer.

Remove the casserole dish from the heat, cover the surface with a sheet of greaseproof paper and put the lid on. Place the casserole in the oven and cook for 1¼–2 hours, or until tender. The meat should be starting to fall off the bone when the rabbit is ready.

When the rabbit is tender, put the casserole dish back on the hob, remove the lid and stir in the cream and the prunes and brandy. Simmer gently for a few minutes until the prunes are hot, stirring carefully so the rabbit doesn't completely fall apart. Adjust the seasoning to taste and serve with some rice or mash to soak up all those creamy juices.

BLANQUETTE DE VEAU

Nearly every French bistro has blanquette de veau – a sort of veal stew – on its menu from time to time. The meat in this much-loved dish is not browned so it stays creamy white and the liquid is finished with a roux of egg yolks and cream. Some purists even discourage the addition of carrots, which are thought to disrupt the pure appearance, but we like a splash of colour.

SERVES 4–6

1kg rose veal shoulder, cut into 4cm chunks
½ tsp sea salt
1 bay leaf
a few sprigs of parsley
a sprig of thyme
a few white peppercorns
2 cloves
1 blade of mace (optional)
200ml white wine
1 leek, cut into chunks
1 carrot, cut into chunks
1 celery stick, sliced
2 garlic cloves, lightly flattened and left whole
15g butter
12 small button onions, peeled
12 baby carrots, peeled
400g button mushrooms, halved if large
150ml double cream
2 egg yolks
60g crème fraiche

Put the chunks of veal in a large saucepan or a flameproof casserole dish and cover them with 1.5 litres of water. Add ½ teaspoon of salt. Bring to the boil, then turn down the heat very slightly so the liquid is still bubbling, rather than gently simmering. Skim off any mushroom-coloured foam that collects on the surface and once this foam has turned completely white, reduce the heat to a gentle simmer.

Loosely wrap the herbs, peppercorns and spices in a piece of muslin and tie it firmly. Add this to the pot together with the wine, leek, carrot, celery and garlic. Simmer gently for about 1½ hours or until the veal is tender – it may take slightly longer depending on your meat. Check the water level in the pot regularly and top it up if necessary. The contents of the pan should be completely covered at all times.

Meanwhile, heat the butter in a lidded frying pan. Add the button onions with a pinch of salt and a ladleful of the cooking liquid from the veal. Cover and simmer for 10 minutes, then add the baby carrots and mushrooms. Cook for a further 10 minutes or until they are tender.

Strain the veal, discarding the leek, carrot, celery and garlic and the bag of herbs and spices, but reserving the liquid. Strain the button onions, baby carrots and mushrooms too and reserve the liquid. To keep the vegetables and veal warm, put them back in the original pan with a splash of the cooking liquid and set them aside.

Pour both the reserved cooking liquids into a saucepan, bring to the boil and reduce to half their original volume. Turn the heat down to a simmer, add the double cream and simmer gently for 5 minutes. Whisk together the egg yolks and crème fraiche in a bowl. Gradually pour in a small ladleful of the cooking liquid, whisking constantly, then slowly pour this mixture into the saucepan. Place the pan on a low heat and whisk until the sauce has thickened slightly and coats the back of a spoon.

Add the button onions, baby carrots, mushrooms and veal to the cream sauce and cook very gently until everything is heated through. Be careful not to let the liquid boil at this stage. Serve with some plain rice and perhaps some greens.

BRAISED FEATHER BLADE BEEF

This is a pretty fancy dish and although it's in the oven for hours it's not hard to prepare. Serve it up for guests and we're sure they will be dead impressed. Feather blade comes from the shoulder of the animal and has a wonderful flavour but is not expensive so is ideal for casseroles and braises.

SERVES 4

1kg feather blade steak,
  trimmed and cut into
  250g pieces
3 tbsp vegetable oil
3 banana shallots or
  1 medium onion, sliced
2 celery sticks, trimmed,
  sliced
2 carrots, thickly sliced
2 garlic cloves, crushed
250ml red wine
500ml beef stock
2 tbsp tomato purée
4–5 sprigs fresh thyme
1 bay leaf
1 tsp English mustard
flaked sea salt
freshly ground black pepper

Preheat the oven to 160°C/Fan 140°C/Gas 3.

Season the steak with salt and lots of black pepper. Heat a tablespoon of the oil in a large heavy-based frying pan and fry the steak pieces over a medium-high heat for 2–3 minutes on each side, or until browned. Do this in batches so you don't overcrowd the pan, transferring each batch of browned meat to a flameproof casserole dish.

Put the frying pan back on the hob and turn down the heat. Add the remaining oil and gently fry the shallots, celery and carrots for 6–8 minutes or until golden-brown and softened. Stir in the garlic, cook for a further minute, then tip everything into the casserole dish.

Deglaze the pan with wine and let it bubble for a few seconds, stirring continuously to scrape up all the sticky bits, then pour this over the meat and vegetables. Put the casserole dish on the hob, stir in the stock and the tomato purée, then add the thyme, bay leaf and mustard and stir until well combined. Bring to the boil and remove the casserole dish from the heat.

Place a piece of greaseproof paper over the meat and liquid, then put the lid on the casserole dish. Cook in the preheated oven for 3–3½ hours or until the meat is really tender.

Take the casserole out of the oven and transfer the meat to a plate. Strain the cooking liquor and vegetables through a sieve into a large non-stick frying pan. Press the vegetables with the bottom of a ladle to extract a rich purée and stir this into the cooking liquor. Add salt and black pepper to taste.

Bring the mixture to a simmer for 3–5 minutes, or until the sauce is well reduced, thick and glossy. Add the steak to the liquid and heat it through for 3–4 minutes, spooning over the sauce to glaze. Serve with some green vegetables and mashed potatoes (see p.352).

BEEF BOURGUIGNON

Another French classic, this needs good-quality meat that's well marbled with fat for the best results. Lean meat will tend to become dry rather than succulent during the long cooking. This has been a go-to favourite of ours for many years and will be for many more years to come.

SERVES 6

1.6kg good-quality braising
  steak (such as chuck)
4–5 tbsp vegetable oil
200g smoked bacon lardons
  or smoked streaky bacon,
  cut into 2cm pieces
1 large onion, finely chopped
2 garlic cloves, crushed
750ml red wine
2 tbsp tomato purée
150ml beef stock
2 large bay leaves
3 bushy sprigs thyme
450g button onions,
  or 24 baby onions,
  unpeeled
25g butter
300g button chestnut
  mushrooms, wiped and
  halved or quartered if large
2 heaped tbsp cornflour
2 tbsp cold water
flaked sea salt
freshly ground black pepper

Cut the steak into chunky pieces, each about 4–5cm, trimming off any really hard fat or sinew. Season with salt and black pepper.

Heat 2 tablespoons of the oil in a large frying pan. Fry the steak in batches over a medium-high heat until it's nicely browned on all sides, turning every now and then and adding more oil if necessary. As soon as the meat is browned, transfer it to a large flameproof casserole dish. Preheat the oven to 160°C/Fan 140°C/Gas 3.

Pour a little more oil into the frying pan and cook the bacon for 2–3 minutes, or until the fat crisps and browns. Scatter the bacon over the steak. Add a touch more oil to the pan and fry the chopped onion over a low heat for 5–6 minutes, stirring often until softened. Stir the garlic into the pan and cook for a minute more.

Add the onion and garlic to the casserole dish with the meat and pour in the wine. Stir in the tomato purée, stock and herbs and bring to a simmer. Stir well, cover with a lid and put the casserole dish in the oven. Cook for 1½–1¾ hours, or until the beef is almost completely tender.

While the beef is cooking, put the button or baby onions in a heatproof bowl and cover them with just-boiled water. Leave them for 5 minutes and then drain and plunge them into a bowl of cold water. When the onions are cool enough to handle, trim off the root and the skins will peel off easily.

A few minutes before the beef is ready, melt half the butter in a large non-stick frying pan with a touch of oil and fry the onions over a medium heat for about 5 minutes, or until golden-brown. Tip them into a bowl. Add the remaining butter to the pan and cook the mushrooms for 2–3 minutes over a fairly high heat until golden-brown, turning often. Mix the cornflour with the water in a small bowl until smooth.

Remove the casserole from the oven and stir in the cornflour mixture, then the onions and mushrooms. Put the casserole back in the oven and cook for 45 minutes more, or until the beef is meltingly tender and the sauce is thick enough to coat the back of a spoon. If the sauce seems thin, add a touch more cornflour, blended with a little cold water, and simmer for a couple of minutes on the hob. Some little new potatoes would be good with this and perhaps a salad on the side.

CORNED BEEF

Home-made corned beef is so different from the canned stuff and we have fond memories of eating it as kids. We used to wonder about the name and apparently the beef was originally preserved with large grains or 'corns' of salt. It's awesome hot, and you can treat yourself to a hash (see page 337) or a Reuben's sandwich (see page 339) with the leftovers. What's not to like? This recipe makes loads, but you can cut the meat into chunks and freeze it.

SERVES 10–12

2.5kg beef brisket
 or silverside
1 onion, sliced
2 carrots, sliced
2 celery sticks, cut into
 chunks
2 garlic cloves, thinly sliced
a sprig of thyme
2 bay leaves

Pickling spice
1 cinnamon stick
2 blades of mace
4 cloves
2 tsp mustard seeds
1 tsp black peppercorns
1 tsp allspice berries
4 bay leaves
1 tsp ground ginger

Brine mixture
300g table salt
200g soft light brown sugar
20g Prague powder #1
 (see tip)
pickling spice (as above)

First make the pickling spice. Toast the whole spices and bay leaves very lightly in a dry frying pan. Cool them immediately, then crush them lightly – you don't want a powder, but you do want to break them up very slightly. Sprinkle in the ground ginger and mix everything together thoroughly.

For the brine mixture, put 2.5 litres of water into a large saucepan and add the salt, sugar, Prague powder and pickling spice. Bring the water to the boil and stir until the salt and sugar have dissolved. Leave to cool.

Put the beef in a large glass, plastic or ceramic container with a lid, or a large, sealable freezer bag. Pour the brine mixture over the brisket and cover with a lid, or seal if using a bag, then place in the fridge. Leave it for 10 days, turning it daily and making sure the meat is completely covered in the brine.

When you're ready to cook the beef, remove it from the brine and throw the brine away. Rinse the meat thoroughly with cold water. Put it into a large saucepan or flameproof casserole dish, cover with water, then add the onion, carrots, celery, garlic and herbs. Bring to the boil, then turn the heat down, cover the pan and leave the beef to simmer very gently for 3–4 hours. The meat is ready when it is very, very tender.

Remove the meat from the cooking liquor and leave it to rest on a board. It can be eaten hot, cut into slices, or chilled and shredded, and it's good served with potato salad (see p.352) and coleslaw (see p.355).

Tip
You can order Prague powder #1 from online suppliers. It's a mix of sodium nitrite and table salt and helps to keep the meat nice and pink, with a springy texture.

BEEF IN GUINNESS WITH HORSERADISH DUMPLINGS

Si's mum made the best dumplings ever and we both copy her method. There's no better place for these little beauties than in a good rib-sticking beef and Guinness stew. Make and enjoy. By the way, you can also use ox cheeks for this, which will make it a much cheaper dish.

SERVES 4–6

2 tbsp plain flour
1kg braising steak, diced
2 tbsp beef dripping or
    vegetable oil
2 onions, thickly sliced
3 large carrots, cut into
    chunks, diagonally
3 celery sticks, cut into
    chunks
200g celeriac, cut into
    chunks
a large sprig of thyme
2 bay leaves
500ml Guinness or stout
flaked sea salt
freshly ground black pepper

Dumplings
250g self-raising flour
125g suet
1 tsp baking powder
1–2 tbsp freshly grated
    horseradish (or horseradish
    sauce)

Season the flour with black pepper and some salt. Toss the beef in the flour, dusting it off thoroughly.

Heat the dripping or oil in a large flameproof casserole dish and brown the steak thoroughly in batches. Remove each batch with a slotted spoon and set it aside. Once all the beef is browned, add the onions, carrots, celery and celeriac and fry them on a fairly high heat until they take on some colour.

Put the beef back in the casserole dish, tuck in the herbs and pour over the Guinness or stout. Bring to the boil, then turn down the heat, cover the casserole dish with a lid and simmer very gently for 1½ hours.

To make the dumplings, mix the flour, suet and baking powder, and season with salt and pepper. Add the horseradish, then gradually add cold water – probably 100–125ml – stirring it in with a knife until you have a soft sloppy mixture. Drop small handfuls of dough on top of the stew and then simmer for 20–25 minutes until the dumplings are well risen and firm.

Alternatively, after adding the dumplings, you can finish cooking this dish in the oven. Preheat the oven to 200°C/Fan 180°C/Gas 6. Bake, with the lid on, for 10 minutes, then remove the lid and cook for another 10–15 minutes until the dumplings are nicely browned.

Serve with some green veg and you have the perfect supper.

BEEF AND APPLE TAGINE

Apple, honey and dried prunes add that moreish flavour to this tagine. We first ate it in Marrakesh and loved it so much that we came home and cooked our own version. It's proof that pork is not the only partner for apples.

SERVES 6

750g chuck steak
4 tbsp vegetable oil
2 onions, halved and sliced
2 garlic cloves, finely
    chopped
2 tsp ground cumin
2 tsp ground coriander
1 tsp hot chilli powder
350ml beef stock
400g can chopped tomatoes
400g can chickpeas, drained
    and rinsed
3 tbsp clear honey
1 cinnamon stick
1 sweet potato (about 400g)
2 large eating apples
25g bunch fresh coriander
75g no-soak dried prunes,
    halved
flaked sea salt
freshly ground black pepper

Garnish

1 large red-skinned
    eating apple
15g butter
1 tbsp clear honey

Trim any hard fat from the beef and cut it into chunks of about 3cm. Season it all over with salt and pepper. Heat a tablespoon of the oil in a large non-stick frying pan and fry the beef over a high heat until lightly browned on all sides, adding a little more oil to the pan when needed. It's best to do this in several batches, transferring each batch to a large flameproof casserole once browned.

Reduce the heat and add 2 more tablespoons of oil to the frying pan. Fry the onions for 5 minutes, or until softened and lightly coloured, stirring regularly. Add the garlic and sprinkle with the cumin, coriander and chilli powder. Cook for 1–2 minutes more, stirring continuously. Preheat the oven to 180°C/Fan 160°C/Gas 4.

Tip the onions and spices into the casserole with the beef. Stir 150ml of cold water into the frying pan and stir vigorously to lift the sticky bits from the bottom. Pour this into the casserole dish.

Add the beef stock, tomatoes and chickpeas to the casserole dish, then the honey and the cinnamon stick and stir well. Bring everything to a simmer on the hob, stirring a couple of times. Cover the dish with a lid, put it in the preheated oven and cook for 1½ hours.

Ten minutes before the 1½ hours is up, cut the sweet potato into chunks of about 2.5cm. Cut the apples into 2cm chunks. Trim the coriander and roughly chop half the leaves.

Take the casserole out of the oven, remove the lid and stir in the sweet potato, apples, prunes and chopped coriander. Cover again and put the casserole back in the oven for another 45–60 minutes, or until the beef is very tender. Roughly chop the remaining coriander leaves just before serving.

To make the garnish, cut the apple into slices and season them with black pepper. Melt the butter in a large non-stick frying pan and fry the apple slices over a high heat for 3–4 minutes, or until lightly browned, turning occasionally. Remove the pan from the heat, drizzle the apple slices with the honey and toss them lightly.

Scatter the fried apples over the tagine and it's ready to go. Good with some crusty bread.

BEEF STIFADO

A traditional Greek meat stew, stifado can be made with pork or rabbit as well as beef. It always contains loads of little onions, cooked whole, and can be served with some short macaroni-style pasta if you fancy.

SERVES 6

1kg chuck steak, cut into large chunks (at least 8cm)
2 tbsp olive oil
500g pickling onions, peeled and left whole
1 tbsp tomato purée
4 ripe tomatoes, peeled and chopped, or 400g can chopped tomatoes
1 tsp honey
fresh oregano or parsley leaves (optional), to serve
flaked sea salt
freshly ground black pepper

Marinade

4 garlic cloves, finely chopped
3 bay leaves
3cm cinnamon stick
1 tsp allspice berries
½ tsp coriander seeds
4 cloves
1 strip of thinly pared orange peel
300ml red wine
50ml red wine vinegar

Put the beef in a glass, ceramic or plastic bowl – metal can react with the marinade – and season with salt and pepper. Add all the marinade ingredients, then cover and marinate for several hours or overnight.

When you're ready to start cooking, heat the olive oil in a large flameproof casserole dish. Add the onions and cook them over a medium heat, shaking regularly, until they have taken on some colour on all sides. Remove them from the casserole.

Strain the beef, reserving the marinade, and pat it dry. Add a splash more olive oil to the casserole if necessary and sear the beef until well browned. You may have to do this in a couple of batches. Return the meat and the onions to the pan.

Add the reserved marinade to the casserole. Mix the tomato purée with a little water, and add this to the casserole, together with the tomatoes and honey. Season with salt and pepper.

Bring to the boil, then turn down the heat to a low simmer. Cover the casserole with a lid and cook the stifado for 1–1½ hours until the meat and onions are tender. Stir at intervals, turning over the meat each time. Sprinkle with fresh oregano or parsley leaves if you like.

BEEF SHORT RIBS

These are sticky, garlicky and spicy and everyone loves them – food that cries out for a cold beer to wash it down. The smoky flavour comes from the smoked garlic powder, which is available in supermarkets now. If you can't find any, use smoked salt instead of ordinary salt. Sounds like a huge amount of meat we know, but there is a lot of bone – and those bones make natural handles!

SERVES 4

2kg beef short ribs, separated and trimmed of excess fat
2 tbsp flour
1 tsp smoked garlic powder (optional)
1 tsp mustard powder
1 tsp dried oregano
1 tsp ground ginger
2 tbsp vegetable oil
1 onion, finely chopped
1 carrot, finely diced
1 celery stick, finely diced
3 garlic cloves, finely chopped
2 tbsp tomato purée
2 bay leaves
a sprig of thyme
250ml red wine
500ml beef stock
a dash of hot sauce such as Tabasco
25ml bourbon (or whisky or brandy)
1 tbsp maple syrup
flaked sea salt
freshly ground black pepper

Put the ribs in a large bowl or bag and season them with salt and pepper. Mix the flour with the smoked garlic powder (if using), mustard powder, oregano and ground ginger, then sprinkle this over the ribs. Mix or shake the ribs to coat them thoroughly, then dust off any excess.

Heat half the oil in a large frying pan and sear the ribs in a couple of batches until they're well browned. Set each batch aside as it is browned.

Heat the remaining oil in a large flameproof casserole dish and add the onion, carrot and celery. Sauté for several minutes until the vegetables are starting to soften, then add the garlic and tomato purée. Stir until the purée starts to separate, then add the herbs and the wine. Bring to the boil and continue to cook until the liquid is reduced by half.

Add the ribs to the casserole dish along with the stock. Season with salt and pepper and bring to the boil, then reduce to a low simmer and cook for 2 hours.

Remove the ribs from the casserole dish and keep them warm. Add the hot sauce, bourbon and maple syrup to the sauce, then simmer for a few minutes until it has reduced to a syrupy consistency. Serve poured over the short ribs.

Good served with mashed potato or polenta.

CHAPTER SIX
PASTIES, PUDDINGS AND PIES

GALA PICNIC PIE

We grew up eating luminous pink gala pie with green egg. We loved it at the time, but this is the gourmet version from two northerners made good, with dinky little quail's eggs down the middle. Great served with salad, pickles and a bit of mustard.

MAKES 12 SLICES

12 quail's eggs
4 pork sausages (about 250g)
200g minced pork
2 rashers streaky bacon,
  cut into 1cm pieces
½ tsp ground ginger
½ tsp ground mace
1 tbsp plain flour, for dusting
freshly ground black pepper

Pastry

225g plain flour, plus extra
  for rolling
½ tsp freshly ground black
  pepper
25g cold butter, cut into
  cubes, plus extra for
  greasing
75g cold lard, cut into cubes
1 tsp sea salt
1 egg, beaten, to glaze

Bring a saucepan of water to the boil. Add the quail's eggs and boil them for 2½ minutes. Drain them and rinse under running water until they're completely cold, then set them aside. Squeeze the sausages out of their skins into a large mixing bowl. Add the mince, bacon, ginger and mace, then season with pepper. Get your hands in there and mix everything together until it's very well combined. Divide the mixture into 2 portions.

Peel the eggs, put them in a bowl and toss them in the flour until they're lightly coated. Preheat the oven to 200°C/Fan 180°C/Gas 6. Line a large, flat metal baking tray with baking parchment.

For the pastry, put the flour and pepper in a food processor with the butter and 25g of the lard. Pulse until the mixture resembles coarse breadcrumbs. Put the remaining lard in a small saucepan and add 4 tablespoons of cold water and a pinch of salt. Bring to a simmer, then add this to the flour mixture with the motor running and blend until the dough comes together. Turn out on to a floured surface and knead lightly to make a smooth, pliable dough.

Dust the baking tin with flour. Shape the dough into a rectangle, and place it on the tray. Dust a rolling pin with flour and roll out the pastry until it is about 6mm thick and makes a rectangle of 30 x 28cm. You'll need to turn the pastry a few times to roll it to the right size.

Place half the pork mixture lengthways down the middle of the pastry, leaving a 1.5cm border at each end. The mixture should be about 25cm long and 10cm wide. Top with the floured eggs, standing them on their ends and placing one next to the other all the way down the length of the pork. Cover with the remaining pork mixture, making sure that all the eggs are enclosed, and press down lightly.

Brush one of the long pastry edges lightly with beaten egg and bring both sides to the middle to encase the filling. Press the edges very firmly together to seal, then trim the top neatly with a sharp set of kitchen scissors, leaving 1cm or so for the crest. Crimp the top edge into a wiggly line on top of the pie.

Brush the pie with beaten egg and bake it for 15 minutes, then remove it from the oven and brush with egg again. Put the pie back in the oven for another 15 minutes or until it's golden-brown and the pastry and filling are completely cooked. Leave to cool before slicing and serving.

PORK, LEEK AND APRICOT RAISED PIE

This is a very special pie and looks quite spectacular when you bring it to the table. It's fab just cut into wedges and served with a bit of mustard and some tasty tomatoes, or it can be part of a grander feast. For an extra treat, make some of our cider and sage jelly (see page 347) to serve alongside. The fresh sage flavour goes beautifully with the rich pork.

SERVES 10–12

400g pork shoulder, fat trimmed, cut into 1.5cm chunks
150g minced pork belly
100g bacon, cut into 1.5cm chunks
100g ready-to-eat apricots, halved
1 leek, trimmed, cut into 1cm slices
½ tsp ground ginger
½ tsp ground allspice
½ tsp finely grated nutmeg
1 egg, beaten
8 ready-to-eat prunes
flaked sea salt
freshly ground black pepper

Pastry
425g plain flour, plus extra for dusting
½ tsp freshly ground black pepper
50g cold butter, cut into cubes, plus extra for greasing
150g cold lard, cut into cubes
2 tsp sea salt
1 egg, beaten, for glazing

To make the pastry, sift the flour into a large mixing bowl and stir in the pepper. Using your fingertips, rub the butter and 50g of the lard into the flour until the mixture resembles fine breadcrumbs. Make a well in the centre of the mixture. Heat the remaining lard with the salt and 150ml of water in a small saucepan. When the mixture is simmering, pour it into the well in the flour and stir with a wooden spoon, gradually drawing the dry mixture into the liquid until it all comes together as a dough.

Tip the dough out on to a lightly floured work surface and knead until it is smooth and pliable. Cover it with clingfilm and set it aside to rest for 30 minutes, but don't put it in the fridge or it will get hard and crumbly.

Meanwhile, make the filling. Mix the pork shoulder, minced pork belly, bacon, apricots, leek, ginger, allspice, nutmeg, egg and a teaspoon of salt in a large bowl until well combined. Season with freshly ground black pepper and mix again.

Once the pastry has rested, unwrap it and cut off one-third to be used as the pie lid. Roll the remaining two-thirds of pastry into a ball and roll it out on a lightly floured surface to a thickness of about 7mm.

Grease a 17.5cm spring-form cake tin with butter. Line the tin with the rolled-out pastry, pressing it into the base and sides of the tin. Leave any excess pastry hanging over the edge of the tin.

Spoon half the filling into the pastry case, pressing it down firmly with the back of a spoon. Flatten the prunes slightly with your hands and arrange them on top of the meat, then cover them with the remaining filling, pressing it down as before.

Roll out the remaining pastry until it is large enough to cover the pie. Brush the overhanging edges of the pie with water and place the pastry lid on top, squeezing it together at the edges to seal. Trim off any excess and crimp the edges neatly. Decorate the pie with pastry trimmings if you like, but keep a few bits for repairs later. Make a small hole in the centre of the lid with a sharp knife, then put the pie in the fridge to chill for 30 minutes.

Preheat the oven to 180°C/Fan 160°C/Gas 4. Place the pie tin on a baking tray and bake in the centre of the oven for 1¼ hours. Remove it from the oven and very carefully release the sides of the spring-form tin. Leaving the pie on the tin base, put it back on the baking tray. Inspect the pie for cracks, patching up any you find with pastry trimmings and smoothing them into place with beaten egg. Then brush the pie all over with a little beaten egg to glaze and put it back in the oven for 15 minutes.

Remove the pie from the oven and glaze it with more beaten egg. If the juices are beginning to run out of the top of the pie, make a small chimney with a piece of foil and stick it into the hole in the pie lid. Put the pie back in the oven for 10–15 minutes, or until the pastry is golden-brown. Set it aside to cool for at least 6 hours before serving and keep it in the fridge once cooled.

Serve the pie in wedges with some salad and cubes of cider and sage jelly (see p.347) if you have some.

Tip
To release the pie from the spring-form tin without breaking it, place the base of the tin on an upturned bowl, release the clip and loosen any sticky edges with a knife. Allow the sides of the tin to drop away.

SWEET AND SAVOURY SUET ROLL

Based on a traditional dish called the Bedfordshire clanger, this is a suet pudding with a savoury filling at one end and a sweet one at the other. What do you reckon to that? Way back, workers used to take a clanger to the fields for their lunch and – lo and behold – they had two courses in one parcel. Not sure if the butter in ours is quite authentic but it tastes good – not a clanger in our book.

SERVES 4

Savoury filling
1 tbsp English or Dijon mustard
100g smoked back bacon, finely diced
1 onion, finely diced
flaked sea salt
freshly ground black pepper

Sweet filling
1 eating apple, peeled and grated
2 tbsp demerara sugar
½ tsp cinnamon or mixed spice

Pastry
350g plain flour, plus extra for dusting
pinch of sea salt
75g cold butter, diced
100g shredded suet

First make the pastry. Put the flour in a large bowl and add a pinch of salt. Rub in the butter until the mixture resembles fine breadcrumbs, then stir in the suet. Using a knife, mix in enough water to make a soft but not sticky dough – 150ml should be about right.

Preheat the oven to 180°C/Fan 160°C/Gas 4. Put a large roasting tin in the oven and fill it with water to about two-thirds up the sides. Put a high rack in the tin, making sure it sits above the water. If you don't have anything high enough, you can balance a lower rack on a few upturned ramekins.

Roll out the dough on a floured surface. It needs to be about 40cm long and 25–30cm wide. Trim this into a rectangle, then roll some of the trimmings into a thin sausage. Put this vertically down the middle to separate the sweet and savoury fillings.

Spread half the pastry with mustard, then sprinkle over the bacon and onion. Season with salt and pepper. Sprinkle the apple, sugar and spices over the other half of the pastry.

Roll it all up into a long sausage, starting at the end closest to you, then wet the edges with water and seal them. Place on a large sheet of buttered foil. Bring the long edges of the foil together and make a loose pleat. Scrunch the short edges together.

Carefully place the roll on the rack, then steam it in the oven for about 1½ hours. If you're not taking your clanger into the fields with you, cut it into slices to serve – it makes a nice lunch with some salad.

PORK WELLINGTON WITH BLACK PUDDING

The classic Wellington is made with beef, but we think pork works well too. A piece of tenderloin is a lot cheaper than beef fillet for a start, and you don't have to worry about getting the meat to the perfect point of pinkness. Pork is more forgiving. The filling is quite moist and juicy but you might like to serve a simple apple sauce alongside or some cider gravy.

SERVES 4

1 tbsp butter
1 onion, finely chopped
50ml Calvados
1 small eating apple, finely diced
1 tsp rubbed sage
150g black pudding, crumbled
1 tbsp olive oil
1 pork tenderloin (500–700g)
500g ready-made puff pastry
6 slices prosciutto (Italian ham)
1 egg, beaten
flaked sea salt
freshly ground black pepper

Heat the butter in a non-stick frying pan. Add the onion and fry it for several minutes until it's soft and translucent. Turn the heat right up, then add the Calvados and let it bubble away until it has almost completely evaporated. Remove the pan from the heat and leave the onion to cool.

Put the cooled onion in a bowl with the apple, sage and black pudding. Season with salt and black pepper and mix everything together well.

Heat the olive oil in the frying pan, add the pork and fry it, turning regularly, until the meat is sealed and well browned on all sides. Remove it from the heat. Preheat the oven to 200°C/Fan 180°C/Gas 6.

Dust a work surface with flour and roll out the puff pastry into a rectangle slightly longer than the pork and wide enough to completely encase it – at least 30 x 40cm.

Lay the slices of prosciutto over the pastry, making sure you leave a pastry border of at least 1cm all round them. Spread the black pudding mixture over the prosciutto. Pat the seared pork dry with kitchen paper, then place it along the centre of the covered pastry.

Brush the edges of the pastry with beaten egg, then wrap the pastry around the pork to form a large sausage shape. Press the ends of the pastry together to make sure the parcel is completely sealed and tuck them underneath. Place the Wellington on a non-stick baking tray, making sure it is seam side down.

Decorate the top with offcuts of pastry if you like, then brush the whole thing with more beaten egg.

Bake the parcel in the preheated oven for 20 minutes, then turn the temperature down to 180°C/Fan 160°C/Gas 4 and cook for another 15–20 minutes, until the pastry is golden-brown. Remove the Wellington from the oven and leave it to rest for at least 10 minutes. Cut into slices and serve with vegetables or salad.

SPANISH SPICY PASTIES

These little pasties are what the Spanish and South Americans call empanadas. We like to use olive oil pastry, which is good and robust and makes the pies very portable – perfect picnic food. This is a meat book, we know, but if you do feel like a veggie version, you could use 400g of cooked diced potato instead of pork.

MAKES 24
small or 12 large pasties

150g cooking chorizo, finely diced
1 onion, finely chopped
½ red pepper, deseeded and finely diced
1 garlic clove, finely chopped
400g minced pork
75g pimento-stuffed olives, finely chopped
1 tsp lemon zest
1 tbsp tomato purée
50ml white wine
2 tbsp finely chopped parsley leaves
olive oil, for brushing
flaked sea salt
freshly ground black pepper

Pastry
500g plain flour
1tsp baking powder
pinch of sea salt
100ml olive oil
100ml white wine or sherry

First, make the pastry. Sift the flour and baking powder into a large bowl and add a pinch of salt. Whisk the olive oil and white wine together, then gradually work this mixture into the flour with a knife. Add 100ml of chilled water a bit at a time, until the dough forms a ball. You may not need all the water.

Lightly knead the dough until it has a smooth, pliable texture. Wrap it in clingfilm and leave it in the fridge to chill while you make the filling.

Put the chorizo in a large frying pan and cook it over a medium heat until it's crisp and has given off lots of fat. Turn the heat down and add the onion and red pepper. Cook for a few minutes, then add the garlic and pork, then continue to cook, stirring regularly, until the pork has browned and is cooked through.

Add the olives, lemon zest, tomato purée and wine. Cook over a high heat for a few minutes, stirring so everything is well combined, then stir in the parsley. Season with salt and pepper, then leave the mixture to cool. Preheat the oven to 200°C/Fan 180°C/Gas 6.

To assemble the pasties, roll out the dough on a floured surface. You will find that this is a very elastic dough and will need to be rolled a number of times before it stops shrinking back. You could roll it in a pasta machine if you have one. Once the dough is nice and thin, cut out 24 circles about 10cm in diameter or 12 circles about 15cm in diameter.

Heap dessertspoonfuls of the cooled filling on to half of a dough circle – use 1 spoonful for the small pasties and 2 for the larger. Wet the edges with water, then bring the uncovered half over the filling. Seal the edge of the pasty and brush it with olive oil. Repeat until you've used all your filling and dough.

Place the pasties on a lined baking tray. Bake them in the preheated oven for 20–25 minutes until golden-brown and crisp. The pasties should puff up to smooth, hard domes.

SQUAB PIE

We first discovered squab pie when we did our *Food Tour of Britain* series and we learned that although squab is a name for a young pigeon, this pie is made with lamb or mutton. It's a traditional dish in southwest England, but not seen much nowadays. We like to make these good old British classics, so we've tweaked our recipe over the years to make it even more delicious.

SERVES 6

1kg lamb neck fillet, cut
　　into bite-sized pieces
1 tbsp plain flour
1 tbsp vegetable oil
15g butter
2 onions, sliced
¼ tsp ground allspice
¼ tsp ground cinnamon
pinch of ground cloves (or
　　1 clove, ground)
grating of nutmeg
2 bay leaves
a sprig of rosemary
a sprig of thyme
500ml chicken or lamb
　　stock
2 eating apples, peeled,
　　cored and thinly sliced
10 soft prunes, pitted
flaked sea salt
freshly ground black
　　pepper

Pastry
300g plain flour, plus extra
　　for dusting
pinch of sea salt
100g butter, chilled
　　and diced
50g lard or vegetable
　　shortening, diced
1 egg, beaten, to glaze
flaked sea salt

Put the pieces of lamb in a bowl and season them with salt and black pepper. Sprinkle over the flour and toss the lamb well, making sure it's all coated with flour.

Heat the oil in a large frying pan and sear the pieces of lamb on all sides, making sure they are well browned. It's best to do this in batches so you don't overcrowd the pan; set each batch aside as it is browned.

Heat the butter in a large flameproof casserole dish. Add the onions and fry them over a gentle heat until they're well softened and translucent. Sprinkle in the spices and stir for a minute, then add the lamb, together with any juices. Add the herbs and the stock.

Bring the stock to the boil, then turn down the heat, cover the casserole and leave it to simmer for 30 minutes. Add the apples and prunes, then simmer for another 30 minutes with the lid on, until the meat is tender and the sauce has slightly thickened. Remove the casserole dish from the heat and set it aside to cool.

Now make the pastry. Sift the flour into a bowl and add a pinch of salt. Rub in the butter and lard or vegetable shortening, then add just enough chilled water to make a firm dough – usually 3–4 tablespoons. Lightly knead the dough until it comes together smoothly, then form it into a ball and wrap it in clingfilm. Chill for half an hour.

Preheat the oven to 200°C/Fan 180°C/Gas 6. Put the lamb mixture in a large pie dish, placing a pie bird or funnel, if you have one, in the centre. Roll out the pastry on a well-floured surface, making sure it is larger than your pie dish, and cut off a 1cm strip.

Wet the rim of the pie dish and line it all the way around with the strip of pastry. Wet the pastry strip, then top it with the rest of the pastry. Press the edges together and trim, crimping decoratively if you like. Brush the pie with beaten egg and bake it in the oven for 30–40 minutes until piping hot and golden-brown.

JAMAICAN PATTIES

When we first saw these bright yellow pasties in Caribbean shops in London, we wondered what they were – and we soon found out that they're so good they're addictive. You need a nice mild curry powder – a yellow one is best rather than a paprika-rich red one. If you like your patties mega hot, add some hot sauce or a Scotch bonnet to taste. The pastry is traditionally made with just lard, but we prefer to use a bit of butter as well to make it easier to handle.

MAKES 8

250g minced lamb,
    beef or pork
150g potatoes, cut
    into small dice
50g frozen peas or petits pois
1 tbsp coconut or
    vegetable oil
4 spring onions, sliced into
    thin rounds
2 garlic cloves, finely chopped
15g fresh root ginger, finely
    chopped or grated
1 tsp thyme
½ tsp allspice berries, finely
    ground
grated zest of 1 lime
1 tsp mild curry powder
50ml creamed coconut
1 tsp hot sauce or a Scotch
    bonnet chilli, deseeded and
    finely chopped (optional)
milk, for brushing
flaked sea salt
freshly ground black pepper

Pastry
300g plain flour
½ tsp turmeric
100g lard
50g butter

First make the pastry. Mix the flour with the turmeric and season it with salt and pepper. Rub in the lard and butter until the mixture has the texture of fine breadcrumbs. Add 2–3 tablespoons of chilled water, a tablespoon at a time, cutting it into the flour mixture until you can form a dough. Knead the dough very lightly until it's smooth, then wrap it in clingfilm and leave it to chill in the fridge.

To make the filling, put the minced meat into a bowl and season it with salt and pepper. Bring a pan of salted water to the boil, add the diced potatoes and peas and blanch them for 3 minutes. Drain them and set them aside to cool.

Heat the coconut or vegetable oil in a frying pan and sauté the spring onions, garlic and ginger for a minute or two, then remove the pan from the heat.

Add the potatoes, peas, spring onions, garlic and ginger to the meat, then sprinkle in the thyme, allspice, lime zest, curry powder, creamed coconut and the hot sauce or Scotch bonnet, if using. Mix everything together thoroughly. Preheat the oven to 200°C/Fan 180°C/Gas 6.

Roll out the pastry and cut it into rounds about 15cm in diameter – the size of a small side plate. Place a couple of tablespoons of filling on half of each round, then wet the edges, fold them over and press them down firmly. Crimp the edges with a fork if you like.

Brush the patties with a little milk. Place them on a non-stick baking tray and bake for 20–25 minutes, until the pastry has started to turn golden-brown around the edges.

LAYERED BEEF AND MUSHROOM SUET PUDDING

This is so British it could be Boudicca's breakfast. A recipe for the suet lover, this has not only a suet crust round the outside but also layers of suet between the meat inside – a bit like a suet pud Viennetta if you can imagine such a thing. It's a taste sensation and as comforting as a great big hug.

SERVES 6

2 tbsp vegetable oil
2 medium onions, chopped
200g button mushrooms, wiped and sliced
4 tbsp plain flour
1 tsp flaked sea salt
2 tsp dried mixed herbs
750g well-marbled braising steak, such as chuck
1 bay leaf
440ml stout
450ml beef stock
2 tbsp tomato purée
2 tsp caster sugar
freshly ground black pepper

Suet pastry
325g self-raising flour, plus extra for dusting
150g shredded suet
25g finely chopped parsley
1 tsp fine sea salt
knob of butter, for greasing

Preheat the oven to 180°C/ Fan 160°C/Gas 4.

To make the filling, heat the oil in a large flameproof casserole dish. Fry the onions and mushrooms over a medium heat for about 5 minutes, or until lightly browned, stirring regularly.

Put the flour, salt and dried herbs in a large bowl. Season with lots of freshly ground black pepper and mix well. Trim any hard fat and sinew off the beef, then cut the meat into cubes about 2.5cm in size. Toss the meat in the flour until coated evenly all over – the flour will help thicken the gravy. Tip the beef and all the flour into the pan with the onions and mushrooms and fry for 3–5 minutes.

Add the bay leaf, stout, stock, tomato purée and sugar, then stir well and bring the mixture to the boil. Cover the casserole dish with a lid, put it in the oven and cook for 2¼ hours, or until the beef is very tender, stirring halfway through the cooking time. If the beef remains a little tough, put the dish back in the oven and cook for longer.

Take 5 ladlefuls (about 450ml) of the cooking liquid and set it aside to use for gravy later. Put the casserole dish on the hob and simmer for 2–3 minutes, or until the sauce is thick enough not to run all over the plate when the pudding is cut. Don't let it get too thick, though, or the pudding will taste dry.

Remove the casserole dish from the heat, tip the contents into a large bowl and leave them to cool completely. Remove the bay leaf.

To make the suet pastry, put the flour in a large bowl and stir in the suet, parsley and salt. Stir in enough water to make a soft, spongy dough – you'll probably need about 250ml. Turn it out on to a floured surface and bring the dough together to form a ball. Knead lightly, then divide it into 4 portions of about 100g, 150g, 200g and 275g.

Butter a 1.5 litre pudding basin and line the base with a small disc of baking parchment – this will make the pudding easier to remove once cooked. Roll out the smallest portion of pastry into a disc about 1.5cm thick. Place this in the base of the pudding basin and cover it with a layer of the beef and mushroom mixture. Roll the 150g portion into a disc large enough to cover the beef and press it down gently, making sure it reaches the sides, then cover with filling. Repeat the process with the remaining pastry and filling until the basin is layered with 4 discs of pastry and 3 layers of beef. Trim the top layer of pastry to fit if necessary.

Take a large piece of foil and fold a pleat into it. Put this over the pudding basin and secure it in place with string or a strong rubber band. Stand the pudding in a steamer over a large saucepan – or if you don't have a steamer, fold up a small tea towel, put it in the saucepan and place the pudding on top of that. Add boiling water to about halfway up the sides of the pudding basin and put a lid on the pan. Steam the pudding in simmering water for 2 hours, checking the water level regularly and making sure the pan doesn't boil dry. Always top up with boiling water.

When the pudding is cooked, turn off the heat and lift the basin from the water. Leave it to stand for 5 minutes. Heat the reserved sauce until it's bubbling, stirring continuously and adding a little extra water if needed.

Remove the foil cover. Run a knife around the top of the basin, to loosen the pudding, then put a serving plate over it. Holding the basin with an oven glove, turn it upside down so the pudding comes out cleanly on to the serving plate. Pour a little of the gravy over the top and then serve in generous wedges with more hot gravy and veg. No potatoes necessary!

STEAK AND KIDNEY PUDDING

A British classic, a good steak and kidney pud is a dish to be proud of. And if you don't like kidneys, use some portobellini mushrooms instead. You'll need a 1.5 litre pudding basin.

SERVES 6

750g braising steak (beef shin is good), trimmed and cut into 3cm chunks
2 lamb's kidneys, cored and quartered (see p.306)
3 tbsp plain flour
1 tsp mustard powder
2 tbsp beef dripping or vegetable oil
1 onion, finely sliced
250ml beer or red wine
600ml beef stock
1 tbsp tomato ketchup
a dash of Worcestershire sauce
a few sprigs of thyme
1 bay leaf
1 small can smoked oysters or mussels, drained (optional)
sea salt
freshly ground black pepper

Suet crust
350g plain flour, plus extra for dusting
2 tsp baking powder
1 tsp dried thyme
175g suet

Pat the steak and the kidneys dry with kitchen paper and put them in a large bowl or a plastic bag. Mix the flour with the mustard powder and season it with salt and pepper. Pour the flour mixture over the meat and toss or shake until all the chunks are completely coated.

Heat the dripping or oil in a large frying pan and brown the steak and kidneys on a high heat. It's best to do this in batches so you don't overcrowd the pan. As each batch is browned, transfer it to a large casserole dish and add more dripping or oil to the pan if necessary.

Once all the meat is browned, add the onion to the frying pan and cook it on a lower heat until softened. Turn up the heat and pour the beer or red wine into the pan. Stir vigorously, scraping up all the nice sticky bits from the bottom of the frying pan. Pour the contents of the pan over the meat in the casserole – the bottom of the frying pan should look clean when you're done.

Add the beef stock, ketchup, Worcestershire sauce and herbs to the casserole dish. Bring to the boil, then turn down the heat and cover the dish with a lid. Simmer very gently for about an hour, stirring every so often. Don't worry if the meat isn't completely tender at the end of the hour, as it will continue to cook when you steam the pudding. Strain the meat from the liquid and leave it to cool. Set the cooking liquid aside – you'll need it later.

Meanwhile, make the suet crust. Put the flour, baking powder, thyme and suet in a bowl and season with salt and pepper. Gradually add water, cutting it in with a knife, until it comes together as dough. You'll probably need around 150–200ml for this, but don't worry if you use a little more.

Shape the dough into a ball and cut it into 2 pieces of unequal size – one should be about two-thirds of the mixture, the other one-third. Roll out the larger piece of dough on a floured surface to make a circle with a diameter of about 25cm. Butter your pudding basin and line it with the rolled-out pastry, letting it overlap the sides slightly. Roll out the smaller piece of dough to fit the top of the pudding basin.

Stir the smoked oysters or mussels, if using, into the steak and kidney, then pile the mixture into the pudding basin. Bring the overlapping edges of pastry down over the filling, then dampen them with cold water. Add the lid, and press firmly around it to seal. Take a large piece of foil and fold a pleat into it. Put this over the pudding basin and secure it in place with string or a strong rubber band.

Stand the pudding in a steamer over a large saucepan – or if you don't have a steamer, fold up a small tea towel, put it in the saucepan and place the pudding on top of that. Add boiling water to about halfway up the sides of the pudding basin and put a lid on the pan. Steam the pudding for 2½ hours, checking the water level regularly and making sure the pan doesn't boil dry. Always top up with boiling water.

When you are ready to serve, heat the reserved cooking liquor until it is piping hot and slightly reduced – the flour should have thickened it slightly. Carefully remove the pudding from the steamer and take off the foil cover. Run a knife around the top of the basin, to loosen the pudding, then put a serving plate over it. Holding the basin with an oven glove, turn it upside down so the pudding comes out cleanly on to the serving plate. Serve with a jug of the hot cooking liquor.

BEEF AND OYSTER PIE

Once upon a time oysters were cheap – not the posh food they are today. They were used as fillers to eke out the filling in meat pies like this one – the original surf and turf! We think the combination works so well and after all, generations of cooks can't be wrong.

SERVES 4–6

900g stewing beef, trimmed
and cut into 3cm cubes
2–3 tbsp vegetable oil
3 long shallots, quartered
125g smoked streaky bacon
rashers, cut into 1cm strips
2 garlic cloves, finely chopped
1 tbsp roughly chopped
thyme leaves
2 bay leaves
330ml stout
400ml beef stock
2 tbsp cornflour, blended with
2 tbsp water to make
a smooth paste
8 oysters, freshly shucked
flaked sea salt
freshly ground black pepper

Pastry
400g plain flour, plus extra
for dusting
¼ tsp sea salt
250g butter, frozen for
at least 2 hours
1 egg, beaten, to glaze

Season the beef cubes with salt and black pepper. Heat a tablespoon of oil in a frying pan and fry the meat over a high heat. Do this in several batches so you don't overcrowd the pan, transferring each batch of meat to a large flameproof casserole dish as it is browned. Add extra oil to the pan if you need it.

Add another tablespoon of oil to the pan and cook the shallots for 4–5 minutes, then add the bacon and fry until it's slightly browned. Add the garlic and fry for another 30 seconds, then tip everything into the casserole dish and add the herbs. Preheat the oven to 180°C/Fan 160°C/Gas 4.

Pour the stout into the frying pan and bring it to the boil, stirring to lift any sticky bits from the bottom of the pan. Tip the stout over the beef and add the stock. Put a lid on the casserole dish and place it in the oven for 2 hours, or until the beef is tender and the sauce has reduced.

Remove the casserole dish from the oven and skim off any surface fat. Taste the sauce and add seasoning if necessary, then stir in the cornflour paste. Put the casserole dish on the hob and simmer the mixture for 1–2 minutes, stirring, until thickened. Leave to cool.

Turn the oven up to 200°C/Fan 180°C/Gas 6. While the filling is cooling, make the pastry. Put the flour and salt in a large bowl. Grate the butter and stir it into the flour in 3 batches. Gradually add about 200ml cold water and stir it in with a round-bladed knife until the mixture comes together. Knead the pastry briefly into a ball.

Roll out the pastry on a floured surface, making sure it is larger than your pie dish, and cut off a 1cm strip. You might have slightly more pastry than you need, but you can freeze any leftovers. Pile the beef into the pie dish and tuck in the oysters.

Wet the rim of the pie dish and line it all the way round with the strip of pastry. Brush the pastry strip with beaten egg, then top it with the rest of the pastry. Press the edges together and trim them, crimping decoratively if you like. Brush the pastry with beaten egg. Put the dish on a baking tray and bake for 25–30 minutes, or until the pie is piping hot and golden-brown on top.

SAVOURY MINCE PIES

Sometimes simple pleasures are the best. We both remember eating little pies like these as kids – very plain but good, with nice flaky pastry. There's nothing exotic about the filling, but it's really tasty and the pies make an ideal family supper.

MAKES 12

1 tbsp vegetable oil
1 onion, finely chopped
1 carrot, finely diced
300g minced beef
1 tbsp flour
250ml beef stock
1 tbsp tomato purée
   or ketchup
a dash of Worcestershire
   sauce
1 egg, beaten, for glazing
flaked sea salt
freshly ground black
   pepper

Pastry
250g plain flour, plus extra
   for dusting
pinch of salt
100g cold butter, diced
50g cold lard or vegetable
   shortening, diced
1 egg, beaten

To make the pastry, put the flour into a bowl and season it with a pinch of salt. Rub in the butter and lard or vegetable shortening with your fingers, then add the beaten egg. Cut this in with a knife, then add just enough chilled water to make a dough – about 2 tablespoons.

Lightly knead the dough until it comes together, then shape it into a ball and wrap it in clingfilm. Put the pastry in the fridge to chill for half an hour while you make the filling.

Heat the oil in a frying pan. Add the onion and carrot and fry them on a gentle heat until they're softened and starting to brown around the edges, then turn up the heat and add the beef. Cook quite briskly until the meat is well browned, then sprinkle in the flour and stir to mix it in.

Add the beef stock, tomato purée or ketchup and Worcestershire sauce and season with salt and pepper. Simmer, stirring regularly, until the gravy has thickened. Remove the pan from the heat and leave the mixture to cool. Preheat the oven to 200°C/ Fan 180°C/Gas 6.

Divide the pastry into 2 pieces, one slightly larger than the other. Roll out the larger piece on a floured surface, and cut out 12 circles about 9cm in diameter. Use these to line a 12-hole fairy cake tin. Press the pastry circles down gently to make sure they fit the holes properly.

Add a heaped dessertspoon of filling to each pie, making sure you leave room for the filling to expand slightly. Roll out the other piece of pastry and cut out slightly smaller rounds. Brush the border of the filled pastry with water, then press the top piece on, pushing it down lightly away from the middle to create a slight dome. Press the edges together and crimp them if you like.

Cut 2 small slits in the top of each pie and brush the pastry with beaten egg. Bake the pies in the preheated oven for 20–25 minutes, until they're crisp, golden-brown and slightly puffed up.

VENISON COBBLER

A cobbler can be sweet or savoury and has a crust made of a scone-like mixture that's placed on top of the filling like little cobblestones. Venison is well worth trying when it's in season, as it's a good healthy meat – lean and low in fat, but with plenty of flavour. You'll need a 2-litre pie dish and a 6cm pastry cutter when making this recipe.

SERVES 6

2 tbsp vegetable oil
2 large onions, sliced
2 celery sticks, trimmed
   and sliced
1 carrot, cut into cubes
2 tbsp plain flour
1 tsp English mustard powder
500ml real ale or stout
1kg venison (ideally shoulder
   or leg), cut into 3cm chunks
2 heaped tbsp redcurrant jelly
1 tbsp fresh thyme leaves,
   roughly chopped
2 bay leaves
1–2 tbsp fresh lemon juice
flaked sea salt
freshly ground black pepper

Cobbler topping
500g self-raising flour,
   plus extra for dusting
½ tsp fine sea salt
100g cold butter, cut into
   cubes
300ml whole milk
beaten egg, to glaze

Preheat the oven to 180°C/ Fan 160°C/Gas 4.

Heat the oil in a flameproof casserole dish and fry the onions, celery and carrot gently for 10 minutes, or until the onion is softened and lightly coloured. Stir occasionally.

Add the flour and mustard and cook for a few seconds, then slowly stir in the ale or stout and 250ml of water. Add the venison, redcurrant jelly, thyme and bay leaves, then stir. Season with a little salt and lots of black pepper. Bring to a gentle simmer, stirring occasionally, then cover the casserole dish with a lid. Transfer the dish to the oven and cook for 1¾–2 hours, or until the venison is very tender and the sauce is thick.

Season to taste and add a little lemon juice to lift the richness. At this point you can cool the venison mixture and keep it in the fridge to finish off later, or the next day if you like.

When you're ready to cook your cobbler, spoon the venison mixture into an ovenproof pie dish. Preheat the oven to 200°C/Fan 180°C/Gas 6.

To make the cobbler topping, put the flour and salt in a bowl and rub in the butter with your fingertips until the mixture resembles breadcrumbs. Add the milk, stirring continuously, until the mixture comes together and forms a soft, spongy dough.

Turn the dough out on to a floured work surface and roll it out to about 2cm thick. Cut out 6cm rounds with a pastry cutter, kneading and re-rolling any leftover dough as necessary.

Place the 'cobbles' over the filling so they nearly cover it and brush them with beaten egg. Bake for 30 minutes, or until the topping is golden-brown and the filling is hot. Some green veg or nice buttery carrots are all you need with this.

CHAPTER SEVEN
MINCED AND CHOPPED MEAT

FAGGOTS

Faggots are a good old-fashioned dish which is creeping back into fashion. There are loads of versions, but faggots are generally made from minced meat and some offal. Traditionally, each faggot is wrapped in caul – known to us as sheep clingfilm. Caul is a thin piece of fat that covers an animal's intestines and looks surprisingly pretty – like a lacy curtain. The caul holds the faggot together and also bastes it with fat to keep it juicy.

MAKES 8 FAGGOTS

250g minced pork
250g minced beef
100g lamb's liver, very
  finely chopped
50g kidneys
150g fine breadcrumbs
1 tsp dried sage
1 tsp dried thyme
1 tsp mustard powder
caul fat or 8 slices of rindless
  streaky bacon, for covering
flaked sea salt
freshly ground black pepper

Gravy
10g butter or beef dripping
1 onion, finely chopped
50g smoked back bacon,
  finely chopped
500ml rich beef stock
200g canned tomatoes,
  puréed or crushed
1 tsp dried sage
a dash of Worcestershire
  sauce or mushroom
  ketchup

Preheat the oven to 180°C/ Fan 160°C/Gas 4.

To make the faggots, put the meat, breadcrumbs, herbs and mustard powder in a large bowl and season with salt and black pepper. Mix thoroughly – the easiest way to do this is with your hands – then shape the mixture into 8 rectangular patties. Each should weigh about 100g.

If using the caul fat, stretch it out and cut 8 pieces large enough to wrap around each faggot. Place a meat patty in the centre of each piece of caul and wrap it up, making sure the edges of the caul overlap slightly.

If using bacon, stretch the rashers out as much as you can lengthways with a knife, then cut them in half. Wrap a piece of bacon lengthways over each patty, and another crossways. It doesn't matter if the bacon doesn't completely cover the patty.

Put the faggots into a lined roasting tin and add a splash of water. Bake them in the oven for about 50 minutes, turning them once, so they are well browned on all sides.

To make the gravy, melt the butter or dripping in a saucepan. Add the onion and bacon and fry gently until the onion has softened, then add the stock, tomatoes and sage. Season with salt and pepper.

Bring the gravy to the boil, then turn the heat down a little and leave it to simmer until it is well reduced – probably about 20 minutes. The gravy should be pourable but thick and not at all watery. Add a dash of Worcestershire sauce or mushroom ketchup to taste and serve it hot with the faggots.

Tip
You can order caul from your butcher but if you can't get any or don't fancy the idea, just wrap the faggots in streaky bacon instead.

PORK-STUFFED CABBAGE LEAVES

These stuffed cabbage leaves are a British take on a popular Romanian dish called sarmale and they make a very tasty and economical supper. They're a bit of a fiddle until you get the hang of the rolling, but they're well worth the effort. Serve them with some sauerkraut on the side if you like.

SERVES 6

3 large green cabbages
1 chicken stock cube
300ml soured cream
paprika, for sprinkling

Stuffing

125g easy-cook long-grain
   rice
2 tbsp vegetable oil
1 onion, finely chopped
3 garlic cloves, finely chopped
1 tsp smoked hot paprika
3 tsp sweet paprika
2 tsp flaked sea salt
500g minced pork
handful of finely chopped
   parsley
freshly ground black pepper

Quick tomato sauce

2 tbsp vegetable oil
1 onion, thinly sliced
2 garlic cloves, finely chopped
400g chopped tomatoes
 2 tbsp tomato purée
1 tsp caster sugar

First make the stuffing. Bring a saucepan of water to the boil, add the rice and cook for 5 minutes. Rinse the rice in a sieve under running water until cold, then drain and set it aside.

Pour the oil into a large saucepan and fry the onion over a medium heat for 3 minutes, stirring, until it's beginning to brown. Add the garlic and cook for 2 minutes more, stirring. Reduce the heat to low and stir in both paprikas, the salt and lots of black pepper. Cook for a further minute, stirring continuously, then remove the pan from the heat and tip the mixture into a bowl to cool.

Now for the cabbage leaves. Remove any really tough or damaged outer leaves from each cabbage. Using a small knife, cut the next few leaves away from the stem at the base of the cabbage. You want as many whole, large leaves as possible, so take care not to tear them. You should be able to get about 12 good leaves from each cabbage. Don't worry about the smaller ones from the heart of the cabbage, as they are too tiny to stuff. Just pop them in the fridge to serve another time.

Wash and drain the cabbage leaves, then using a small knife, carefully shave a thin sliver off the thickest central vein on the outside of each leaf. This will make it easier to roll the leaves. Put 1.2 litres of water in a large saucepan and bring it to the boil. Blanch the leaves in the boiling water for 5 minutes – it's best to do this in a few batches. Remove each batch with a slotted spoon and rinse in a colander under running water until cold. Drain and set the leaves aside in a bowl. Stir the stock cube into the cooking water in the saucepan until dissolved, then pour this liquid into a large measuring jug.

To finishing the stuffing, add the rice, minced pork, chopped parsley and lots of seasoning to the spiced onions and mix with your hands until they are thoroughly combined. Place a blanched leaf on a board with the inner part of the leaf facing upwards.

Take a small handful of the pork stuffing and roll it into a little sausage shape. Place it at the base of the leaf and roll once. Tuck in the left-hand side of the leaf and continue rolling to the top of the leaf. Then tuck in the right-hand side of the leaf to secure the parcel. Repeat with all the other leaves and stuffing.

Place the stuffed cabbage leaves in a large saucepan or a flameproof casserole – they should fit fairly snugly and they will need to be in at least 2 layers. Pour the reserved chicken stock over the top, until it almost covers the cabbage parcels. Bring the stock to the boil and then reduce the heat. Cover the pan with a tight-fitting lid and leave it to simmer gently for 45 minutes, or until the stuffing is cooked and tender.

Meanwhile, make the quick tomato sauce. Heat the oil in a large non-stick frying pan and gently fry the sliced onions for 5 minutes, or until they're softened and beginning to brown, stirring regularly. Add the garlic and cook for 2 minutes more, stirring.

Tip the tomatoes into the pan and add the tomato purée and sugar. Fill the tomato can with cold water and stir it into the pan (you'll need about 400ml water). Bring the sauce to a gentle simmer and cook for 25 minutes, stirring occasionally, until thick. Remove from the heat and leave it to stand.

When the stuffed leaves have finished cooking, take off the lid and scoop 4 ladlefuls of their cooking liquor into the pan containing the tomato sauce. Bring the sauce to the boil and cook for 2–3 minutes, or until it is well reduced and thick once more, stirring regularly.

Meanwhile, use a pair of tongs to transfer the stuffed cabbage leaves to a large warmed platter or a heatproof dish. Pour the hot tomato sauce over the top. Spoon half the soured cream over the tomato sauce and sprinkle with a little paprika. Serve with the remaining soured cream.

SAGE AND ONION TOAD IN THE HOLE

A classic dish – we never tire of this. We still reckon Dave's mum's Yorkshire pud batter is the best ever, but we now like to add a bit of sage for extra flavour and we also pile some lovely onions in with the sausages. Use the best sausages you can find – we cook them in a bit of goose fat or lard, but you can use oil if you prefer.

SERVES 4

1 heaped tbsp lard or goose
   or duck fat
8 pork sausages
1 large onion, sliced

Batter
150g plain flour
½ tsp salt
1 tsp rubbed dried sage
2 eggs, beaten
275 whole milk

Start by making the batter. Put the flour in a bowl, whisk it lightly to get rid of any lumps, then add the salt and rubbed sage. Make a well in the middle and add the eggs. Work the eggs into the flour, then gradually add the milk. Or if you like, put everything in a food processor and blitz until it's smooth. Leave the batter to stand for an hour.

Preheat the oven to 180°C/Fan 160°C/Gas 4. Put the lard or goose or duck fat into a rectangular roasting tin or oven dish, about 30cm x 20cm in size, and heat until it's smoking. Add the sausages and cook in the oven for 10 minutes.

Meanwhile, bring a small saucepan of water to the boil. Add a pinch of salt and the sliced onion, simmer for 3 minutes, then drain thoroughly.

Add the onions to the sausages, spreading them evenly around the tin or dish and turning the sausages. Put them back in the oven for a further 20 minutes, stirring regularly to ensure the onions cook evenly.

Turn the oven up to 200°C/Fan 180°C/Gas 6. Pour the batter around the sausages and onions, making sure everything is well spaced out. Bake for another 30 minutes until the batter has risen and is a dark golden-brown on top. Enjoy at once.

ITALIAN-STYLE STUFFED COURGETTES

We originally used marrow in this recipe, but then we saw the little round courgettes in the shops and thought they would work even better. Feel free to use a marrow, though, if you prefer – this is delicious with either vegetable. Italian-style sausages are usually seasoned with fennel and garlic and work particularly well, but you can use other kinds of sausages if you prefer.

SERVES 6

1 tbsp vegetable oil
1 onion, chopped
2 medium carrots, diced
2 celery sticks, trimmed
  and diced
2 garlic cloves, crushed
12 Italian-style sausages,
  meat removed from skins
1 tsp dried chilli flakes
1 tsp dried oregano
1 tsp caster sugar
1 tbsp plain flour
150ml red wine
400g can cherry tomatoes
300ml beef stock
1 bay leaf
12 small round courgettes

Cheese sauce
15g butter
15g plain flour
250ml milk
25g Parmesan cheese,
  finely grated
125g mozzarella, drained
flaked sea salt
freshly ground black pepper

To make the filling, heat the oil in a large non-stick frying pan and fry the onion, carrots and celery for 6–8 minutes until the onion is softened and beginning to brown. Add the garlic and sausage meat and cook for another 3–4 minutes, stirring continuously with a wooden spoon to break up any large clumps of meat.

Stir in the chilli flakes, oregano, sugar and flour and cook for a minute. Add the wine to the pan, followed by the tomatoes, stock and bay leaf. Bring everything to a gentle simmer and cook for 30–40 minutes, until the meat is tender and the sauce has thickened, stirring occasionally.

For the cheese sauce, melt the butter in a large heavy-based saucepan and stir in the flour. Cook over a low heat for about 30 seconds, stirring continuously, then gradually add the milk. Increase the heat a little and bring to a gentle simmer. Cook the sauce for 5 minutes, stirring continuously, then sprinkle in the grated Parmesan and simmer for 1–2 minutes more until the cheese has melted.

Season the sauce with salt and black pepper. Remove the pan from the heat and cover the surface of the sauce with clingfilm to prevent a skin forming. Preheat the oven to 190°C/ Fan 170°C/Gas 5.

Cut the tops off the courgettes and set them aside to use as 'lids' later, then spoon out the seeds to make room for the stuffing. Place a sheet of foil in a large roasting tin and put the courgettes on top, with the scooped-out sides facing upwards. Spoon meat mixture into the hollow in each one and top with some cheese sauce. Tear the mozzarella into pieces and arrange some on each courgette. Top with the lids.

Bring the foil up around the courgettes and pinch the edges to seal them. Bake in the centre of the oven for 45 minutes or until the courgettes are tender and the filling is hot. Unwrap the foil, remove the lids from the courgettes and pop the roasting tin under the grill for 5–10 minutes or until the cheesy tops are golden and bubbling.

Transfer the courgettes to a platter or board and pop the lids back on if you like. Serve with a fresh green salad.

WILD BOAR RAGÙ

Wild boar used to be common in this country, but they were hunted so much that they were wiped out. Now the meat is popular again and British farmers are raising boar. They're woodland creatures so we've used ingredients such as juniper berries and herbs that they might snuffle up in the woods to flavour this rich meat sauce. The secret to success with this sauce is to cook it long and slow, until the meat is falling apart.

SERVES 6

700g boneless wild boar shoulder

4–5 tbsp vegetable oil

4 rashers smoked streaky bacon or pancetta, cut into 1cm slices

1 large onion, finely chopped

4 garlic cloves, crushed

75g pitted black olives, rinsed and drained

2 tsp juniper berries, lightly crushed in a pestle and mortar

500ml red wine

400g can chopped tomatoes

2 tbsp tomato purée

500ml beef stock

2 large bay leaves

3 bushy sprigs of thyme

1 rosemary stalk, about 12cm long, leaves finely chopped

2 tsp caster sugar

freshly cooked pappardelle pasta, to serve

shavings of Parmesan cheese, to serve

flaked sea salt

freshly ground black pepper

Cut the boar into chunky pieces, each about 2.5cm. Trim off any really hard fat or sinew as you go – this is important, as boar sinew is very tough. Season the meat well with salt and pepper. Heat 2 tablespoons of the oil in a large frying pan.

Fry the chunks of boar over a medium-high heat until nicely browned on all sides, turning them every now and then. Do this in a couple of batches so you don't overcrowd the pan, adding more oil if necessary. As the meat is browned, transfer it to a large flameproof casserole dish or a large saucepan.

Add a little more oil to the pan in which you browned the boar and fry the bacon for 2–3 minutes, or until the fat crisps and browns, then scatter it over the meat. Add a touch more oil and fry the chopped onion over a low heat for 5 minutes, stirring often.

Stir the garlic, olives and crushed juniper berries into the pan and cook for 2 minutes more, stirring. Add them to the meat in the casserole dish, then pour in the wine.

Stir in the tomatoes, tomato purée and beef stock. Add all the herbs and the sugar and bring the mixture to a simmer. Stir well and cover the casserole loosely with a lid, then turn the heat down low and leave the ragù to simmer very gently for 2½ hours, or until the meat is completely tender and falling apart.

Remove the lid every now and then and stir. If the liquid reduces too much, add a little extra water. The sauce should be fairly thick at the end of the cooking time, but not at all dry. Remove the thyme and rosemary stalks and bay leaves, then season to taste with salt and pepper.

Serve with freshly cooked pappardelle pasta and Parmesan shavings. Any leftover sauce makes great ravioli or arancini (see p.333).

WILD BOAR MEATBALLS

Wild boar makes cracking meatballs, spiced up with a little nutmeg and allspice. The gravy is an essential part of this recipe and the strange thing is that it doesn't taste that great on its own, but once it has been simmered with the meatballs it works very well. Good with lots of mash (see page 352) or some chips (see page 351) to soak up the sauce.

SERVES 4–6

1 tbsp olive oil
1 onion, finely chopped
1 garlic clove, finely chopped
600g minced wild boar
4 anchovy fillets, finely
   chopped
100g breadcrumbs
1 egg
50ml milk or single cream
½ tsp allspice
¼ tsp nutmeg
fresh dill, to serve
1 tsp salt
freshly ground black pepper.

Gravy
25g butter
25g flour
100ml white wine
500ml well-flavoured beef
   stock
2 tbsp single cream
1 tbsp lingonberry jam (or
   redcurrant or cranberry
   jelly), plus extra to serve

Preheat the oven to 200°C/Fan 180°C/Gas 6.

Heat the oil in a frying pan and gently fry the onion until it's soft and translucent. Add the garlic and cook for another minute. Remove the pan from the heat and allow the onion and garlic to cool.

Put all the meatball ingredients, including the onion and garlic, in a large bowl and mix them thoroughly – it's easiest to do this with your hands. Shape the mixture into balls somewhere between the size of a walnut and a golf ball – they should be about 40g in weight and you'll have about 24. Put the balls on a baking tray and bake them for 12–15 minutes until they are cooked through.

To make the gravy, melt the butter in a pan large enough to hold the meatballs. Add the flour, and stir to combine, then cook until the mixture has turned golden-brown – give this a few minutes, as you want the flour to cook out a little. Add the white wine and stir vigorously until it's well mixed in. Gradually add the beef stock, stirring thoroughly between each addition to avoid lumps, until you have a slightly thickened gravy. Add the cream and the jam or jelly, then stir to combine. Taste for seasoning and add salt and pepper as necessary.

Remove the meatballs from the oven, put them in the pan with the gravy and simmer gently for a few minutes to allow all the flavours to combine. Serve with a sprinkling of dill and some more jam or jelly on the side if you like.

Tip
This dish is also good made with minced pork.

MOUSSAKA

One of the best-known of all Greek dishes, moussaka is a kind of Mediterranean shepherd's pie. Layers of cinnamon-spiced lamb and tender aubergines, all topped with a creamy sauce, make this a luxurious and delicious dish. We've included potatoes, but you can use an extra aubergine instead if you prefer.

SERVES 6

2 aubergines, cut into
    1cm slices
1 tbsp fine sea salt
750g minced lamb
1 onion, finely chopped
2 garlic cloves, crushed
1 tsp dried oregano
1½ tsp dried mint
2 bay leaves
1 cinnamon stick
1 tbsp plain flour
200ml red wine
400g can chopped tomatoes
2 tbsp tomato purée
7 tbsp olive oil
500g Maris Piper potatoes,
    cut into ½ cm slices
flaked sea salt
freshly ground black pepper

White sauce
50g butter
50g plain flour
400ml whole milk
25g Parmesan cheese,
    finely grated
1 tsp finely grated nutmeg
1 egg, beaten

Place the aubergine slices in a colander and sprinkle them with salt, then set them aside for 10 minutes.

Put the lamb mince, onions, garlic, oregano, mint, bay leaves and cinnamon in a large heavy-based frying pan and cook over a medium heat for 10 minutes, stirring with a wooden spoon to break up the meat.

Mix in the flour and season with salt and black pepper. Add the wine, tomatoes and tomato purée, then bring everything to a simmer. Cook for 30 minutes, stirring occasionally until the lamb is tender and the sauce has thickened. Check the seasoning and set aside.

Rinse the aubergine slices in cold water and pat them dry with a clean tea towel. Heat 3 tablespoons of oil in a heavy-based frying pan and fry a batch of aubergines for 2–3 minutes on each side. Remove them from the pan and put them on kitchen paper to drain. Fry the rest of the aubergine slices in batches, adding more oil as necessary and setting each batch on kitchen paper.

Cook the potatoes in boiling water for 5 minutes, then drain in a colander and cool them under running water until cold. Preheat the oven to 180°C/ Fan 160°C/Gas 4.

For the white sauce, melt the butter in a large saucepan and stir in the flour. Cook for a few seconds, then gradually stir in the milk. Add half the Parmesan and the grated nutmeg, then simmer the sauce gently for 4–5 minutes, stirring regularly. Season to taste with salt and black pepper. Remove the saucepan from the heat and quickly stir in the beaten egg. Cover the surface of the sauce with clingfilm to prevent a skin forming.

Spoon one-third of the meat sauce into a large, shallow ovenproof dish. Cover with a layer of potatoes and a layer of aubergines. Repeat the layers twice more, finishing with the aubergines. Pour over the white sauce, making sure it covers the aubergines in a thick, even layer, then sprinkle with the remaining Parmesan. Bake the moussaka in the oven for 45 minutes, or until deep golden-brown on top and bubbling.

LAMB MEATBALLS WITH BROAD BEANS AND CHARD

This is based on Egyptian and Israeli meatball dishes and makes a lovely green and fresh bowlful. If you use fresh broad beans, it's best to remove the outer grey skins to reveal the bright green beans inside. Baby frozen ones should be fine whole. You can also make the meatballs with beef.

SERVES 4

1 tbsp olive oil
1 onion, finely chopped
2 garlic cloves, finely chopped
500g minced lamb
50g breadcrumbs
50g pine nuts, toasted and
    lightly crushed
2 tbsp each of parsley,
    coriander and mint,
    finely chopped
1 tbsp dill, finely chopped
1 tsp ground cumin
½ tsp ground allspice
a grating of nutmeg
1 egg
1 lemon
extra herbs, for garnish
flaked sea salt
freshly ground black pepper

Sauce

1 tbsp olive oil
1 onion, finely chopped
200g Swiss chard, stems
    and leaves separated,
    both shredded
3 garlic cloves, finely chopped
500ml chicken stock
250g broad beans (frozen
    are fine)
2 tbsp coriander leaves,
    finely chopped
1 tbsp mint leaves, finely
    chopped
1 tbsp dill, finely chopped

Heat the olive oil in a frying pan and add the onion. Fry gently until it is soft and translucent, then add the garlic and cook for another couple of minutes. Allow to cool.

Preheat the oven to 220°C/ Fan 200°C/Gas 7. Put the mince in a large bowl and season it with salt and pepper. Add the breadcrumbs, pine nuts, herbs and spices to the meat, then the cooled onion and garlic and mix thoroughly. Break the egg into the mixture and stir to combine.

Shape the meatballs into rounds the size of golf balls – you should have about 20. Place them on a baking tray and bake them in the preheated oven for 10 minutes – they will finish cooking in the sauce.

To make the sauce, heat the olive oil in a large saucepan or casserole. Fry the onion and chard stems for a few minutes, then add the garlic and cook for another minute.

Pour in 400ml of the chicken stock, then add the broad beans and the meatballs. Simmer for 5 minutes.

Put the remaining chicken stock in a separate saucepan and add the chard leaves and chopped herbs. Simmer for a couple of minutes, then blitz with a stick blender until roughly puréed. Add this to the broad beans and meatballs, just before you serve. Squeeze over plenty of lemon juice, then garnish with extra coriander, mint and dill.

PELMENI

These are a Russian version of ravioli – little nuggets of tasty filling wrapped in a thin dough – and they are epic. You can get pelmeni moulds, but it's fairly easy to fold them by hand once you get the hang of it. There are loads of different fillings, but we've suggested a meat one or a potato and cheese variation. When serving, melted butter is essential but you may also like to add some soured cream or even some tomato sauce (see page 239).

SERVES 4

Dough
250g plain flour, plus
   extra for dusting
½ tsp sea salt
1 egg
2 tbsp soured cream
2 tbsp water

Meat filling
250g minced beef
150g minced lamb
100g minced pork
1 onion, finely grated
flaked sea salt
freshly ground black pepper

Potato filling
25g butter
1 onion, finely diced
300g floury potatoes, cut
   into chunks
100g cottage cheese
50g feta, crumbled
30g Parmesan cheese, grated

To serve
melted butter
crumbled fried bacon
soured cream
chopped dill

To make the dough, sift the flour and salt into a large mixing bowl, then make a well in the middle. Lightly whisk the egg with the soured cream and 2 tablespoons of water and pour this into the well.

Using a fork, start working the flour into the wet ingredients, until you have a rough, floury dough. Turn the whole lot out on to a lightly floured work surface and knead until the dough is smooth. It should not be sticky – if it is, add a little more flour. Cover the dough with clingfilm and leave for an hour while you make the filling. Each filling recipe makes enough to fill this quantity of dough so you only need to make one.

To make the meat filling, mix together all the ingredients and season well. Traditionally, the meat for pelmeni should be very finely minced, so put the mixture in a food processor and pulse a few times. This also helps to combine the ingredients thoroughly.

To make the potato filling, melt the butter in a frying pan, add the onion and fry gently until it's very soft and translucent. Meanwhile, boil or steam the potatoes until they are tender. Drain and mash them, then mix with the buttery onions and all the cheeses. Season and mix thoroughly.

Now for the assembly. Cut the dough in half and put one piece aside. Roll out the other piece on a floured surface – you want to roll it as thin as you can without it tearing, so not quite translucent.

Cut out rounds of dough with a 5–6cm cutter. Put a generously heaped teaspoon of filling into the centre of each round, then brush the edges with water or lightly beaten egg white. Stretch one side of the dough over the filling and press down firmly all round the edges, sealing it tightly into a half moon shape. Turn the corners inwards and squeeze together. Put the finished pelmeni on a floured surface until you are ready to cook them. Do exactly the same with the other piece of dough.

To cook, bring a large pot of salted water to the boil. Cook the pelmeni a few at a time – adding too many at once will crowd the pan and lower the temperature too much. Boil for between 5–7 minutes, then remove them with a slotted spoon and toss gently in melted butter to stop them sticking together. Serve with crumbled fried bacon and chopped dill and some soured cream on the side.

PICADILLO

A spicy mix of minced meat with sweet raisins and salty olives, this flavoursome stew is much loved in many parts of the Caribbean and Latin America. Enjoy it with pasta or rice or use it instead of beef chilli to stuff tacos. We've suggested pitted olives here, but pimento-stuffed ones would also be good.

SERVES 4–6

2 tbsp coconut or
  vegetable oil
1 large onion, finely chopped
1 red and 1 green pepper,
  deseeded and finely diced
2 garlic cloves, finely chopped
750g minced beef or pork
1 Scotch bonnet chilli, finely
  chopped, or 2 tsp hot sauce
1 tsp cumin
pinch of cinnamon
4 tomatoes, peeled and
  chopped or 200g chopped
  canned tomatoes
25g raisins
25g pitted olives, thinly sliced
25g capers, well rinsed
squeeze of lime juice
2 tbsp finely chopped parsley,
  to garnish
flaked sea salt
freshly ground black pepper

Heat the oil in a large heavy-based saucepan and add the onion and peppers. Cook them over a gentle heat until the onion is soft and translucent, then add the garlic, minced meat, Scotch bonnet or hot sauce, and the spices. Continue to cook over a slightly higher heat until the meat is well browned.

Season with salt and pepper, then add the tomatoes and raisins. Cook uncovered for about 20 minutes, then add the olives and capers and simmer for a further 5 minutes. Taste for seasoning and adjust accordingly. Add a squeeze of lime juice and garnish with finely chopped parsley.

CLASSIC BURGERS

For us, this is the perfect burger. The beauty is in its simplicity – just chuck steak instead of mince and a little seasoning. If you are up for it, the bone marrow does give extra flavour and juiciness. The burger sauce is lip-smacking good and you can serve the burgers as they are, with bacon and/or cheese as well as lettuce, slices of red onion, tomatoes, pickles and so on. The choice is yours, so enjoy.

SERVES 4

800g chuck steak, trimmed of any gristle or hard pieces of fat
50g bone marrow, finely diced (optional)
4 burger buns, split
flaked sea salt
freshly ground black pepper

Burger sauce
100g mayonnaise
2 tbsp tomato ketchup
a squeeze of lemon juice
1 large gherkin, finely chopped
1 tsp garlic powder
½ tsp chipotle paste or other hot sauce

First prepare the meat. Make sure it's well chilled – in fact, you can freeze the meat, then let it thaw partially and you'll find it much easier to cut. Put the meat through a coarse mincer, or chop it very finely by hand. It should be fine enough to stick together when you squeeze a handful. Add the bone marrow, if using.

Season the mixture with salt and a little black pepper, then divide the mixture into 4 and shape into round patties 2–2.5 cm thick. The mincing and chopping will help bring the meat to room temperature, but if it's still cold, leave the burgers to stand for a while.

Heat a non-stick frying pan or your barbecue. When the pan or grill is too hot to hold your hand over, add the burgers – there's no need for oil, as some fat will render out of the meat. Leave for 4 minutes, by which time the burgers should be very well seared and have a thick crust. Flip them and cook for another 3 minutes for rare meat, 4 minutes for medium rare, 5 for medium and up to 6 for well done.

If you want a cheesy topping, add it once you've flipped the burgers. Once the burgers are cooked to your liking, leave them to rest for a couple of minutes. Meanwhile, put the burger buns cut side down on the pan or barbecue to toast very slightly and take up some of the meaty flavours. Serve with your choice of toppings.

To make the burger sauce, mix all the ingredients together and season with salt and pepper.

BEEF MINCHI

This minced meat dish comes from the Chinese province of Macau, once a Portuguese colony. It's a sort of Chinese version of mince and tatties and is usually served topped with a fried egg. Something green on the side is good too. Traditionally, minchi is made with beef or pork or a mix of the two, but there are also chicken, fish and veggie versions.

SERVES 4

1 large potato (about 250g),
  cut into 1cm cubes
1 tbsp vegetable oil
1 onion, finely chopped
2 bay leaves
2 garlic cloves, finely chopped
600g minced beef
1 tsp Chinese five-spice
  powder
1 tsp ground cumin
½ tsp ground white pepper
¼ tsp soft light brown sugar
2 tbsp light soy sauce
2 tbsp dark soy sauce
a dash of Worcestershire
  sauce

Garnish
1 tbsp vegetable oil or butter
4 eggs
cayenne pepper (optional)
4 spring onions, cut into
  rounds

Bring a saucepan of water to the boil and add the cubes of potato. Blanch them for a minute, then drain.

Heat the vegetable oil in a wok. When it's hot and shimmering, add the potatoes and stir-fry them until they're golden brown and just cooked through. Remove the cubes with a slotted spoon and drain them on kitchen paper.

Add a little more oil if the pan is looking dry, then add the onion and bay leaves. Stir-fry on a medium heat until the onion is starting to take on some colour, then add the garlic and meat. Sprinkle over the spices and sugar. Cook, stirring continuously, until the meat has browned, then pour in the soy sauces and Worcestershire sauce. Cook for another 3–4 minutes, adding a splash of water if the mixture starts looking too dry.

Put the potatoes back in the wok to heat through. Meanwhile, heat a tablespoon of oil or butter in a frying pan and fry the eggs. Serve the minchi topped with a fried egg and a sprinkling of cayenne, if using, and the spring onions.

Tip
For a change, make this with 300g each of minced beef and pork.

MEATBALLS WITH TOMATO SAUCE

Everyone loves meatballs and these are baked, Italian style, with tomato sauce and topped with grated cheese for a wonderful family supper. If you like, replace 100g of the mince, with finely chopped smoked bacon or chorizo and fry this with the onion. Or try making the meatballs with lamb and use dried mint and cinnamon instead of oregano and nutmeg. Replace the milk with some crumbled feta. All good.

MAKES ABOUT
20 meatballs

1 tbsp olive oil
1 onion, very finely chopped
2 garlic cloves, finely chopped
600g minced beef or
   400g minced veal and
   200g minced pork
2 tsp dried oregano
a few gratings of nutmeg
grated zest of 1 lemon
100g fine breadcrumbs
50ml milk or single cream
1 egg
flaked sea salt
freshly ground black pepper

To serve
25g Cheddar, Gruyère or
   Parmesan cheese, grated

Tomato sauce
2 tbsp olive oil
1 onion, finely chopped
3 garlic cloves
1 tsp dried oregano
1 bay leaf
1 piece of thinly pared lemon
   peel
200ml red or white wine
2 x 400g cans chopped
   tomatoes
pinch of cayenne pepper
   (optional)
pinch of sugar (optional)
handful of chopped basil

Preheat the oven to 220°C/ Fan 200°C/Gas 7. Line a baking tray with non-stick baking parchment.

Heat the olive oil in a frying pan, then add the onion and fry it gently on a low heat until it's soft and translucent. Add the garlic and cook for a further minute, then take the pan off the heat.

Put the mince in a bowl and add the oregano, nutmeg, lemon zest, breadcrumbs, milk or cream and egg, then the cooked onion and garlic. Season generously with salt and black pepper. If you want to check the seasoning, fry a small piece of the mixture on both sides until it's just cooked through, then taste and adjust the seasoning accordingly.

Shape the mixture into rounds about the size of golf balls and weighing roughly 50g each. Place them on the baking tray, allowing space between each one. Cook them in the oven for 15–18 minutes until browned and just cooked through.

Transfer the meatballs to a baking dish and pour the tomato sauce over them. Sprinkle with grated cheese and bake in the oven for about 10 minutes until the cheese has melted.

Tomato sauce
Heat the olive oil in a saucepan. Add the onion and fry it gently on a low heat until it's very soft and translucent. Add the garlic, oregano, bay leaf and lemon peel, then cook for another couple of minutes.

Pour the wine into the pan, then boil until it has reduced by half. Add the tomatoes and season well with salt and pepper and add the cayenne, if using. Taste the sauce, and if the tomatoes are a bit too acidic, add a pinch of sugar. Bring the sauce back to the boil, then reduce the heat and simmer for 30 minutes, until it is reduced and thickened. Taste for seasoning and stir in a handful of chopped basil.

ITALIAN MEAT SAUCE

This recipe makes a lot of sauce, but it's well worth making a big batch like this and freezing some in portions to enjoy another day. Serve it up with a bowl of pasta, use it to stuff pancakes or arancini (see page 333) or make it into a shepherd's pie – the choices are endless. And for very economical version, try replacing half the meat with some cooked brown lentils, adding them at the same time as the tomatoes.

SERVES 8–10

1kg minced beef
3 tbsp olive oil
1 large onion, finely chopped
2 large carrots, finely chopped
3 celery sticks, finely chopped
4 garlic cloves, finely chopped
200g chicken livers, finely chopped (optional)
1 tsp dried oregano
2 bay leaves
1 sprig of thyme
250ml milk
500ml red wine
1 tbsp tomato purée
600g canned tomatoes or passata
400ml beef stock or water
flaked sea salt
freshly ground black pepper

First brown the beef – it's best to do this in batches, as if you overcrowd the pan the meat will steam rather than brown. Heat a large frying pan and put in some of the beef – no need for oil. Press it down with a wooden spatula and leave it to seal for 3–4 minutes until a brown crust has formed. Turn the meat over, and seal the other side, then start breaking up the meat. Once the meat is nicely browned, transfer it to a plate and brown the next batch.

Heat the olive oil in a large flameproof casserole dish or a heavy-based saucepan. Add the onion, carrots and celery and fry them gently on a medium heat for about 10 minutes. You can do this while the beef is browning. When the vegetables have started to soften and brown around the edges a little, add the garlic, chicken livers, if using, and oregano and cook for a further minute.

Add the browned meat to the vegetables, and cook for a minute or so longer, making sure the meat is just cooked through. Season with salt and pepper and add the bay leaves and thyme. Pour in the milk, then simmer on a very low heat until the milk has completely evaporated.

Pour in the red wine and allow it to boil until reduced by about two-thirds. Stir in the tomato purée, then add the tomatoes or passata and the beef stock or water. Bring to the boil, then turn down the heat, cover the pan with a lid and simmer the sauce for as long as you can, preferably at least 1½ –2 hours. Remove the lid and continue to cook for at least another 20–30 minutes to reduce the sauce.

Serve the sauce with pasta, or leave it to cool, then batch up into portions and freeze.

CHAPTER EIGHT
HOT, HOT, HOT

KOREAN BRAISED RIBS

Everyone loves ribs and these are really sticky and meaty. Not a genteel dish, we have to admit, but it's dead good and will bring a smile to your face. Easy to put together too, but make sure you allow time to marinate the ribs.

SERVES 4

1kg pork ribs (as meaty
  as possible)
2 tbsp vegetable oil
1 onion, finely chopped
3 garlic cloves, sliced
500ml light beer (Asian beer
  such as Tsingtao is ideal)
2 tbsp soy sauce
2 tbsp soft light brown sugar
4 spring onions, sliced finely
  lengthways

Rub

2 tbsp chilli powder
1 tbsp sweet smoked paprika
1 tsp garlic powder
1 tsp black peppercorns
½ tsp salt
2 tbsp soft light brown sugar
2 tbsp soy sauce
2 tbsp vegetable oil
1 tbsp sesame oil
1 tsp rice vinegar

Mix together all the rub ingredients to make a bright red, smooth, runny paste. Put the ribs in a large plastic, glass or ceramic container – not metal – and pour over the paste. Mix thoroughly so that all the ribs are completely covered, then leave to them to marinate for at least 2–3 hours, or overnight if possible.

To cook the ribs, heat a tablespoon of the vegetable oil in a large frying pan. Scrape off any excess marinade from the ribs, then brown them thoroughly in the oil – you'll need to do this batches so you don't overcrowd the pan. Don't be tempted to rush this stage – the ribs should be well caramelised.

Meanwhile, heat the remaining oil in a large flameproof casserole dish and gently fry the onion and garlic over a medium heat until they are starting to brown. As the ribs are browned, add them to the casserole, then when they're all done, deglaze the base of the frying pan with some of the beer. Pour this over the ribs, then pour the rest of the beer into the casserole dish.

Add the soy sauce and sugar, then bring to the boil. Turn down the heat, cover the casserole with a lid and leave to simmer for 2½–3 hours, until the ribs are very tender.

Serve the ribs garnished with the spring onions, with perhaps some steamed rice on the side.

PORK MOLE

Just to reassure you – this has nothing to do with small brown creatures! Mole is an amazing Mexican dish, flavoured with chillies, lime and a little dark chocolate, and it's a taste sensation. Try any combo of chillies, such as mulatto, pasilla, ancho, guajillo, but use a mixture of mild and hot so the sauce doesn't blow your head off. You can make the sauce ahead of time if you like and heat it up when you're ready to serve.

SERVES 6

1.5kg pork loin, boned,
    skinned and rolled
juice and grated zest
    of 2 limes
1 lime, thinly sliced
flaked sea salt
freshly ground black pepper

Sauce
40g dried chillies,
    preferably a mixture of
    Mexican types or 2 tbsp
    chipotle en adobo sauce
4 cloves
4 allspice berries
½ tsp white peppercorns
½ tsp anise or fennel
2cm cinnamon stick
20g lard, butter or
    vegetable oil
1 onion, finely chopped
3 garlic cloves, thinly sliced
2 tsp soft light brown sugar
50g ground almonds
50g breadcrumbs, preferably
    made from lightly toasted
    brioche
2 tbsp sesame seeds
½ plantain or banana
2 tomatoes, peeled and
    deseeded or 150g canned
    tomatoes
500ml chicken stock
15–30g dark chocolate

Put the pork in a non-metallic bowl and season it with salt and pepper. Pour the lime juice over the meat, add the lime zest, then stir to combine. Leave the pork to marinate in the fridge for at least a few hours or overnight.

Remove the meat from the fridge at least an hour before you want to cook it so it can come to room temperature. Preheat the oven to 220°C/Fan 200°C/Gas 7.

Put the slices of lime in the base of a roasting tin and put the pork on top. Pour over the marinading juices and add about 200ml water to the tin. Roast the meat for 20 minutes, then turn the oven down to 200°C/Fan 180°C/Gas 6 and continue to roast for another hour and 20 minutes, basting regularly with the pan juices. Remove the pork from the oven and leave it to rest for 10 minutes.

While the pork is roasting, make the sauce. If using dried chillies, take off the tops and remove the seeds. Dry-fry the chillies in a saucepan for a couple of minutes, then cover with water and bring to the boil. Simmer them until soft, then drain.

Put all the whole spices into a frying pan and toast them until you smell their fragrant aroma. Remove them from the heat and let them cool, then grind to a fine powder.

Heat the lard in a saucepan. Add the onion and fry it gently on a medium high heat until golden-brown and softened. Reduce the heat, add the garlic and cook for a further minute, then remove the pan from the heat and allow the onion and garlic to cool.

Put the onion and garlic in a blender with the rest of the sauce ingredients, except the chocolate. Blitz to make an ochre-coloured sauce the consistency of double cream – you can put this through a sieve if you want to make sure it is completely smooth. Pour the sauce into a pan and simmer it for about 20 minutes, then stir in the chocolate, adding it a little at a time and tasting until you get the flavour you want.

Pour any juices from the roasting tin and the resting pork into the mole sauce. Slice the pork and serve it with the sauce poured over it and the sticky lime slices on the side.

INDONESIAN SPICED PORK

The proper name for this dish of pork simmered in hot, sweet sauce is babi kecap and one of the ingredients is kecap manis, an Indonesian soy sauce that contains palm sugar. Good served with some rice and Asian greens.

SERVES 4–6

1.5kg boned pork shoulder, cut into 5cm chunks
½ tsp ground black pepper
1 tsp ground coriander
½ tsp ground ginger
¼ tsp ground cinnamon
½ tsp salt
1 tbsp groundnut or vegetable oil
1 large onion, or 6 shallots, thinly sliced
5 garlic cloves, crushed
20g fresh root ginger, peeled and grated
4 red bird's-eye chillies, deseeded and finely chopped
500ml chicken stock
4 tbsp kecap manis sauce
2 tbsp light soy sauce
2 tbsp tamarind paste (the non-concentrated sort)

Garnish
2 tbsp groundnut oil
4 shallots, thinly sliced
2 mild red or green chillies, thinly sliced

Put the pieces of pork in a bowl. Mix the spices and salt, then sprinkle them over the pork, turning the meat to make sure it is all well covered.

Heat the oil in a large flameproof casserole dish, then add the onion or shallots. Fry them gently over a gentle heat until soft and translucent. Add the garlic, ginger and chillies and cook for a further minute.

Add the pork to the casserole dish and cook on a medium heat for a few minutes, turning the pieces of meat until they are browned all over. Mix the chicken stock with the kecap manis, soy sauce and tamarind paste and pour this over the pork.

Bring to the boil, then turn the heat down and cook, uncovered, for 1½–2 hours, until the meat is very tender and the sauce has reduced. Stir regularly and turn up the heat a little towards the end of the cooking time if the sauce is still quite liquid.

To make the garnish, heat the oil in a frying pan and add the shallots. Fry over a medium to high heat, stirring frequently, until the shallots are golden-brown and crisp. Remove them from the pan, drain on kitchen paper and allow them to cool. Serve the pork garnished with the shallots and sliced chillies.

LAMB VINDALOO

We love our curries and a good hot vindaloo has long been a great favourite. It comes from the Goa region of India, which was once a Portuguese colony, and the cooking there has lots of Portuguese influences. Vindaloo has become a curry house classic.

SERVES 6

1.3 kg boneless lamb
  shoulder, cut into chunks
  of about 4cm
100ml red wine vinegar
2 tbsp vegetable oil
2 bay leaves
500g potatoes, peeled and
  cut into 2.5cm chunks
flaked sea salt

Sauce

125ml vegetable oil
4 onions, 3 thinly sliced
  and 1 chopped
6 garlic cloves, roughly
  chopped
3 long red chillies (do not
  deseed), roughly chopped
25g fresh root ginger, peeled
  and roughly chopped
1 tbsp English mustard
  powder
1 tbsp ground cumin
1 tbsp ground coriander
1 tbsp ground paprika
2 tsp ground turmeric
2 tsp cayenne pepper
1 tsp ground cinnamon

Trim the lamb, discarding any really hard lumps of fat and sinew. Mix the vinegar and vegetable oil with 2 teaspoons of sea salt in a non-metallic bowl until well combined, then add the lamb and turn it to coat in the marinade. Cover and leave in the fridge for 2 hours to marinate.

For the sauce, heat 3 tablespoons of the oil in a large heavy-based frying pan. Cook the sliced onions very gently over a medium-low heat for 15 minutes until they're softened and lightly browned, stirring occasionally.

While the onions are cooking, put the remaining chopped onion with the garlic, chillies, ginger, mustard powder, cumin, coriander, paprika, turmeric, cayenne pepper and cinnamon in a food processor and blend to a purée. Stir this purée into the fried onions. Add 2 tablespoons of oil and cook together for 5 minutes, or until the sauce has thickened and is beginning to colour. Tip the mixture into a flameproof casserole dish.

Drain the lamb in a colander over a bowl, reserving the marinade. Return the frying pan to the heat and add 2 tablespoons of the remaining oil. Fry the lamb over a medium high heat, turning occasionally until lightly browned – do this in 4 or 5 batches, adding a little extra oil if necessary. Add each batch of lamb to the casserole as it is browned. Preheat the oven to 180°C/160°C Fan/Gas 4.

Pour the reserved marinade and 500ml water into the casserole dish, then add 2 teaspoons of salt and the bay leaves and bring to a simmer. Cover the surface of the curry with a piece of greaseproof paper, then put a lid on the dish. Cook in the oven for 45 minutes.

Remove the casserole from the oven and stir the potato chunks into the curry. Replace the greaseproof paper and the lid and continue to cook for a further hour or until the lamb and potatoes are very tender. Check the seasoning and add salt to taste.

Serve with some rice or warmed naan bread and a bowl of cooling yoghurt on the side.

MUTTON SAAG

This is the curry Dave loves best. Saag dishes are all based on leafy greens such as spinach, as well as other vegetables and sometimes meat. You can use lamb, but mutton gives a richer, deeper flavour and works really well with the iron-rich spinach. You might need to ask your butcher to bone the leg of mutton for you – you'll need about 1.7g in weight to get 900g of meat.

SERVES 6

5 tbsp vegetable oil
4 large onions, sliced
10 cardamom pods
1 tbsp cumin seeds
2 tsp mustard seeds
¼ cinnamon stick
2 long red chillies, sliced
6 garlic cloves, roughly
    chopped
1 tbsp ground coriander
2 tsp ground turmeric
500g spinach leaves
    (preferably not baby
    spinach), stalks removed,
    washed and drained
900g boneless mutton leg
    meat, cut into 4cm pieces
1 bay leaf
2 tbsp tomato purée
flaked sea salt
freshly ground black pepper

Heat 3 tablespoons of the oil in a large heavy-based frying pan. Cook the onions gently for about 20 minutes, or until they're softened and golden-brown.

Meanwhile, place the cardamom pods in a pestle and mortar and pound them lightly to split the pods. Tip them on to a board, open each pod and scrape the seeds back into the mortar. Add the cumin, mustard seeds and cinnamon stick and grind them to a fine, dry powder.

Transfer half the onions to a plate and set them aside. Put the pan back on the heat, stir the chillies and garlic into the remaining onions and cook them for 3 minutes. Add the cardamom mixture, the coriander and turmeric, then fry, stirring continuously, for 2 minutes. Preheat the oven to 160°C/ Fan 140°C/Gas 3.

Add 300g of spinach to the pan, cover and cook for 2–3 minutes. Remove the pan from the heat, tip the contents into a heatproof bowl and set aside to cool.

Return the pan to the heat and add a tablespoon of oil. Season the mutton all over with salt and black pepper. Working in 2 or 3 batches, brown the mutton over a medium-high heat until it's nicely browned on all sides, adding a little more oil if necessary. Transfer each batch to a flameproof casserole dish as it is browned.

Put the spiced onions and cooked spinach in a food processor and blend to a thick green paste. Stir this into the casserole dish with the meat and add the bay leaf, tomato purée and 800ml cold water. Season with a teaspoon of sea salt, stir well and bring to a simmer.

Cover the surface of the curry with a piece of crumpled baking parchment, then put a lid on the casserole dish. Place it in the oven and cook for 2–3 hours or until the mutton is very tender and the sauce is thick.

Stir in the reserved onions and the remaining spinach. Cover with the lid and put the dish back in the oven for 15–20 minutes or until the onions are hot and the spinach has wilted. Serve with rice or warm naan bread.

LAMB KOFTA CURRY

Serve these golden balls of heaven in curry sauce with a few dollops of cooling yoghurt on the side. Start the day before you want to eat this if possible, so the mixture can marinate overnight and the flavours can develop fully. Yes, there are quite a few ingredients, but this is not difficult to make and it's a good way of feeding six people for not much money.

SERVES 6

1 onion, roughly chopped
2 plump green chillies
  (deseed first if you prefer)
15g fresh root ginger, peeled
  and roughly chopped
4 garlic cloves, roughly
  chopped
1 tsp flaked sea salt
2 tsp garam masala
¼ tsp hot chilli powder
1 tbsp tomato purée
600g lean minced lamb
3 heaped tbsp finely chopped
  fresh coriander leaves
thick natural yoghurt and
  fresh coriander, to serve
  (optional)
freshly ground black pepper

Sauce
3 tbsp ghee or vegetable oil
2 onions, roughly chopped
4 garlic cloves, finely chopped
25g fresh root ginger, peeled
  and finely chopped
½–1 tsp hot chilli powder
1 tbsp garam masala
4 large ripe tomatoes,
  roughly chopped
1 tbsp tomato purée
1 tsp flaked sea salt
½ tsp caster sugar
500ml lamb stock
1 cinnamon stick
2 bay leaves

To serve
cooked rice
thick natural yoghurt
fresh coriander leaves

Put the onion, chillies, ginger, garlic, salt, garam masala, chilli powder and tomato purée in a food processor. Season with lots of pepper. For a great flavour, add more pepper than you think you'll need – it works.

Blend the ingredients to a paste that's as smooth as you can get it. You'll need to remove the lid of the food processor and push the mixture down with a spatula 2–3 times. Add the lamb and blend once more, then transfer the mixture to a bowl and stir in the coriander. Cover the dish with clingfilm and chill for 1–3 hours, or overnight, to allow the mixture to stiffen and the meat to absorb all the wonderful spices.

To make the sauce, heat the ghee (or oil) in a large non-stick saucepan and gently fry the onions, garlic and ginger for 10 minutes, or until they are softened and lightly browned, stirring regularly. Add the chilli powder and garam masala and cook for 20–30 seconds, stirring continuously.

Stir in the roughly chopped tomatoes and cook for 3–4 minutes over a high heat, or until they soften and release their juice, stirring continuously. Add the tomato purée and sprinkle with the salt and sugar and pour over the lamb stock. Season with lots of black pepper, add the cinnamon and bay leaves and bring to a simmer. Cover the sauce loosely with a lid and cook for 20 minutes, stirring occasionally.

While the sauce is simmering, make the meatballs. Take a small portion of the mixture and roll it into a smooth ball – a little smaller than a walnut in its shell. You should be able to make about 24 balls. If your mixture gets a little sticky, either roll the meatballs with damp hands or dust your hands with plain flour as you roll.

Remove the pan of sauce from the heat when the 20 minutes are up and fish out the cinnamon stick and bay leaves. Blitz the sauce with a stick blender until it's as smooth as possible – be careful, as the sauce will be hot. If you don't have a stick blender, leave the sauce to cool for a few minutes then transfer to a food processor and blend to a purée.

Put the pan back on the heat and stir up to 200ml water into the sauce – you might not need all of this. Bring the sauce to a gentle simmer, gently drop in the meatballs and bring back to a simmer. Cook, uncovered, for 30–35 minutes, or until the meatballs are tender and the sauce is thick, stirring regularly. If the sauce reduces too much or begins to stick on the bottom of the pan, add a little extra water and continue cooking. Adjust the salt and pepper to taste. Serve with rice and some yoghurt and coriander.

CORIANDER AND SOUR ORANGE LAMB

This punchy, citrus-flavoured stew is based on a Peruvian dish. We know it seems like a lot of peas, but you need them for the right balance of flavours, so trust us – this works. You do have to precook the potatoes in a separate pan, but otherwise it's a one-pot wonder and makes a tasty supper.

SERVES 4—6

25g bunch of fresh coriander, plus extra to serve
2 hot red chillies, deseeded if you prefer
1 head of garlic, cloves separated and peeled
3 tbsp olive oil
1 large onion, finely chopped
1kg lamb neck fillet or boned shoulder, cut into 3cm chunks
250ml Seville orange juice or 150ml orange juice and 100ml lime juice
750g new or waxy potatoes, thickly sliced
500g frozen garden peas or petits pois
1 large red pepper, deseeded and cut into strips
flaked sea salt
freshly ground black pepper

Roughly chop the coriander, chillies and garlic, then put them in a food processor with a tablespoon of the olive oil. Blitz until you have a paste, adding a little water if necessary.

Heat the remaining oil in a large flameproof casserole dish, then add the chopped onion and fry gently until it is soft. Add the paste, quickly followed by the meat, then stir for several minutes until the meat has browned and is completely coated with the paste.

Pour the orange juice, or the orange and lime juice combo, into the pan, then add enough water just to cover the lamb. Season with salt and black pepper. Bring to the boil, then turn down the heat, cover the pan and leave it to simmer for about an hour.

Meanwhile, bring a large saucepan of water to the boil, add the potatoes and blanch them for 5 minutes, then drain. When the lamb has been cooking for 45 minutes, add the drained potato slices, then the peas and red pepper. Cook for another hour until the peas are soft and sweet and the potatoes and lamb are tender. Serve garnished with extra coriander.

CURRY GOAT

Goat is a favourite meat in the Caribbean and curry goat is nearly always on the menu at family gatherings and parties. For the best flavour, buy a West Indian curry powder mix or make your own from the recipe below. If you buy your goat on the bone, get 1.5kg to give you about 1kg of meat – you can also use mutton. Rice and peas (see page 355) are the traditional accompaniment.

SERVES 4–6

1kg boned goat or mutton, cut into large dice

2 tbsp curry powder, either a West Indian brand, medium strength, or see below

3 spring onions, including the green part, finely chopped

a branch of thyme, separated into sprigs

2 garlic cloves, finely chopped

1–2 Scotch bonnet chillies, deseeded and very finely chopped

2 tbsp coconut or groundnut oil

2 large onions, sliced

2 large tomatoes, skinned, deseeded and chopped

300g floury potatoes, peeled and cut into chunks

2 tsp brandy or rum

a squeeze of lime juice

flaked sea salt

freshly ground black pepper

West Indian curry powder

2cm cinnamon stick

2 bay leaves

4 cloves

2 tbsp coriander seed

1 tbsp black peppercorns

1 tbsp allspice berries

1 tbsp fenugreek seeds

a couple of mace blades

1 tsp cardamom pods, seeds only

1 tbsp mustard seeds

2 tsp ground turmeric

2 tsp ground ginger

Put the goat in a large bowl and season it with salt and pepper. Sprinkle over the curry powder, then add the spring onions, thyme, garlic and Scotch bonnets. Leave for at least an hour to marinate or put the bowl in the fridge and leave it for longer – overnight if you like.

Remove the meat from the fridge at least an hour before you want to start cooking it. Heat half the oil in a large flameproof casserole dish and gently cook the sliced onions until they are soft. Remove the meat from its marinade, brushing off as much as possible and reserving it for later. Heat the remaining oil in a frying pan, then fry the meat, in batches if necessary, until it is well browned. Transfer each batch to the casserole dish as it is browned.

Add a little water to the frying pan and let it sizzle as you scrape up all the sticky bits, then pour this over the meat. Add the tomatoes and a small amount of water – about 300ml – then bring it to the boil. Don't worry if the water doesn't cover everything, as the meat will give out quite a lot of liquid during the cooking. Turn the heat down, then put a lid on the casserole dish and leave it to simmer until the meat is tender; about 1½ hours.

After the first hour, add the potatoes and the reserved marinade. Continue to cook until everything is tender and the sauce has reduced. Check for seasoning, then add the brandy or rum and a squeeze of lime. Serve with rice and peas (see p.355).

West Indian curry powder

Place all the whole spices, except the mustard seeds, in a dry frying pan and toast them over a medium heat, shaking the pan gently from time to time. When the aroma starts to intensify, add the mustard seeds. When they start to pop, the spices will be ready to grind. Grind the toasted spices together in a spice grinder or with a pestle and mortar, then mix them with the ground turmeric and ground ginger.

BEEF BIRYANI

This is a really special dish and although it does take a while to prepare, it is perfect for a celebration feast and makes a splendid centrepiece. If you like a bit more heat, don't deseed the chillies. And don't forget to infuse the milk with the saffron the night before you make your biryani.

SERVES 6

100ml whole milk
1 heaped tsp saffron strands
135ml vegetable oil
1kg braising steak, trimmed
  of hard fat and cut into bite-
  sized chunks
4 onions
4 garlic cloves
25g fresh root ginger, peeled
  and roughly chopped
2 fresh red chillies, deseeded
  and roughly chopped
5 cloves
2 tsp cumin seeds
2 tsp coriander seeds
¼ cinnamon stick
12 cardamom pods
½ whole nutmeg, finely
  grated
200ml natural yoghurt
2 bay leaves
2 tsp caster sugar
325g basmati rice
4 tbsp chopped fresh
  coriander
50g butter
flaked sea salt
freshly ground black pepper

To serve

3 hard-boiled eggs, cut
  into quarters
40g flaked almonds
50g sultanas
fresh coriander

Pour the milk into a small saucepan, add the saffron strands and heat gently for 2 minutes without letting the milk boil. Remove the pan from the heat and set it aside for 2–3 hours, preferably overnight, for the flavour to infuse.

Heat 2 tablespoons of the oil in a frying pan. Season the beef with salt and pepper, then brown it a batch at a time so you don't overcrowd the pan. As each batch is browned, transfer it to a large, lidded saucepan.

Roughly chop 2 of the onions and put them in a food processor with the garlic, ginger and chillies. Add 50ml cold water and blend to a smooth paste. Put the cloves, cumin, coriander, cinnamon, 1½ teaspoons salt and the seeds from the cardamom pods into a pestle and mortar and grind them to a fine powder. Grate the nutmeg into the mixture and tip it all into the onion paste. Add plenty of black pepper and mix well.

Add 3 more tablespoons of oil to the frying pan and fry the spiced onion paste over a medium heat for about 10 minutes until it is lightly browned, stirring often. Tip this into the pan with the beef, then stir in the yoghurt, 450ml water and the bay leaves. Place the pan over a low heat and bring to a gentle simmer. Cover with a lid and simmer gently for 1½ hours or until the beef is tender, stirring occasionally.

Take the lid off the pan and stir in the sugar, then turn up the heat and simmer the sauce for 10 minutes, or until it is reduced and thick. Add a little more salt and pepper to taste.

Cut the remaining 2 onions in half and slice them thinly. Pour 2 tablespoons of oil into a frying pan and fry the onions for 6–8 minutes over a fairly high heat until they are softened and golden-brown, stirring frequently. Set aside. Preheat the oven to 180°C/Fan 160°C/Gas 4.

Bring a saucepan of water to the boil and add a teaspoon of salt. Put the rice in a sieve and rinse under plenty of cold water, then stir the rice into the hot water and bring it back to the boil. Cook for 5 minutes, then drain well. Add the coriander and stir until well combined.

Transfer half the meat and sauce into a large ovenproof dish. Spoon over half of the part-cooked rice and drizzle with half the milk and saffron mixture. Top with half the fried onions. Repeat the layers once more, then dot with the butter. Cover the dish with a couple of layers of tightly fitting foil and bake for 30 minutes.

Toast the almonds in a non-stick frying pan over a medium heat for 4–6 minutes, watching them carefully to make sure they don't burn. Stir the sultanas into the almonds and immediately tip them all into a bowl. Set aside to cool.

Remove the dish from the oven, take off the foil and lightly fluff the rice with a fork. Garnish with the eggs and scatter the toasted almonds and sultanas on top. Add a few fresh coriander leaves, then serve up your biryani with pride.

BEEF RENDANG

An Indonesian speciality, beef rendang is a glorious curry made with coconut and was one of the most popular dishes we featured on our *Best of British* series. Serve with jasmine rice and greens for a slap-up supper. Chuck steak works well for this, but you can use any good braising beef.

SERVES 6

2 lemon grass stalks, dry
outer leaves removed,
roughly chopped

3 red onions, quartered

6 garlic cloves

25g fresh root ginger, peeled
and roughly chopped

75g galangal, peeled and
roughly chopped

3 plump red chillies, roughly
chopped without deseeding

3 tbsp vegetable oil

2 tsp ground cumin

1 tbsp ground coriander

1 tsp ground turmeric

1.5kg chuck steak, trimmed
and cut into 3cm cubes

400ml can coconut milk

4 fresh kaffir lime leaves

1 cinnamon stick

1 tbsp soft light brown sugar
or palm sugar

2 tsp tamarind paste or
freshly squeezed juice
of 1 lime

2 tbsp dark soy sauce

toasted coconut flakes,
to serve (optional)

flaked sea salt

freshly ground black pepper

Put the lemon grass, onions, garlic, ginger, galangal and chillies in a food processor and blend them to a fine paste. You may need to remove the lid and push the mixture down a couple of times with a spatula until you get the right consistency.

Heat the oil in a large flameproof casserole and fry the paste gently for 3–4 minutes, stirring continuously. Add the cumin, coriander and turmeric and cook for another 2 minutes.

Add the beef to the pan and stir to coat it in the paste and spices. Cook for 5 minutes, stirring continuously, until the meat is very lightly coloured all over. Pour the coconut milk and 400ml cold water into the casserole dish, then add the lime leaves, cinnamon stick, sugar, tamarind paste or lime juice, soy sauce and 2 teaspoons of salt and bring to a simmer.

Reduce the heat and leave the rendang to simmer gently for 2½–3 hours, uncovered, or until the meat is meltingly tender and the sauce is thick and glossy. Stir the beef occasionally towards the beginning of the cooking time, then more often later on as the coconut milk reduces so the sauce doesn't stick to the bottom of the pan. Season to taste with more salt and black pepper.

Pick out the kaffir lime leaves and cinnamon stick, and serve the rendang sprinkled with the toasted coconut, if using.

Tip
This curry is even better made the day before it's eaten, so cook it for 15 minutes less and cool quickly in a large, shallow dish. Cover and keep it in the fridge. Next day, reheat the rendang slowly in a large casserole dish until piping hot, stirring just enough to distribute the heat, but not so often that the meat breaks up.

BEEF CHILLI WITH BITTER CHOCOLATE

There's nothing like a gutsy chilli on a winter's evening. This recipe is really good and a bit different from the usual chilli in that we use some diced steak as well as mince to give extra texture and a more luxurious feel. Don't be scared about the chocolate – it just adds richness and isn't sickly. You must use proper bitter dark choc though, not an Easter bunny.

SERVES 6–8

4 tbsp vegetable oil

500g good-quality braising steak such as chuck, finely diced

500g good-quality minced beef

1 white onion, finely chopped

1 red onion, finely chopped

2 celery sticks, chopped

1 dried chipotle chilli

1 tbsp dried chilli flakes

½ tbsp chilli powder

2 tsp dried oregano

3 tbsp soft light brown sugar

2 x 400g cans chopped tomatoes

500ml beef stock

400g can kidney beans, drained and rinsed

400g can black-eyed beans, drained and rinsed

75g plain chocolate, minimum 70% cocoa solids, roughly chopped

handful of fresh coriander, chopped

8 tbsp soured cream, to serve

4 spring onions, trimmed and thinly sliced, to serve

flaked sea salt

freshly ground black pepper

Heat 2 tablespoons of the oil in a large heavy-based pan with a tight-fitting lid.

Fry the diced steak in batches until it's browned all over, setting each batch aside on a plate. Add another tablespoon of oil to the pan and fry the mince until it's browned, then set it aside with the steak.

Add the remaining tablespoon of oil to the pan and fry the onions and celery for 3–4 minutes, or until the onions have softened but not browned. Stir in the chipotle chilli, chilli flakes, chilli powder and oregano and cook for a further 2 minutes.

Return the diced and minced beef to the pan, then stir in the sugar, chopped tomatoes, beef stock, kidney beans and black-eyed beans. Bring the mixture to the boil, then reduce the heat until it is simmering. Cover the pan and continue to simmer over a low heat for 2–3 hours.

Alternatively, you can transfer the mixture to an ovenproof dish and cook it in a preheated oven at 140°C/ Fan 120°C/Gas 1, for the same amount of time.

Just before serving, season the chilli with salt and black pepper. Stir in the chocolate until melted, then add the chopped coriander.

Serve the chilli with steamed rice and top each serving with a dollop of soured cream. Garnish with the sliced spring onions.

Tip

This recipe makes a large amount, but freezes well. Leave any leftovers to cool completely, then batch up into portions and pop them in the freezer.

BURMESE CURRY

This continues our round the world curry quest – it's a curry jungle out there. We've suggested beef here, but you can make this curry with lamb or goat if you like. The flavours are lovely and mellow and you can add extra chillies if you want more heat. The shallots are an authentic touch. The trick is to cook them quite briskly so they go a lovely deep golden-brown, but not black.

SERVES 4–6

750g stewing steak,
  cut into large chunks
½ tsp turmeric
½ tsp red chilli powder
3 tbsp vegetable or
  groundnut oil
3cm galangal, grated
  (or 1 tbsp ready-grated)
4 garlic cloves, crushed
750ml chicken stock or water
100g tomatoes, chopped
  (fresh or canned)
1 tbsp fish sauce (nam pla)
4 shallots, thinly sliced
2 tbsp torn coriander leaves
1 tbsp peanuts, lightly roasted
  and crushed, to serve
sliced red or green chillies
  (optional), to serve
flaked sea salt
freshly ground black pepper

Put the chunks of beef in a bowl and season them with salt and black pepper. Mix the turmeric and chilli powder, add them to the bowl and toss the beef until it's all covered in spice. Set it aside for about an hour.

Heat a tablespoon of the oil in a large flameproof casserole dish, add the meat and sear it on all sides. Turn down the heat, add the galangal and garlic and fry them gently for a couple of minutes, until you can smell the aroma.

Add the stock or water, tomatoes and fish sauce. Bring the mixture to the boil, then turn down the heat and partially cover the pan with a lid. Leave the curry to simmer gently for an hour and a half, stirring every so often.

Meanwhile, heat the remaining oil in a frying pan. Add the shallots and fry them quite briskly on a medium-high heat until they're quite crisp and golden-brown, stirring regularly. Remove them from the pan and drain them on kitchen paper.

Add half the shallots to the beef curry and simmer for a further 15 minutes. Taste for seasoning and add salt and pepper if needed. Serve garnished with the remaining shallots and the coriander leaves, peanuts and chillies, if using.

CREOLE SPICED BEEF

Another wonderful Caribbean recipe, this is lovely served with coconut rice – you can use the rice and peas recipe on page 355, but leave out the peas. You'll notice that there is no liquid to speak of in this, other than the tomatoes and tot of rum, but that's fine – the meat releases lots of liquid as it cooks. And as Kingy always says: anything with pineapple chunks is worth eating.

SERVES 4–6

1kg stewing steak, cut
   into 5cm cubes
juice of 2 limes
3 garlic cloves, finely chopped
15g fresh root ginger, peeled
   and grated
1 Scotch bonnet chilli,
   deseeded and finely
   chopped
1 tsp dried oregano
½ tsp black peppercorns,
   ground
½ tsp ground allspice
½ tsp ground cinnamon
1 tbsp coconut oil or
   15g butter
2 onions, thinly sliced
3 bay leaves
2 tomatoes, finely chopped
   (about 150g)
1 tbsp dark rum
a grating of nutmeg
   (about ¼ tsp)
200g pineapple, cut into
   chunks (optional)
flaked sea salt
freshly ground black pepper

Put the beef in a bowl and season it with half a teaspoon of salt and lots of freshly ground black pepper. Put the lime juice, garlic, ginger, Scotch bonnet, oregano and spices into a food processor or blender and blitz. You won't get a completely smooth result, but that's fine. Pour this mixture over the beef and mix thoroughly, then leave to marinate for at least a couple of hours – overnight if you wish.

Heat the coconut oil or butter in a large flameproof casserole dish. Add the onions and fry them gently until they are well softened. Strain the cubes of beef, reserving any marinade, and add them to the onions. Cook for a few minutes, until the beef is well coated with the oil or butter and onions, then pour in the reserved marinade.

Add the tomatoes with the bay leaves, rum and nutmeg. Bring to the boil, then turn down the heat and simmer, uncovered, for 1½–2 hours. Stir regularly, turning over the pieces of meat. If you're including the pineapple, add the chunks to the casserole for the last 30 minutes of cooking time. Taste for seasoning and adjust if necessary before serving.

ARGENTINIAN BEEF AND CHILLI STEW

Known as chupi in its native Argentina, this dish isn't quite a soup and isn't quite a chilli, but something in between. It has plenty of veg so makes a good one-pot dinner, with some bread on the side to soak up the juices.

SERVES 4

1 tbsp olive oil

1 large onion, finely chopped

1 large red pepper, deseeded
   and finely diced

1 celery stick, finely diced

1 red chilli, deseeded and
   finely chopped

2 garlic cloves, finely chopped

500g minced beef or very
   finely diced chuck steak

250g potatoes, diced

1 tsp dried oregano

1 tbsp tomato purée

pinch of sugar

1 litre beef stock

4 tomatoes, peeled and diced

2 tbsp finely chopped parsley
   leaves, to serve

hot sauce, to serve

flaked sea salt

freshly ground black pepper

Heat the oil in a flameproof casserole dish or a heavy-based saucepan. Add the onion, pepper, celery and chilli, then a splash of water and cover the pan with a lid. Leave to cook on a low heat for 10 minutes or so until the vegetables soften, stirring every so often.

Add the garlic and cook for a further 2 minutes, then turn up the heat, add the beef and stir until it is browned. Add the potatoes and oregano, then stir in the tomato purée and continue stirring until it coats everything.

Season with salt, pepper and the pinch of sugar, then pour the beef stock into the pan. Simmer for 10 minutes, then add the tomatoes and simmer for another 10 minutes. Taste for seasoning, then serve the stew with chopped parsley and a dash of hot sauce.

CHAPTER NINE
A LITTLE GOES A LONG WAY

SPAGHETTI CARBONARA

We reckon this is one of the best quick suppers going. Everyone loves it – it's basically bacon and eggs with pasta so what's not to like – and you can make the sauce in the time it takes to cook the spaghetti. Pecorino, by the way, is an Italian cheese made from sheep's milk. It works well in this dish, but if you can't find any, use extra Parmesan instead.

SERVES 4

400g spaghetti
2 tbsp olive oil
200g pancetta, thickly
  sliced, then diced
2 garlic cloves, crushed
50ml vermouth, such as
  Noilly Prat, or white wine
2 eggs
50g Pecorino cheese,
  finely grated
50g Parmesan cheese,
  finely grated
2 tbsp finely chopped parsley,
  to serve
flaked sea salt
freshly ground black pepper

First get the spaghetti going. Bring a large saucepan of water to the boil and add salt. Once the water is boiling, add the spaghetti and cook for 10–12 minutes until al dente.

Meanwhile, heat the olive oil in a large frying pan. Add the pancetta and cook it on a medium heat until it's nicely crisped. Add the garlic and fry gently for a couple more minutes.

Pour in the vermouth or white wine and let it bubble for a couple of minutes until well reduced. Remove the pan from the heat.

Crack the eggs into a bowl large enough to hold the pasta and beat them well, then stir in the cheeses. Season with a small amount of salt and lots of black pepper.

Strain the pasta in a colander. Don't do this too thoroughly as you don't want the pasta to be completely dry. Add the pasta to the egg and cheese mixture and mix thoroughly, making sure all the pasta is well coated. Then add the pancetta and garlic to the spaghetti and mix thoroughly again. Serve at once sprinkled with parsley.

Tip
Italian pasta recipes often suggest not draining the pasta too thoroughly, as it's good to have a little of the cooking water to lubricate the sauce.

CHORIZO, CLAMS AND WHITE BEANS

Spicy chorizo sausage and black pudding both go extraordinarily well with clams and other shellfish and their sock-it-to-me flavour really brings this dish alive. If you can't get clams, mussels are good too and usually very cheap. Morcilla is a Spanish version of black pudding and available in some delis in this country.

SERVES 4

1 fat chorizo sausage, cut into diagonal slices
1 red onion, cut into thin wedges
2 garlic cloves, finely chopped
½ tsp sweet smoked paprika
a large sprig of thyme
50ml dry sherry
250ml chicken stock
400g can tomatoes
2 x 400g cans cannellini beans, drained and rinsed
500g clams (or mussels)
100g black pudding, or Spanish morcilla, skinned and broken up
3 tbsp finely chopped parsley (optional)
flaked sea salt
freshly ground black pepper

Place a large flameproof casserole dish or a saucepan with a lid on the hob. Add the slices of chorizo and cook them on a medium heat until the slices start to brown and the fat is coming out. Chorizo can burn quite easily so keep a close eye on it. Remove the chorizo from the pan and set it aside.

Turn down the heat. Strain off most of the fat and reserve it, then add the wedges of onion. Fry them on a medium heat for several minutes until they're starting to colour, then add the garlic, paprika and thyme. Cook for another minute.

Add the sherry and allow it to sizzle for a minute or so, then pour in the chicken stock. Add the tomatoes and beans and season with salt and pepper. Bring to the boil, then turn the heat down to a gentle simmer and cover the pan. Leave to cook for 20 minutes while you prepare the clams or mussels.

Wash the clams in cold water. If using mussels, wash them well, pull off any beards and scrape off barnacles. For both clams and mussels, discard any that don't close when sharply tapped.

When the beans have finished simmering, put the chorizo back in the pan to warm through. Arrange all the clams or mussels on top, then cover the pan again and let them steam for 3–4 minutes. Meanwhile, heat some of the reserved chorizo fat in a frying pan and quickly fry the black pudding. Remove it from the pan and drain on some kitchen paper.

Check that the clams or mussels have opened and chuck out any that haven't. Sprinkle over the black pudding and garnish with lots of finely chopped parsley, if using, then serve at once.

SAUSAGE AND WHITE WINE RISOTTO

This is a risotto with attitude. It makes a good family supper and although you do have to stand over risotto while it cooks, it can be quite soothing to stir and inhale the delicious aromas. It's up to you how many sausages you use and it's good to brown them in the pan you're going to use for the risotto to add flavour. The caramelised onions give a lovely sweetness to the dish.

SERVES 4

1 tbsp olive oil

2–4 sausages, preferably Italian

1 litre warm chicken stock

30g butter

1 large onion, sliced

2 garlic cloves, finely chopped

1 sprig of thyme

1 sprig of rosemary

300g risotto rice

150ml white wine or vermouth (such as Noilly Prat)

50g Parmesan cheese, freshly grated, plus extra to serve

2 tbsp finely chopped parsley, to serve

flaked sea salt

freshly ground black pepper

Preheat the oven to 200°C/Fan 180°C/Gas 6. Heat the olive oil in a large, shallow pan, then add the sausages and brown them thoroughly. Transfer the sausages to a roasting tin and put them in the oven for 20 minutes. Pour the stock into a saucepan and keep it on a low heat.

Meanwhile, add half the butter to the pan. Add the onion and fry it gently on a medium to high heat until it starts to take on some colour – the aim is to lightly caramelise it to add sweetness. Add the garlic, herbs and rice, then cook for a further minute, stirring continuously, until the rice is glossy. Season with salt and pepper.

Pour in the wine or vermouth and bring it to the boil, then allow it to bubble until it's reduced by at least two-thirds. Add a ladleful of warm stock, then stir over a medium heat until all the liquid has been absorbed. Keep adding the stock, a ladleful at a time, making sure each one is absorbed before adding the next. Continue until you have used up all the stock – this should take about 20 minutes. The rice by this time should be swollen but still have a little bite.

Remove the sausages from the oven and cut them into small pieces. Check the consistency of the risotto – it should fall back in waves when you drag your spoon through it. Add the sausage to the risotto, then beat in the remaining butter and 50g of the grated Parmesan. Fish out the sprigs of thyme and rosemary. Sprinkle with parsley and serve with a bowl of freshly grated Parmesan.

BOSTON BAKED BEANS

We like a bit of bacon in our beans as the smokiness balances the sweetness well and makes a more flavoursome dish. Never have beans been better dressed. This recipe makes a bumper bundle of beans, which is good, as everyone loves them and they freeze well. Enjoy these on their own or with some sausages and greens – whatever you fancy. Just remember to put the dried beans in a big bowl of water to soak the night before you want to cook this.

SERVES 6–8

500g haricot beans, soaked
    overnight.
300g pork belly, cut into
    thick chunks
100g smoked streaky bacon
    or pancetta, cut into thick
    slices
1 large onion, finely chopped
100ml red wine, sherry or
    bourbon (optional)
4 cloves
1 blade of mace
1 bay leaf
1 sprig of thyme
400g can chopped tomatoes
3 tbsp black treacle or
    molasses
1 tbsp English mustard
a dash of Tabasco
a dash of Worcestershire
    sauce (optional)
flaked sea salt
freshly ground black pepper

Drain the soaked beans, put them in a flameproof casserole dish and add 1.5 litres of cold water. Bring the water to the boil and skim off any starch that collects on the top, then boil fiercely for 20 minutes. Turn the heat down and simmer the beans for another 40 minutes. Preheat the oven to 150°C/ Fan 130°C/Gas 2.

Place a frying pan on the heat and add the chunks of belly pork and bacon. Dry fry them until the fat starts to run out and the meat is browned, then tip it all into the casserole dish with the beans. Fry the onion in the same pan until it's softened and starting to caramelise, then add this to the beans and meat. Deglaze the pan with the red wine, sherry or bourbon, if using, or with a little water, scraping up any brown bits from the bottom of the pan. Pour this into the casserole dish, too.

Place the cloves, mace, bay and thyme on a small piece of muslin and tie it up to make a little bag, then drop this into the beans. Add the tomatoes, black treacle, mustard and Tabasco and the Worcestershire sauce, if using, then season well with salt and pepper.

Put a lid on the casserole dish and transfer it to the preheated oven. Cook for 3 hours, then remove the lid and cook for a further hour. The beans should be very tender and the sauce should be well reduced. Remove the bag of herbs and spices before serving.

If you're not using all the beans, let them cool completely, then divide into portions to freeze for another time.

SAUSAGE PASTA

This makes a nice change from tomato-based pasta sauces and it's a very good-tempered dish. You can use fewer sausages if that's what you have, or you can add extras such as 100g peas along with the white wine. We also like piling some shredded greens into the pasta pan for the last minute of the cooking time. Just drain them with the pasta and stir them through the sauce.

SERVES 4

1 tbsp olive oil
1 onion, finely chopped
400g sausages, preferably
   Italian, skinned and broken
   into chunks
2 garlic cloves, finely chopped
½ tsp dried oregano or sage
pinch of chilli flakes
½ tsp fennel seeds (if not
   using Italian sausages)
250ml white wine
50ml double cream
300g short tubular pasta,
   such as rigatoni or penne
grated Parmesan cheese,
   to serve
torn basil leaves, to serve
flaked sea salt
freshly ground black pepper

Heat the olive oil in a large frying pan, then add the onion and chunks of sausage meat. Cook over a medium heat, stirring regularly, until the onion has softened and the meat is cooked through.

Add the garlic, oregano or sage, chilli flakes and fennel seeds, if using, and stir for another minute. Season with salt and freshly ground black pepper.

Turn up the heat and pour over the wine. Simmer until the wine has reduced by half but the sauce still looks very liquid, then stir in the cream and take the pan off the heat and set aside.

Meanwhile, cook the pasta in plenty of boiling, salted water until just al dente. Drain, then add the pasta to the pan with the creamy sausage sauce. Stir to combine, then put the pan back on a low heat for a minute or so – the sauce should thicken and coat the pasta well.

Serve with plenty of grated Parmesan and a few torn basil leaves.

BACON JAM

Everyone loves bacon, so when we discovered bacon jam we knew we were on to a winner – bread and jam has never been better. This is a bit different from the other recipes in this chapter, as it uses a lot of bacon, but it's here because a small amount of it can transform your snack or supper. The coffee is essential for some reason. Ordinary instant isn't strong enough, but coffee made with instant espresso powder is fine. Give this a try, we beg you.

MAKES 1 LARGE POT

500g smoked streaky bacon, finely diced
2 medium onions, very finely chopped
3 garlic cloves, finely chopped
a sprig of thyme, left whole
75ml cider vinegar
75g soft light brown sugar
50ml maple syrup
100ml strong coffee
100ml bourbon (or use whisky or brandy)
1 tbsp chipotle paste, or 1 tsp chilli powder

Put the bacon in a large saucepan and fry it over a medium heat until it's starting to crisp up and brown. Add the onion and continue to cook until it has softened and is slightly caramelised. Add the garlic and thyme and cook for a further minute or so.

Add the cider vinegar, sugar, maple syrup, coffee and bourbon to the saucepan. Cook over a low heat, stirring continuously to dissolve the sugar, then leave to simmer gently for about an hour, until the mixture is thick and syrupy.

Using a stick blender if you have one, blend the bacon jam roughly – a couple of very short whirrs of the blade should be enough, as you want to keep plenty of texture in there. Stir again to mix.

Transfer the jam to a clean, sterilised jar and store it in the fridge. It keeps for up to a month. It's great on hot buttered toast, but is also very good in a roly poly – do a half portion of the sweet and savoury suet roll (see p.193) and spread it thickly with bacon jam.

WARM BACON AND LENTIL SALAD

Bacon and lentils are made for each other and you don't need a lot to flavour this hearty salad, which is just right for a quick midweek supper. You can buy bacon lardons in the supermarket – they're just little chunks of smoked bacon – but if you don't have any, just dice some rashers of streaky instead.

SERVES 4

250g green or puy lentils,
   well washed and drained.
2 bay leaves
2 garlic cloves, sliced
150g bacon lardons
1 tbsp olive oil
4 banana shallots, sliced into
   crescents
12 celery sticks, finely sliced
2 carrots, diced
2 garlic cloves, finely chopped
100ml dry sherry
1 tsp mustard
1 tsp red wine vinegar
12 cherry tomatoes,
   quartered
chopped parsley, to serve
flaked sea salt
freshly ground black pepper

Put the lentils in a large saucepan and add water to cover. Add the bay leaves and sliced garlic, then bring the water to the boil and simmer the lentils for 25–30 minutes until they are al dente. Take care not to overcook them, as you don't want them mushy. Drain them in a colander, reserving the cooking water, and set both aside.

While the lentils are cooking, heat a flameproof casserole dish or a large sauté pan with a lid, then fry the bacon lardons. Cook them on a medium heat until they're crisp and browned, then remove them with a slotted spoon and set them aside.

Add the olive oil to the bacon fat in the dish or pan, then put in the shallots, celery and carrots. Fry them on a medium heat for a few minutes until they're starting to take on some colour. Add the chopped garlic and fry for another couple of minutes. Pour in the sherry and allow it to reduce, then add a small ladleful of the lentil cooking water. Cover the pan and simmer the vegetables until tender.

Stir the mustard and red wine vinegar into the veg, then add the lentils, bacon and tomatoes. Season with salt and pepper to taste, then heat gently – the tomatoes need to be warmed through but don't let them disintegrate.

Sprinkle with parsley, then serve with salad leaves – preferably something with a touch of bitterness such as frisée or endive.

RABBIT AND ARTICHOKE PAELLA

We both love rabbit and think we should all eat it more often. Try this recipe and we're sure you'll agree. You can buy diced rabbit in some supermarkets now, or you can ask your butcher to prepare some for you, and you only need a small amount for this dish. In fact, rabbit is a traditional ingredient in paella and goes beautifully with artichokes. We like to use those chargrilled ones you see at the deli counter.

SERVES 4

3 tbsp olive oil
350g rabbit, diced into
  3cm cubes
1 large Spanish onion, finely
  chopped
4 garlic cloves, finely chopped
grated zest of 1 lemon
300g paella rice
150ml sherry (amontillado
  or fino)
pinch of saffron, soaked
  in a little warm water
1 litre chicken stock
250g small artichoke hearts,
  halved
a few sprigs of fresh oregano,
  leaves only
lemon wedges, to serve
flaked sea salt
freshly ground black pepper

Heat the olive oil in a large shallow pan. Quickly sear the cubes of rabbit over a high heat until they're lightly browned on all sides, then remove them and set them aside. Add the onion and cook it gently until very soft and very lightly coloured – this will take at least 15 minutes.

Add the garlic and lemon zest to the pan, then pour in the rice. Stir until the rice looks glossy, then turn up the heat a little and pour in the sherry. Cook for a minute, then add the saffron and its soaking water and the chicken stock. Tuck the rabbit and artichokes into the rice and sprinkle over some of the oregano. Season with salt and black pepper.

Simmer the paella for 10 minutes on a medium heat, shaking the pan every so often to make sure the rice isn't sticking on the bottom. Turn the heat down and continue to cook for another 5 minutes. By this point, most of the liquid should have been absorbed into the rice. Remove the pan from the heat, cover, and leave the paella to stand for another 5 minutes. The rice should be cooked through.

Serve sprinkled with more oregano and with lemon wedges on the side.

Tip
It is important to use short-grain paella rice, which absorbs lots of liquid, not long-grain. You'll see packs labelled Spanish paella rice in the supermarket or look for Bomba or Calasparra rice.

SHAKSHUKA WITH MERGUEZ SAUSAGES

Another sausage celebration – does the sausage know no bounds? Merguez are little spicy sausages, usually made from lamb and flavoured with harissa. They're a North African speciality but very popular here now too. They're ideal with shakshuka – also a North African dish – which is a simple little stew of peppers, onions and tomatoes with some fried eggs. Ideal for brunch, lunch or whenever you feel peckish.

SERVES 2
or 4 with a side dish

2 tbsp olive oil
6 merguez sausages
2 red onions, sliced into
   wedges
1 large red pepper, deseeded
   and sliced into strips
1 large green pepper,
   deseeded and sliced
   into strips
2 garlic cloves, finely chopped
1 tsp ground cumin
½ tsp sweet smoked paprika
½ tsp cayenne pepper
   (optional)
400g can tomatoes
4 eggs
4 dessertspoons Greek
   yoghurt
chopped coriander, parsley
   and mint, to serve
flaked sea salt
freshly ground black pepper

Heat a tablespoon of the olive oil in a large, shallow pan that has a lid. Add the sausages and cook them quickly on a high heat until browned all over, then remove and set them aside. When the sausages are cool enough to handle, cut them into chunks 3–4cm long.

Add the remaining olive oil to the pan. Gently fry the onions and peppers on a medium heat for about 10 minutes, until they've softened and started to brown slightly. Add the chopped garlic and the spices, then cook for another minute.

Put the sausages back in the pan, then pour in the can of tomatoes and 200ml water. Season with salt and black pepper. Simmer for another 10–15 minutes until the sauce has reduced down – it needs to hold its shape a bit so make sure it isn't too runny.

Make 4 evenly spaced 'wells' in the sauce. Carefully crack an egg into each one, then top each egg yolk with a dessertspoon of yoghurt.

Cover the pan with a lid, and cook for another 5 minutes or so until the whites of the egg have set. The yoghurt should prevent the yolks from firming up too much so they should still be runny. Serve at once, sprinkled with coriander, parsley and mint.

LAMB AND AUBERGINE TRAYBAKE

Feta, lamb, mint and aubergine are a very Mediterranean combo and this lovely one-pot dish smacks of sunshine and Greek islands. It feeds four generously with only two lamb steaks – a green salad to follow is all you need. Hardly any washing-up either and we always think that's a bonus.

SERVES 4

2 aubergines, cut into rounds
1 red pepper, deseeded
  and cut into thick strips,
  lengthways
1 red onion, cut into wedges
8 new potatoes, halved
2 tbsp olive oil
2 tsp red wine vinegar
2 garlic cloves, thinly sliced
1 tsp dried oregano
a few sprigs of rosemary
2 lamb leg steaks
handful of cherry tomatoes
150g feta cheese, cut into
  chunks
small bunch of mint,
  leaves only
flaked sea salt
freshly ground black pepper

Preheat the oven to 200°C/Fan 180°C/Gas 6. Put the aubergines, pepper, onion and potatoes in a large roasting tin and drizzle them with the olive oil and red wine vinegar. Sprinkle the garlic, oregano and rosemary on top, then season with salt and pepper. Cover the dish with foil, then put it in the oven for 40 minutes.

After 40 minutes, remove the roasting tin from the oven and check the vegetables – they should feel tender when pierced with a knife. Turn the oven up to 220°C/Fan 200°C/Gas 7.

Tuck the tomatoes and feta around the vegetables, making sure they are evenly spaced. Season the lamb steaks with salt and pepper, then put them on top of the veg.

Put the dish back in the oven and cook, uncovered, for 15–20 minutes, depending on how well done you want your lamb. Remove and allow the lamb steaks to rest for at least 5 minutes. Slice the lamb and serve with the vegetables, strewn with fresh mint.

BEEF AND MUSHROOM TERIYAKI NOODLES

Get all your ingredients prepped – just like we do on the telly – and you can make this in the time it takes the noodles to cook. Wok on! Most supermarkets stock shiitake mushrooms and some have enoki too – the ones that look like a brush but have a great savoury flavour. If you can't find any, use ordinary mushrooms instead.

SERVES 4

200g soba noodles (or any
   Japanese-style noodles)
1 tbsp groundnut or
   vegetable oil
200g rump steak (fat
   removed), cut into
   thin slices
200g shiitake mushrooms,
   sliced
1 punnet of enoki
   mushrooms, separated
15g fresh root ginger, peeled
   and finely chopped
2 garlic cloves, finely chopped
50ml sake
50ml mirin
25ml dark soy sauce
200g Asian greens,
   such as baby pak choi
5 spring onions, sliced
   into rings
flaked sea salt
freshly ground black pepper

Cook the noodles in plenty of salted water according to the instructions on the packet.

Meanwhile, heat the oil in a wok. When it's very hot and shimmering, add the slices of steak. Sear them very quickly until browned, stirring continuously, then remove them with a slotted spoon and set them aside. Add all the mushrooms and cook them very quickly, then set them aside with the beef.

Pour in a little more oil if necessary, then add the ginger and garlic. Stir-fry them for a minute, then put the beef and mushrooms back in the wok. Pour over the sake, mirin and soy sauce, then season with salt and pepper.

Add the greens and spring onions to the noodles for the last minute of cooking, then drain them thoroughly and toss everything into the wok. Make sure the greens and noodles are well coated with the sauce, then serve immediately.

CHAPTER TEN
LOVELY OFFAL

PEA AND PIG'S TROTTER SOUP

Si: It always bothered me that Dave wasn't a fan of pig's trotters, as I knew he was missing out on a real treat. So I came up with this fab soup which is gorgeously green and fresh and brought to life by the crispy crackling and meat from the roasted trotters. I'm glad to say that he loves it and is now a convert.

SERVES 4

4 pig's trotters
1 tbsp olive oil

Soup

1 tbsp olive oil
10g butter
1 onion, finely chopped
1 carrot, finely diced
1 celery stick, finely chopped
1 leek, finely chopped
1 garlic clove, finely chopped
1 litre chicken stock
2 bay leaves
bunch of fresh mint, stems and leaves separated
400g peas, fresh or frozen
2 tbsp double cream (optional)
flaked sea salt
freshly ground black pepper

Garnish

1 tbsp olive oil
3 garlic cloves, very thinly sliced

Preheat the oven to 150°C/Fan 130°C/Gas 2. Rub the pig's trotters with olive oil, then season them with salt. If possible, stand the trotters upright on a baking tray or in a roasting tin; otherwise, lay them on a well-oiled rack inside a tin. Roast the trotters in the oven for about 2 hours, then turn up the heat to 200°C/Fan 180°C/Gas 6 and cook for another 20 minutes to crisp up the skin. Remove the trotters from the oven and leave them to cool a little.

When the trotters are cool enough to handle, remove the crackling and break it into thin shards. Remove any meat too and set aside both the meat and the crackling. Chuck everything else away.

To make the soup, heat the olive oil and butter in a large saucepan. Add all the vegetables and the garlic with a splash of water. Fry very gently for at least 10 minutes, until the vegetables have softened and are taking on a little colour. Stir regularly to make sure they aren't sticking.

Add the stock and the bay leaves. Tie the mint stems together loosely (this will make them easier to remove later) and add them to the saucepan as well, then season with salt and pepper. Simmer for 10 minutes until the vegetables are completely tender, then add the peas.

Simmer for another couple of minutes, until the peas are just cooked, but still very fresh and green in appearance. Remove the bay leaves and mint stems from the saucepan and add the mint leaves. Allow the leaves to wilt very slightly, then blitz the soup with a stick blender or in a food processor until smooth.

To make the garnish, heat the olive oil in a frying pan, then add the slices of garlic. Fry them briskly for just 1 minute until they've crisped up but have not taken on much colour. Remove them from the pan and drain them on kitchen paper.

Stir the reserved trotter meat through the soup. Serve garnished with the crackling and crisp garlic slices.

STUFFED LAMBS' HEARTS

Your butcher will prep the lambs' hearts for you or if you buy them in the supermarket they should be ready to cook. It's still worth checking them over for any particularly prominent bits of ventricle and sinew, though, and snipping them out with scissors. If the hearts have very thick layers of fat on them, particularly around the opening, trim it but leave some, as it will melt into the sauce and improve the texture.

SERVES 4

8 lambs' hearts, trimmed
  (see above)
2 tbsp plain flour
½ tsp cayenne pepper
1 tbsp olive oil
15g butter
1 large onion, thinly sliced
2 garlic cloves, finely
  chopped
250ml white wine
250ml chicken stock
4 tomatoes, peeled and
  chopped
flaked sea salt
freshly ground black pepper

Stuffing
1 tbsp olive oil
1 onion, finely chopped
2 garlic cloves, finely
  chopped
100g breadcrumbs
grated zest of 1 lemon
½ tsp cayenne pepper
1 tsp dried mint
pinch of cinnamon
small bunch of parsley
  (or dill or coriander)
1 egg

First make the stuffing. Heat the olive oil in a frying pan and add the onion. Fry it gently for several minutes until it's very soft and translucent, then add the garlic and cook for another couple of minutes. Remove the pan from the heat and leave the onion and garlic to cool.

Put the breadcrumbs in a bowl and add the lemon zest, cayenne, mint, cinnamon, parsley and the contents of the frying pan. Finally, add the egg and mix thoroughly. Put some stuffing into each heart.

Mix the plain flour with the cayenne in another bowl and season with salt and pepper. Toss the hearts in the flour, then shake off any excess.

Heat the olive oil and butter in a large flameproof casserole dish. Add the onion and fry it gently over a medium heat until it's started to soften and caramelise. Add the garlic and cook for another couple of minutes. Remove the onion and garlic from the dish with a slotted spoon and set them aside. Turn up the heat, add the stuffed hearts and brown them on all sides – you may have to do this in a couple of batches. Put all the browned hearts back in the dish, together with the onion and garlic.

Pour over the wine and bring it to the boil, then add the chicken stock and tomatoes. Season with salt and pepper, then reduce the heat and cover the casserole with a lid. Simmer for 1½–2 hours, until the hearts are tender. Remove the lid and reduce the sauce slightly if necessary.

Alternatively, preheat the oven to 150°C/ Fan 130°C/Gas 2 while browning the hearts, then cook them in the oven for about 2 hours or until tender. Serve with new potatoes, rice or crusty bread.

SWEETBREADS

Sweetbreads are the thymus glands of a calf or a lamb – not the nuts – and they're really tender and tasty. Chefs are divided on how best to prepare them. Some say to remove all the membrane, while others advise only to take off some of it, otherwise the sweetbread will fall apart. We suggest that the best option is to take off what you can. Whatever you do, don't skip the soaking step, as this greatly improves the flavour of the sweetbreads.

SERVES 4

400g sweetbreads
1 tbsp white wine vinegar
1 bay leaf
2 cloves
1 tbsp plain flour
2 tbsp olive oil
15g butter
50ml dry sherry (fino is good)
4 fresh tomatoes, finely chopped (peeling optional)
pinch of sugar
1 tsp sherry vinegar
¼ tsp hot paprika
2 tbsp capers, well rinsed
grated zest of 1 lemon
a small bunch of parsley, chopped
flaked sea salt
freshly ground black pepper

To prepare the sweetbreads, soak them in cold water for several hours, changing the water regularly – you can leave them overnight if you like. The longer you leave them, and the more frequently you change the water, the milder the flavour will be.

Bring a large saucepan of cold water to the boil, season it with salt and pepper, then add the vinegar, bay leaf and cloves. Add the sweetbreads, immediately turn the heat right down and simmer them very gently for 5 minutes. Drain the sweetbreads, discarding the bay leaves and cloves, and run some cold water over them to cool them down.

When the sweetbreads are cool enough to handle, take a sharp knife and cut or scrape off any obvious bits of fat, gristle and membrane (the very thin skin surrounding each sweetbread). Pat them as dry as possible with kitchen paper.

Season the flour, then toss the sweetbreads in the seasoned flour, shaking off any excess.

Heat the butter in a large frying pan with the olive oil. Fry the sweetbreads for 2–3 minutes on each side until they're golden-brown. The centres should be soft, almost like thick custard.

Remove the sweetbreads from the pan and keep them warm. Turn up the heat and add the sherry to the pan to deglaze it, scraping up all the sticky bits. When the sherry has bubbled up and reduced – this should take a matter of seconds – add the tomatoes, sugar, sherry vinegar and paprika. Season with salt and pepper.

Continue to cook on a medium high heat for a couple of minutes – just until the tomatoes have started to break down – then add the capers, lemon zest and parsley. Cook for another 2 minutes. Put the sweetbreads back in the pan to warm through briefly, then serve them with some of the sauce spooned over and perhaps some rice or pasta on the side.

LAMB'S LIVER AND BULGUR WHEAT SALAD

There's more to liver than bacon and onions. This is a lighter than usual way of serving liver and teams it with a fresh, herby bulgur wheat salad. It's so delicious it might even tempt the offal haters among you. Go on – give it a go.

SERVES 4

400g lamb's liver,
  thinly sliced
1 tbsp flour
½ tsp allspice
½ tsp cayenne pepper
¼ tsp cinnamon
1 tbsp olive oil
150g bulgur wheat,
  soaked in warm water
  for 10 minutes
2 tomatoes, finely chopped
½ cucumber, deseeded and
  finely diced
½ red onion, finely chopped
a large bunch of parsley,
  very finely chopped
a small bunch mint, finely
  chopped
salad leaves, to serve
flaked sea salt
freshly ground black pepper

Dressing
1 tbsp olive oil
juice of 1 lemon
1 tbsp pomegranate
  molasses
pinch of cinnamon

Pat the slices of liver dry with kitchen paper. Mix the flour with the spices and season with salt and pepper. Toss the liver in the spicy flour and shake off any excess.

Heat the olive oil in a large frying pan. When it's hot, add the slices of lamb's liver, and cook them for 2 minutes on each side. Remove the liver from the pan and leave it to rest. Add a small amount of water to the pan to deglaze it, scraping up all the sticky bits, and let it reduce.

Drain the bulgur wheat and put it in the frying pan. Stir the bulgur over a low heat, until it starts to smell slightly nutty and looks drier, then remove the pan from the heat and tip the bulgur into a bowl. Add the tomatoes, cucumber, onion and herbs and mix well, then season with salt and pepper.

Arrange the bulgur salad on plates and top with slices of liver and some leaves. Whisk the salad dressing ingredients together and season, then drizzle this over each serving. Serve at room temperature.

DEVILLED KIDNEYS

Be a demon and give these little devils a go – they're so good they made Dave's tache curl. Kidneys are one of those things you either love or hate and we love 'em. Devilled kidneys on toast were a popular breakfast dish in the old days and we think they make an excellent brunch, lunch or starter. Be sure to prepare the kidneys carefully as we describe here and you'll have a nice little treat.

SERVES 4

8 calves' or lambs' kidneys
2 tbsp plain flour
1 tsp cayenne pepper
   or hot paprika
15g butter
50ml dry sherry
50ml chicken stock
a dash of Worcestershire
   sauce
1 tsp Dijon or English
   mustard (depending how
   much heat you want)
hot buttered toast, to serve
flaked sea salt
freshly ground black pepper

First prepare the kidneys. If they are whole, you may need to remove the very thin membrane that surrounds them. Cut into the kidney with a sharp knife and peel the membrane away – it should come off very easily and cleanly.

Now look at the core of the kidney (where it dimples) and you will see white gristle or tendons, the tough, central bit of which should be removed. The easiest way to do this is to snip the centre out with sharp scissors – see opposite. Cut the kidneys in half and pat them dry.

To devil the kidneys, mix the flour with the cayenne and season well with salt and pepper. Toss the kidneys in the flour.

Melt the butter in a large shallow frying pan over a medium-high heat. When it has melted, add the kidneys and cook them for a couple of minutes on each side.

Add the sherry, stock and Worcestershire sauce, then whisk in the mustard. Allow everything to bubble, then turn the heat down and simmer for another 3–4 minutes. The kidneys should still be slightly pink inside. Taste and add salt and black pepper if necessary.

Serve the kidneys and sauce on hot buttered toast.

LIVER AND BACON WITH PEAS

For a change from liver with onion gravy, we like to make this recipe in which the liver is bathed in a sweet sauce containing a bit of booze and some apple or redcurrant jelly. If you'd like slightly less sweetness, use red wine instead of the Madeira; perfect with buttery mash to soak up all the juices.

SERVES 4

1 tbsp olive oil
100g smoked bacon lardons
1 onion, thickly sliced
600g lamb's or calf's liver, cut on the diagonal into thick slices
1 tbsp plain flour
1 tsp mustard powder
1 sprig thyme
1 bay leaf
100ml Madeira (or sherry or port)
200ml chicken or beef stock
1 tsp apple or redcurrant jelly
300g frozen peas or petits pois
flaked sea salt
freshly ground black pepper

Heat the olive oil in a large, shallow pan. Add the bacon lardons and fry them quite briskly until plenty of the fat runs out. Add the onion and cook for a few minutes longer until the slices have started to take on some colour.

Blot the slices of liver with kitchen paper, making sure they are dry. Mix the flour with the mustard powder and season it with salt and pepper, then dust the liver with this mixture, patting off any excess.

Add the slices of liver to the pan and sear them for a minute on each side until well browned. Add the herbs, then pour over the Madeira. Allow the wine to bubble up and cook for a couple of minutes, then pour in the stock. Simmer for another couple of minutes.

Whisk in the jelly until it has dissolved, then add the peas. Cook for another few minutes. The sauce should be quite well reduced and the liver should still be slightly pink in the middle. Best served with a pile of mashed potato (see p.352).

CALF'S LIVER VENEZIANA

Simple, quick and utterly delicious, this is the classic way of preparing calf's liver, which is pricier than lamb's but has a more delicate flavour. Use Spanish onions if you can, as they are sweeter and cook into a lovely gooey mass much more successfully than smaller, more pungent onions. Ask your butcher to cut the liver into really thin slices for you. Offally delicious, that's our verdict.

SERVES 4

3 tbsp olive oil
30g butter
2 large Spanish onions,
   thinly sliced
a sprig of thyme
500g calf's liver, thinly sliced
50ml Marsala wine
100ml chicken stock
2 tbsp finely chopped
   parsley (optional)
flaked sea salt
freshly ground black pepper

Heat 2 tablespoons of the olive oil and half the butter in a large, shallow pan. Add the onions and thyme and season with salt and pepper. Cook the onions slowly on a low heat for at least 20 minutes, until they are really soft and sweet. Remove them from the pan and set them aside.

Add the remaining oil and butter to the pan and turn up the heat. When the butter is foaming, add the slices of liver, in batches if necessary so you don't overcrowd the pan, and fry them for a minute on each side. The aim is to get a good brown crust on the outside, but keep the liver pink on the inside.

Remove the liver from the pan and keep it warm. Pour the Marsala into the pan to deglaze, scraping up all the sticky bits and letting the alcohol bubble. Put the onions and liver back in the pan and add the chicken stock.

Simmer for a couple of minutes to make sure everything is hot, then serve immediately with salad or green veg. Garnish with chopped parsley if you like.

ROASTED BONE MARROW

Our grans would be gobsmacked to know that smart restaurants now serve up roasted bone marrow – the gooey stuff in the middle of bones. Back in the old days bone marrow was seen as a super-cheap food for the family, then it fell out of favour for a long time. It is very nutritious and it's good to see marrow bones appearing in the shops again. This recipe makes a cracking snack or starter.

SERVES 4

4 beef marrow bones,
  split lengthways
4 tbsp breadcrumbs
1 tbsp capers, chopped
2 tbsp finely chopped
  parsley
grated zest of 1 lemon
flaked sea salt
freshly ground black pepper

To serve
mixed greens – watercress,
  lamb's lettuce, spinach
a few radishes, thinly sliced
1 shallot, very thinly sliced
2 tbsp walnut oil
1 tsp cider vinegar
1 tsp Dijon mustard
hot buttered toast,
  preferably sourdough

Preheat the oven to 220°C/ Fan 200°C/Gas 7. Arrange the marrow bones on a baking tray.

Mix together the breadcrumbs, capers, parsley and lemon zest, then season with salt and pepper. Divide this mixture between the marrow bones.

Roast the bones in the oven for 12–15 minutes, but start checking after 10 minutes to make sure the topping isn't burning. The marrow needs to soften, but it may melt away if you overcook it, so be vigilant. When the crust is lightly brown, remove the bones from the oven.

Put the greens, radishes and shallot in a bowl. Whisk the oil, vinegar and mustard together and thin it with a very little water. Season this dressing with salt and pepper and drizzle it over the salad ingredients. Serve with the bone marrow and the buttered toast. You can also scoop out the marrow and serve it on toast.

OX HEART
KEBABS

Ox heart on skewers is a popular dish all over South America and can be cooked on a barbecue as well as on a griddle pan. It might sound odd, but we promise you that ox heart tastes just like steak and makes a good, cheap alternative to beef or lamb for kebabs. Serve with a salad of red onions, peppers and tomatoes.

SERVES 4

1 ox heart, trimmed
  and cut into 3cm pieces
  or long strips
flaked sea salt
freshly ground black pepper

Marinade

2 tbsp olive oil
2 jalapeño chillies, chopped
3 garlic cloves, chopped
2 tsp ground cumin
¼ tsp cinnamon
1 tsp ground oregano
50ml red wine vinegar
1 tbsp tomato purée
1 tbsp soy sauce

Red onion salad

1 red onion, sliced into
  crescents
1 red pepper, deseeded and
  thinly sliced
2 tomatoes, diced
small bunch of coriander,
  leaves only
1 tbsp olive oil
juice of ½ lime

Put all the marinade ingredients into a blender and blitz until fairly smooth. Place the strips of ox heart in a glass or plastic bowl or a plastic bag and season well with salt and pepper. Pour over the marinade and stir to make sure all the meat is covered, then leave to marinate in the fridge for several hours or overnight. Take the meat out of the fridge half an hour before you want to cook the kebabs.

Prepare a barbecue or heat a griddle until very hot. If you're using bamboo skewers, soak them in warm water for half an hour.

Strain the ox heart, reserving the marinade, and thread the pieces of meat on to the skewers. Grill for 2–3 minutes on each side, basting with the reserved marinade until the meat is glossy and well charred.

To make the salad, mix the onion, red pepper, tomatoes and coriander. Season with salt and pepper, then drizzle with olive oil and lime juice.

Serve the kebabs with the red onion salad on the side.

TONGUE

Another good old-fashioned dish, tongue is creeping back into fashion. Your butcher will supply tongue, but you may need to order it in advance and say whether you want the tongue brined ('pickled') or not. It's usual to brine a tongue before cooking, so say yes, but check whether you should soak the tongue before cooking. Ox tongue is the most commonly sold but you can also buy calf or sheep tongue.

SERVES 4–6

1 ox tongue
2 onions, cut into chunks
2 carrots, cut into chunks
2 celery sticks, cut into
  chunks
2 bay leaves
a few sprigs of parsley
½ head garlic, left whole
1 tsp peppercorns
3 cloves
2 blades of mace
1 star anise

Salsa verde
2 shallots, chopped
2 garlic cloves, chopped
2 tbsp capers, rinsed
2 anchovies, chopped
juice of ½ lemon
small bunch of parsley
small bunch of basil leaves
200ml olive oil
flaked sea salt
freshly ground black pepper

If the tongue needs soaking, put it in a large bowl of cold water and leave it overnight. Next day, rinse the tongue thoroughly in lots of cold water, then put it in a large saucepan.

Add water just to cover, bring it to the boil, and skim off any mushroom-coloured foam. When the foam turns white, turn down the heat and add the onions, carrots, celery, herbs and spices.

Simmer, with a lid partially covering the pan, for 2½–3 hours, until the tongue is very tender. Keep an eye on it while it cooks and top up the liquid with boiling water if necessary.

When the tongue is cooked through, strain it, reserving the cooking liquid as this makes very good stock. Set the tongue aside until it is cool enough to handle, then peel off the skin and the gristly bit underneath towards the back of the tongue.

Cut the tongue in half. Serve half of it warm, cut into thick slices, with the salsa verde. Allow the rest to cool, then put it in the fridge. To make the tongue easier to slice for sandwiches, put it between 2 plates and weigh it down with something heavy such as a can of tomatoes. This will press the tongue and make the flesh denser.

Salsa verde
Put the shallots, garlic, capers, anchovies and lemon juice in a small food processor. Season with salt and pepper, then pack in the herbs as well. Blitz until you have a fairly coarse paste, then, while the motor is running, gradually drizzle in the olive oil until you have a smoother sauce. Serve with the warm tongue.

CHAPTER ELEVEN
LEFTOVERS

CROQUETAS

If you have some leftover ham hock (see page 21) these croquetas are a lovely way of using it up and they make a fab starter or snack. Otherwise you can use Parma or Serrano ham instead. Traditionally, croquetas are deep-fried, but we suggest oven baking as an alternative, which makes them lighter – and is easier to do. BTW, if you've cooked a ham hock and have some stock, you can replace 200ml of the milk with stock for extra flavour.

MAKES ABOUT 30

700ml milk
½ onion
3 cloves
2 bay leaves
1 blade of mace
100g butter
100g plain flour
200g leftover ham hock
    or Parma or Serrano ham,
    diced
vegetable oil, for frying
    (optional)
flaked sea salt
white pepper

Coating
75g plain flour
2 eggs, beaten
100g very fine breadcrumbs

First infuse the milk. Pour the milk into a saucepan, then stud the onion half with the cloves and add it to the milk, together with the bay leaves and mace. Place the pan on the heat and bring the milk almost to boiling point, then remove the pan from the heat and leave the milk to infuse until it's cool. Strain.

Melt the butter in a saucepan, add the flour and stir to combine. Keep stirring for several more minutes to cook out the raw flavour of the flour. Gradually start to add the milk, making sure you stir in each ladleful thoroughly until it has completely combined with the butter and flour mixture. You should end up with a fairly thick, pourable béchamel sauce.

Season the béchamel with salt and white pepper, then stir in the diced ham. Line a shallow baking tray (about 30cm x 20cm) with oiled clingfilm, making sure the clingfilm goes over the sides. Spread the béchamel evenly over the tray. Oil another piece of clingfilm and use this to cover the béchamel, making sure the clingfilm touches the sauce, as this will stop a skin forming. Chill this mixture for several hours at least and for up to 3 days if you like.

When you're ready to make the croquetas, preheat the oven to 220°C/Fan 200°C/Gas 7 and line a baking tray with non-stick baking parchment. If you're deep-frying the croquetas, heat some vegetable oil to 180°C in a deep-fat fryer.

Remove the top layer of clingfilm, then cut the béchamel into about 30 strips. Put half the flour and half the breadcrumbs on separate plates and beat one of the eggs in a bowl. Shape a strip of béchamel into a sausage, dip it into the flour and dust it off, then dip it in egg, then lastly in the breadcrumbs, making sure it is completely coated. Repeat until you've coated half the béchamel strips.

Put the rest of the flour and breadcrumbs on the plates and beat the second egg, then repeat to coat the rest of the béchamel strips. Coating them in 2 batches like this keeps the egg and breadcrumbs from getting too messy!

To bake the croquetas, lay them on the prepared baking tray and cook them in the preheated oven for about 15 minutes.

To deep-fry, carefully lower them a few at a time into the hot oil for 3 minutes. Be careful and never leave the deep-fat fryer unattended. Allow the croquetas to cool slightly before eating.

PULLED PORK SALAD

If you manage to save some pulled pork (see page 147), try making this salad. In fact, this is so good that it's worth cooking extra pulled pork so you have leftovers. The tortilla makes the salad more substantial and the grilled peaches are a refreshing addition.

SERVES 4

1 tbsp olive oil
about 250g pulled pork, plus
  some cooking liquor
½ tsp chilli powder or hot
  sauce
2 peaches, halved
large bag of salad leaves
150g canned black beans,
  drained and rinsed
1 large corn tortilla, toasted
  and cut into strips (optional)
handful of fresh coriander
  leaves
handful of fresh basil leaves
flaked sea salt
freshly ground black pepper

Dressing
1 tbsp olive oil
juice of 1 lime

Heat the olive oil in a frying pan. Add the pulled pork, a ladleful of the cooking liquor and the chilli powder and cook over a high heat until the meat is well caramelised around the edges. Remove the frying pan from the heat.

Heat a griddle pan until it's very hot. Add the peaches and cook them for a couple of minutes on the cut sides until they're marked with dark char lines. Cut the peach halves into wedges.

Now assemble the salad. Spread the leaves on plates. Arrange the black beans, pulled pork and tortilla strips, if using, over the salad leaves, then add the coriander and basil and wedges of grilled peach.

Deglaze the frying pan with a couple of tablespoons of water, adding any juices from grilling the peaches. Whisk in the olive oil and lime juice and season with salt and pepper. Pour this dressing over the salad and serve immediately.

BREADED PIG'S CHEEKS WITH SAUCE GRIBICHE

If you have any pig's cheeks left from making the casserole (see page 149), fry them up into deliciously porky little morsels to serve as a starter or snack. They're seriously good dipped into sauce gribiche, which is a classic little French goody that's a bit like tartare sauce. You can cut the cheeks into strips instead of halves if you like – makes them a bit more dainty.

SERVES 4

4 pig's cheeks, cooked
   and chilled
50g plain flour
1 tsp mustard powder
½ tsp garlic powder
½ tsp dried oregano
1 egg, beaten
50g fine breadcrumbs
flaked sea salt
freshly ground black pepper

Sauce gribiche
2 hard-boiled eggs
1 tsp Dijon mustard
150ml olive oil
1 tsp red wine vinegar
2 tbsp capers, rinsed and
   chopped
2 tbsp cornichons, finely
   chopped
3 tbsp finely chopped parsley
   leaves
1 tbsp finely chopped
   tarragon leaves

Preheat the oven to 200°C/Fan 180°C/Gas 6.

Take the pig's cheeks and scrape off the layer of fat which runs along the side and discard it. Cut the cheeks in half, lengthways, to make 2 thinner pieces from each.

Mix the flour with the mustard powder, garlic powder and oregano. Season with salt and pepper.

Line a baking tray with non-stick baking parchment. Put the flour and breadcrumbs on separate plates and beat the egg in a shallow bowl. Dip a piece of cheek in the flour, then brush off any excess and dip it into the egg, then coat it completely in the breadcrumbs. Place it on the baking tray and repeat to coat the rest of the cheeks. When they're all on the baking tray, cook them in the preheated oven for 20 minutes until they're golden-brown.

To make the sauce, separate the egg yolks from the whites. Finely chop the whites and set them aside. Mash the yolks with the mustard in a bowl until smooth, then start beating in the olive oil, slowly at first, as if making mayonnaise, then at a faster rate once the sauce starts to thicken and emulsify. Stir in the red wine vinegar, capers, cornichons, herbs and egg whites, then season with salt and pepper. Add a little warm water if the sauce is too thick – it shouldn't be runny, but not quite as thick as mayonnaise.

Serve the gribiche as a dipping sauce for the pig's cheeks.

PORK SCRATCHINGS

If you're cooking pork loin without the skin – for instance, the Italian-style pork in milk on page 122 – this is a good way to use the skin. And everyone loves pork scratchings. They're great seasoned just with salt and pepper or with paprika, cayenne or herbs such as dried thyme – whatever takes your fancy. You'll want to eat them straight out of the oven, but they keep in an airtight container for a few days and you can crisp them up in the oven for a few minutes.

MAKES LOTS

large piece of pork skin, about
    500g, with a layer
    of up to ½ cm of fat
2 tbsp cider vinegar
flaked sea salt
freshly ground black pepper

Preheat your oven to its hottest setting.

Cut the pork skin into strips about 1cm wide. If the skin has been scored, this will be much easier – just cut along the score lines. Cut the strips into pieces 6–8cm long. The easiest way to do this is with sharp kitchen scissors.

Put the pork skin in a colander. Bring a kettle of water to the boil, then carefully pour the contents over the pork skin. Pat it dry with some kitchen paper.

Sprinkle the pork skin with the vinegar and some salt. Put a rack over a baking tray and lay the pork skin on it so the fat will drip through, leaving the scratchings drier and less greasy. Put the baking tray in the oven and immediately turn the heat down to 200°C/Fan 180°C/Gas 6. Cook the scratchings for 25–30 minutes, until the skin is a deep golden-brown and has bubbled or popped in places.

Remove the baking tray from the oven and toss the scratchings in salt and pepper or whichever dried herbs or spices you want to use. Or just enjoy them as they are. Pour the fat into a bowl, store it in the fridge once cool and use it for frying potatoes.

MUFFALETTA

A super-butty and a proper feast of a sandwich, the muffaletta originated in New Orleans where it's made with a special muffaletta loaf. Away from the Big Easy you can use focaccia or ciabatta – you just need something that the juices from the filling can soak into. Use pitted or stuffed olives, but don't buy the bitter brined ones, which make everything too sour. You'll find mortadella sausage at the deli counter of most supermarkets.

SERVES 2–4

1 large focaccia or 2 ciabatta
olive oil for drizzling
200g Italian salami
200g thinly sliced leftover
   ham hock or gammon (or
   some cooked ham)
200g sliced mortadella
   sausage
12 slices of Provolone cheese
   or a mild hard cheese such
   as Manchego
a small bunch of basil, finely
   shredded
2 large roasted red peppers,
   skinned and cut into strips

Olive salad

200g pitted olives, finely
   chopped
2 tbsp capers, rinsed and
   drained
1 shallot, finely chopped
1 celery stick, finely chopped
2 hot pickled red peppers,
   finely chopped (optional)
½ tsp dried oregano
3 tbsp olive oil
2 tsp red wine vinegar
freshly ground black pepper

Cut the bread in half horizontally. Pull out a little of the dough from both halves, leaving a good 2cm border all the way round – this helps the olive salad sit better and makes it less likely to fall out.

Mix together the olive salad ingredients and taste for seasoning – you will probably find it is salty enough, and as the meats are also salty, you may just need pepper.

Divide the olive salad between the two pieces of bread. Layer the salami and ham on one side, and the mortadella and cheese on the other. Finally, put the red peppers and basil on the bottom half.

Very carefully turn the top piece of bread over the bottom half to complete your sandwich. You can eat it immediately, but it's a good idea to wrap the sandwich in clingfilm and weigh it down with something for 30 minutes to an hour so the flavours meld together properly. Cut it into large sections to serve.

Tip
You can use a jar of roasted, skinned peppers if you want to save time.

SHEPHERD'S OR COTTAGE PIE

The best shepherd's and cottage pies are made with leftover roast meat, not mince. In fact, the whole purpose of these pies was to eke out the leftovers and make a meal for another day. Use beef or lamb and if you've got some slow-roast lamb shoulder (see page 129) that would make an extra tasty pie. For another variation, try using sweet potato for the topping instead of ordinary potatoes. If you don't have any leftovers, use finely diced fresh meat.

SERVES 4

about 600g leftover
   roast meat
1 tbsp olive oil
1 large onion, finely diced
2 carrots, finely diced
1 celery stick, finely diced
2 garlic cloves, finely chopped
1 large sprig of rosemary,
   leaves finely chopped
1 sprig of thyme, leaves
   finely chopped
300ml red wine
1 tbsp tomato purée
   or ketchup
300ml leftover gravy or stock
a dash of Worcestershire
   sauce
flaked sea salt
freshly ground black pepper

Topping

1kg floury potatoes, cut
   into chunks
large knob of butter, plus
   extra for dotting on top
   of the pie

Chop the meat into small dice. This is best done by hand, but if you want to use a food processor, cut the meat into slices first, then process it very carefully, as you don't want it chopped too fine.

Heat the olive oil in a large saucepan or a flameproof casserole dish. Add the onion, carrots and celery, then fry them gently on a medium heat for up to 10 minutes, until they are softening and just starting to take on some colour.

Turn up the heat, add the meat and cook it on a medium heat for a few minutes. Keep the stirring to a minimum at first until the underside is well browned, then stir until it's well coloured. Add the garlic and herbs and season with salt and pepper.

Pour in the red wine and let it bubble until it has reduced almost completely, then add the tomato purée or ketchup, gravy or stock and the Worcestershire sauce. Bring the mixture to the boil, then turn down the heat and simmer for about 20 minutes. Keep an eye on it and if the mixture looks in danger of drying out, add a little more stock or water. Preheat the oven to 200°C/Fan 180°C/Gas 6.

Meanwhile, put the potatoes in a large saucepan and cover them with cold water. Bring to the boil, then turn down the heat slightly and simmer for about 20 minutes. When the potatoes are tender, drain and tip them back into the pan, then season with salt and add the butter. Mash until smooth, adding a very little milk if they appear dry – they shouldn't be.

Pour the filling into an ovenproof dish (about 30cm x 20cm x 5cm). Using a spatula, spread the potatoes over the top in as even a layer as possible, then rough up the surface with a fork. Dot with butter.

Put the dish on a baking tray and bake the pie in the oven for 25–30 minutes until it's piping hot inside and well browned on top. Serve with some green veg.

ARANCINI

Arancini means 'little oranges' in Italian, presumably because that's what these little balls of deliciousness look like when fried. This is the perfect use for leftover risotto – it's worth making extra specially – and if you've got some Italian meat sauce as well, you're laughing. You could also use shredded ham with the mozzarella if you don't have any meat sauce. If you like, you can open freeze these once they're assembled and cook them from frozen.

MAKES 8

about 400g of leftover risotto (see p.356)
4 tbsp grated Parmesan cheese
a few basil leaves, finely chopped
100g mozzarella, diced
about 65g of leftover Italian meat sauce (see p.241) or wild boar ragù (see p.223)
2 eggs
50g flour
100g breadcrumbs
vegetable oil for deep-frying
olive oil spray (optional)

Make sure the risotto is well chilled, as this makes it much easier to handle. Stir in the Parmesan and basil, making sure they are evenly distributed through the rice.

Wet the palms of your hands, take a heaped tablespoon of the risotto (about 50g) and mould it into a ball. Make an indentation in the ball with your thumb and push in a small square of mozzarella, followed by a scant teaspoon of the meat sauce. Smooth the rice over the filling to mould it back into a ball. Repeat to use up all your risotto, mozzarella and sauce.

Beat one of the eggs in a bowl. Spread half the flour over a plate and half the breadcrumbs over another plate – this way the coating mixtures don't get too messy.

Roll the arancini in the flour, then dust off the excess, dip them into the egg, then roll them in the breadcrumbs and set aside. When you've used up all the flour, egg and breadcrumbs, put the rest of the flour and breadcrumbs on the plates, beat the second egg, then prepare the rest of the arancini.

You can deep-fry the arancini or bake them in the oven. To deep-fry, pour vegetable oil into a deep-fat fryer or a large saucepan, filling it to the half way point. Heat the oil to 170°C – always be very careful when deep-frying and never leave hot oil unattended. To test whether the oil is at the right temperature, drop in a cube of bread – it should immediately start to bubble and will turn a light brown in about 30 seconds. When the oil is ready, fry the arancini a few at a time for 4–5 minutes. If cooking from frozen, fry them for 10–12 minutes.

Alternatively, preheat the oven to 180°C/Fan 160°C/Gas 4. Spread out the arancini on a baking tray and give them a quick blast with olive oil spray if you have some. Bake them for about 20 minutes until they are crisp and golden. If cooking the arancini from frozen, bake for 30 minutes at 200°C/Fan 180°C/Gas 6.

CRISPY PANCAKES

If you're about the same age as us you might have fond memories of Findus Crispy Pancakes, which first appeared back in the 1970s. We loved them, but now we like to make our own, using leftover meat sauce. It's best to keep the pancakes quite small or they are a bit tricky to work with. We've made this batter slightly thicker than usual so it holds the filling well.

SERVES 4

Pancakes
125g plain flour
pinch of salt
2 eggs
300ml milk
butter or oil, for greasing

Filling
about 450g leftover meat
   sauce (see p.241)

Coating
2 eggs, beaten
75g plain flour
100g breadcrumbs
flaked sea salt
freshly ground black pepper

To make the batter, put the flour in a bowl with a pinch of salt. Whisk it briefly to get rid of any lumps, then make a well in the middle. Add the eggs and gradually work them into the flour, then drizzle in the milk, whisking constantly until you have a smooth batter. Alternatively, put the whole lot in a food processor and whizz. Leave the batter to stand for half an hour.

Heat a small frying pan – 14–16cm diameter is about right – and add a small amount of butter or oil, then wipe it over with kitchen paper. Add a ladleful of batter and swirl it around until the base of the pan is covered. Cook until the batter has set on the underside, then flip the pancake. Remove and repeat until you have used up all the batter – you should be able to get about 12 pancakes from this quantity of mixture. Preheat the oven to 200°C/Fan 180°C/Gas 6.

Now, assemble the pancakes. Put 2 generous tablespoons of filling on one half of a pancake, then fold the other half over the filling to make a semi-circle. Brush the edges with water, then seal them. Repeat until you've used all your pancakes and filling.

For the coating, beat one of the eggs in a shallow bowl and put half the flour and half the breadcrumbs on separate plates. Season the flour with salt and pepper. Dust each pancake with flour, then dip it in the egg and finally coat it in the breadcrumbs and place it on a baking tray. When you've used up all the coating ingredients, beat the remaining egg and spread the rest of the flour and breadcrumbs on the plates – this way the egg and breadcrumbs don't get too messy.

Bake the pancakes in the preheated oven for 20 minutes until they're golden-brown.

CORNED BEEF HASH

Corned beef hash is always good, but with home-made corned beef it is the bees' knees. If you happen to have any leftover gravy you could add some with the ketchup. It takes a little longer to cook this way, as you need to reduce the liquid, but it tastes really good. You could also use this recipe with a can of corned beef.

SERVES 4

600g floury potatoes, diced
1 tbsp oil or 15g dripping
    or butter
1 large onion, chopped
400g corned beef (see p.177),
    chopped
1 tbsp tomato ketchup
1 tsp Dijon mustard
a dash of Worcestershire
    sauce
2 tbsp finely chopped parsley
fried eggs, for serving
    (optional)
flaked sea salt
freshly ground black pepper

Put the potatoes in a saucepan and add water to cover them. Bring the water to the boil, then add salt and simmer for 2–3 minutes. Drain the potatoes and set them aside.

Heat the oil, dripping or butter in a large frying pan. Add the onion and fry gently until it has until softened and is turning a golden-brown. Add the potatoes and the corned beef, then press the mixture down in the pan with a spatula and leave it to cook for 5 minutes.

Add enough water to the ketchup and mustard to make a pourable mixture, then add this to the corned beef and potato. Add the parsley and season with pepper – be careful with salt as the corned beef will already be salty – then stir. The underside should have started to turn a deep golden-brown.

Continue to cook, stirring and pressing down the mixture, until it is all completely heated through, the potatoes are tender, and a lot of the mixture has taken on some colour. Good served with fried eggs.

REUBEN SANDWICH

There are many stories about how, why and where this famous sandwich originated, but the bottom line is that it's dead good – possibly the best sandwich in the world. There are variations, but basically it's made with corned beef, Swiss cheese, sauerkraut and Russian dressing on rye bread. The quantities below make a hearty sandwich for one, but if you're generous enough to share this delight, multiply the quantities accordingly.

SERVES 1

several slices of corned beef
(see p.177)
2 slices light rye bread
butter, for spreading
a few slices of Swiss cheese
(such as Emmental or
Gruyère)
2–3 tbsp sauerkraut
dill pickles, for serving

Russian dressing
1 tbsp mayonnaise
1 tbsp ketchup
1 tsp horseradish
a dash of hot sauce
(Frank's is best for this)
a dash of Worcestershire
sauce
1 tsp finely chopped shallot
2 cornichons or ½ dill pickle,
finely chopped
pinch of hot paprika
flaked sea salt
freshly ground black pepper

First make the Russian dressing. Simply mix all the ingredients together in a small jug and season with salt and pepper.

Put the corned beef on a piece of foil and sprinkle it with water, then fold the foil into a parcel. Put some water in a frying pan or saucepan and bring it to the boil. Add the foil parcel and cover the pan with a lid, then steam for a few minutes just to warm the meat through.

Butter both slices of bread. Put the corned beef on one slice, then top it with the cheese and sauerkraut. Spread the Russian dressing over the remaining slice of bread and place it on top of the sauerkraut.

Heat a frying pan and fry the sandwich, pressing it down well with a spatula, for 3–4 minutes on each side until the bread is well browned and the cheese has melted. Alternatively, you can toast it in a toasted sandwich maker – the flat sort, not the kind that shapes the sandwich into triangles. Serve with dill pickles.

Tip
If you're making lots of sandwiches, you could warm the meat (wrapped in foil as above) in the oven at 200°C/Fan 180°C/Gas 6 for 15 minutes.

CHAPTER TWELVE
BASICS AND SIDE DISHES

BEEF STOCK

MAKES ABOUT
2 litres

1.5 kg beef bones, including
   marrow bones if possible,
   cut into small lengths
500g piece of beef shin or
   any cheap, fairly lean cut
2 onions, unpeeled and
   roughly chopped
1 leek, roughly chopped
2 celery sticks, roughly
   chopped
2 carrots, roughly chopped
2 tomatoes
½ tsp peppercorns
a bouquet garni made of large
   sprigs of thyme, parsley and
   2 bay leaves

This tasty stock is a good basis for any broth or consommé. You'll also have a couple of side products – the beef and the fat. The beef should be left in one piece and taken out at the end of the cooking time. Seasoned well, it's excellent in sandwiches or can be sliced, fried and added to salads. The fat you collect from the top of the chilled stock is ideal for roasting veg or cooking Yorkshire puds. The first two photos opposite show the making of the stock. The other two show the final stages of preparing consommé.

Put the bones and meat into a large stockpot and cover them with cold water – at least 3–3.5 litres. Bring the water to the boil and when a starchy, mushroom-grey foam appears, start skimming. Keep on skimming as the foam turns white and continue until it has almost stopped developing.

Add the vegetables, peppercorns and bouquet garni, turn down the heat until the stock is simmering very gently, then partially cover the pan with a lid. Leave the stock to simmer for 3–4 hours.

Line a sieve or colander with 2 layers of muslin or a tea towel, and place it over a large bowl or saucepan. Ladle the stock into the sieve or colander to strain it. Remove the meat and set it aside, then discard everything else.

Pour the strained stock into large container and chill it thoroughly. The fat should solidify on top of the stock and will be very easy to remove. Keep the stock in the fridge for 2 or 3 days or freeze it.

CONSOMMÉ

2 egg whites
shells from 2 eggs, quite
   finely crushed
1 onion, finely chopped
1 carrot, finely diced
1 celery stick, finely chopped
200g lean beef, finely diced
   (not minced)
½ tsp peppercorns
1.5 litres beef stock (see
   above), chilled
flaked sea salt

You can use your beef stock to make consommé. Lightly whisk the egg whites in a bowl until they are starting to foam. Mix in the egg shells, then the vegetables, beef and peppercorns – this mixture will capture all the impurities that would otherwise cloud the consommé. Put the mixture into a large saucepan.

Pour in the stock, then place the pan on a high heat. Slowly bring the stock to the boil, whisking constantly. When it boils, a white crust should start to form – don't stir or you will disturb this crust. Turn the heat down to a very low simmer, and leave the stock to cook for an hour.

Line a sieve with 2 layers of wet muslin or a clean tea towel and place it over a bowl or saucepan. Carefully break through the crust and ladle the stock into the sieve to strain it. You should end up with a well-flavoured, crystal-clear consommé. Season with salt before eating.

CHICKEN STOCK

MAKES 1 LITRE

at least 1 chicken carcass,
  pulled apart
4 chicken wings (optional)
1 onion, unpeeled, cut into
  quarters
1 large carrot, cut into large
  chunks
2 celery sticks, roughly
  chopped
1 leek, roughly chopped
1 tsp black peppercorns
3 bay leaves
a large sprig of parsley
a small sprig of thyme
a few garlic cloves, unpeeled
  (optional)

Put the chicken bones and the wings, if using, into a saucepan, just large enough for all the chicken to fit quite snugly. Cover with cold water, bring to the boil, then skim off any foam that collects. Add the remaining ingredients and turn the heat down to a very low simmer. Partially cover the pan with a lid.

Leave the stock to simmer for about 3 hours, then remove the pan from the heat. Line a sieve or colander with muslin and place a bowl underneath it then ladle the stock through the muslin to strain it. Decant the stock into a container and leave it to cool.

The stock can be used right away, although it is best to skim off most of the fat that will collect on the top. If you don't need the stock immediately, chill it in the fridge. The fat will set on top (and can be used for frying) and will be much easier to remove.

You can keep the stock in the fridge for up to 5 days, or freeze it. If you want to make a larger amount of stock, save up your chicken carcasses in the freezer or add more chicken wings.

HORSERADISH SAUCE

SERVES 4

4 tbsp grated horseradish
1 tbsp white wine vinegar
pinch of English mustard
  powder
1 tsp caster sugar
150ml double cream

Mix all the ingredients together in a bowl until well combined and slightly thickened. Serve with roast beef.

MINT SAUCE

SERVES 4

3 tbsp finely chopped fresh
  mint leaves, plus extra small
  whole mint leaves, to serve
2 tsp caster sugar
2 tbsp white wine vinegar
splash of extra virgin olive oil

Mix the chopped mint leaves and sugar in a small bowl. Using the back of a spoon, crush the leaves for 1–2 minutes to extract their flavour. Add the white wine vinegar and a dash of olive oil, then stir until well combined.

GUACAMOLE

SERVES 4

flesh of 2 ripe avocados,
  finely diced
½ small red onion, finely
  chopped
2 medium tomatoes, finely
  chopped
a few sprigs of coriander,
  finely chopped
1–2 garlic cloves, finely
  chopped
1 jalapeño, finely chopped
juice of 1 lime
flaked sea salt
freshly ground black pepper

Put the diced avocado flesh in a bowl and mash it very lightly with the back of the fork to break it down a little. You don't want it to be too smooth.

Add all the remaining ingredients, season with salt and pepper, then stir until thoroughly combined. Taste and adjust the seasoning, chilli and lime juice quantities if necessary.

APPLE AND HERB JELLY

MAKES ABOUT 1KG

or 4 small jars

1.5kg Bramley apples,
    washed and roughly
    chopped
large sprigs of fresh herbs,
    such as rosemary, mint,
    thyme, sage, tarragon
4 tbsp finely chopped herbs
granulated or preserving
    sugar, see method for
    quantity

First sterilise the jars. Put them through a hot cycle on your dishwasher and leave them to dry completely, or wash them thoroughly in hot soapy water, then put them in a low oven to dry.

Put the apples in a large saucepan or preserving pan with the herb sprigs, then pour a litre of water into the pan. Bring the water to the boil, then turn down the heat and simmer until the apples have completely collapsed. Squash them with the back of a spoon every so often to extract all the juice. Remove the pan from the heat.

If you have a jelly bag and stand, scald the jelly bag and arrange it on the stand with a bowl underneath. If you don't have a jelly stand, line a large colander or a sieve with a layer of muslin and place it over a large bowl. Ladle in all the apples with their liquid and leave them to strain. Don't be tempted to push the liquid through or you'll get a very cloudy jelly. Leave the apples to strain for several hours or overnight if you wish – just cover with a large tea towel. When the apple pulp is very dry, discard it. Put a couple of saucers in the freezer to chill.

Measure the strained liquid. For every 600ml liquid, add 450g sugar. Put the liquid and the sugar in a large saucepan or preserving pan and stir over a low heat until all the sugar has dissolved. Bring to the boil and keep at a rolling boil for 5 minutes, then remove the pan from the heat. To check if the jelly has reached setting point, spoon a little of the mixture on to one of the chilled saucers and leave it for a minute. Push the mixture lightly with your finger – if the jelly has set, it will wrinkle a little. If it is too runny, put the pan back on the heat, boil for another couple of minutes, then test again.

Spoon off any scum from the jelly with a slotted spoon, then leave it to cool for a few minutes. Stir in any finely chopped fresh herbs at this point, then ladle the jelly into jars. Cover immediately with lids, then leave to cool. The jellies will keep indefinitely unopened and will last for months in the fridge once opened.

If you like, add spices such as chillies or star anise to your jelly instead of herbs.

CIDER AND SAGE JELLY

MAKES 60 CUBES

6 sheets of leaf gelatine
75g caster sugar
100ml cold water
300ml dry sparkling cider
1 tbsp finely chopped sage
    leaves

Line a 15cm x 25cm x 5cm roasting tray or heatproof dish with clingfilm.

To soften the gelatine leaves, place them in a bowl, cover them with cold water and set aside for 5 minutes..

Put the sugar and 100ml of water in a saucepan and stir until the sugar has dissolved. Bring the mixture to the boil for 30 seconds, then remove the pan from the heat and set it aside for 5 minutes.

Squeeze any excess water from the gelatine leaves and add them to the saucepan of warm sugar syrup. Stir with a wooden spoon until the gelatine has dissolved.

Slowly pour the cider into the pan and mix gently. Then pour the mixture into a jug and chill it in the fridge for 1½–2 hours, or until the jelly has started to set.

When the jelly has set a little but not too much, remove it from the fridge. Using a fork, whisk the chopped sage into the jelly until you can see some bubbles and the jelly looks fizzy. Pour the half-set jelly into the lined roasting tray or dish, cover with clingfilm and put it back in the fridge for at least 3 hours, or until it is fully set. Cut into 2.5cm cubes to serve – it's great with the raised pork pie on p.190.

ROAST POTATOES

SERVES 4–6

1.5kg potatoes (Maris Pipers
  or King Edwards are good)
100g goose fat
2 tbsp semolina or polenta
flaked sea salt
freshly ground black pepper

Cut the potatoes into large chunks. Put them in a saucepan of cold, salted water, bring to the boil and boil for about 5 minutes. Drain well in a colander, then tip the potatoes back into the saucepan and shake them to scuff up the surfaces. This helps to make lovely crispy roasties.

Meanwhile, preheat the oven to 200–220°C/Fan 180–200°C Fan/Gas 6–7 and melt the goose fat in a roasting tin. It must be good and hot. Sprinkle the semolina or polenta over the potatoes and carefully tip them into the sizzling goose fat. Season liberally and roast them until golden. This will take 45–50 minutes, depending on the size of the potatoes.

SAUTÉ POTATOES

SERVES 2

650g potatoes, preferably
  Maris Pipers
50g butter
2 tsp vegetable oil
1 small bulb of garlic
1 tsp finely chopped fresh
  thyme leaves
flaked sea salt
freshly ground black pepper

Cut the potatoes into chunks of about 2.5cm. Put them in a pan, add water to cover, then bring to the boil. Reduce the heat slightly and leave to simmer for 5 minutes.

Drain the potatoes in a colander and leave them to stand for 2 minutes. Bash the edges of the potatoes a little by shaking the colander from side to side. This will help make them extra crisp.

Melt the butter with the oil in a large non-stick frying pan or sauté pan, then tip the potatoes into the pan and season them with salt and lashings of black pepper. Fry them over a medium to low heat for 10 minutes, stirring occasionally.

Separate the cloves of garlic and scatter them, unpeeled, into the pan with the potatoes. Continue to cook for 15 minutes, turning regularly until the potatoes are golden-brown all over and the garlic has softened. Sprinkle over the thyme leaves and cook for 5 minutes more, stirring and turning the potatoes as before.

DAUPHINOISE POTATOES

SERVES 4–6

1 garlic clove, cut in half
25g butter
1kg salad/waxy potatoes such
  as Charlotte, thinly sliced
300ml double cream
400ml milk
1 tsp plain flour
grating of nutmeg (optional)
flaked sea salt
freshly ground black pepper

Preheat the oven to 180°C/Fan 160°C/Gas 4.

Rub a shallow gratin dish with the cut halves of garlic, then take a small piece of the butter and rub this around the dish as well.

Rinse the potatoes to get rid of excess starch, then dry them as thoroughly as you can. Layer them in the gratin dish, seasoning with salt and pepper as you go.

Put the double cream and milk in a jug and whisk in the flour – this helps stop the cream curdling. Pour the mixture over the potatoes, then dot the remaining butter on top. Grate over some nutmeg, if using.

Bake in the preheated oven for an hour, then turn the heat up to 220°C/Fan 200°C/Gas 7 and bake for a further 10 minutes or until the top layer of potatoes has turned a crisp golden-brown.

BOULANGÈRE POTATOES

SERVES 6

2 tbsp olive oil, plus extra
  for greasing
1 large onion, thinly sliced
3–4 sprigs of fresh thyme,
  plus extra to garnish
3 garlic cloves, thinly sliced
1.2 kg floury potatoes, such
  as Maris Pipers, thinly sliced
  to the thickness of a £1 coin
400ml chicken or vegetable
  stock
flaked sea salt
freshly ground black pepper

Heat the oil in a large non-stick frying pan. Add the onion and thyme sprigs and fry gently, stirring occasionally, for 8–10 minutes, until the onion has softened and browned slightly. Add the garlic and continue to fry for 2–3 minutes, then season to taste with salt and freshly ground black pepper.

Preheat the oven to 200°C/Fan 180°C/Gas 6. Grease a 20cm x 30cm roasting tin or ovenproof dish with a little oil. Arrange a layer of potato slices to cover the base of the dish. Sprinkle over a third of the fried onions. Continue layering the potato slices and onion mixture, ending with a layer of potatoes.

Pour over the stock until it just reaches the top layer of potatoes. Season again with black pepper and garnish with a few sprigs of thyme. Cook for about 1¼ hours or until the potatoes are tender and lovely and brown on top.

POTATO LATKES

MAKES 12

1 egg
1 egg yolk
1 large onion
1.2kg potatoes, preferably
  Maris Pipers
25g plain flour
2 tbsp finely chopped fresh
  parsley or chives
6 tbsp vegetable oil, for frying
flaked sea salt
freshly ground black pepper

Whisk the egg and egg yolk together in a small bowl. Grate the onion and potatoes coarsely, then place them in a large colander. Mix well.

Take handfuls of onion and potato and squeeze out as much liquid as possible into the sink, putting each handful in a clean bowl as you go. When the veg are as dry as possible, add the beaten eggs, flour, parsley or chives, if using, and 1 teaspoon of salt. Season with lots of black pepper and mix well.

Heat 2 tablespoons of the oil in a large non-stick frying pan over a low to medium heat. Take a handful of the potato mixture and shape it into a loose ball. Place it in the pan and flatten it with a spatula until it's about 1.5cm thick. Repeat with 3 more balls of the mixture, until you have 4 latkes cooking at the same time.

Cook the latkes for 6–8 minutes on each side until golden-brown and cooked through. Don't be tempted to increase the heat or the latkes will be burnt on the outside before they are ready in the middle. Put them on a baking tray and set aside while you cook the remaining 8 latkes in the same way. Add an extra 2 tablespoons of oil to the pan between batches.

Preheat the oven to 200°C/Fan 180°C/Gas 6. When you're almost ready to serve the latkes, place them in the oven for 10–15 minutes, or until they're hot and crisp.

TRIPLE-COOKED CHIPS

SERVES 4

1kg potatoes, preferably
  Maris Pipers
groundnut or sunflower oil,
  for deep frying
flaked sea salt

Cut the potatoes into thick batons about 1.5 x 1.5 x 6cm. Rinse them in cold water to remove as much starch as possible, then put them in a large saucepan – make sure the chips have plenty of room so you can take them out easily.

Cover the chips with cold water and slowly bring to the boil. Simmer gently for 20–25 minutes, until the potatoes are knife tender and you can see lines and cracks start to develop. Yes, it does sound like a long time, but it works. Using a slotted spoon, remove the chips very, very carefully from the saucepan – don't tip them into a colander, or they will fall apart. Drain the chips on some kitchen paper, then gently pat them dry.

Half fill a deep-fat fryer or a large saucepan with oil and heat it to about 130°C. Take care when deep-frying and never leave the pan unattended. Fry the chips in a couple of batches, until they have developed a crust but not taken on any colour – this will take about 5 minutes. Remove each batch when it's ready and set it aside.

Now heat the oil to 180°C. Return the chips to the pan, again in a couple of batches, and fry for 1–2 minutes until they are very crisp and a deep golden-brown.

Drain on kitchen paper, then sprinkle the chips with salt and serve them immediately. You could also use beef dripping for cooking the chips. You'll need about 1.5kg.

POTATO SALAD

SERVES 4

400g new potatoes, unpeeled
3 tbsp mayonnaise
1 tbsp crème fraiche
2 tbsp baby capers, drained
50g baby gherkins, drained
   and sliced
2 tsp lemon juice
grated zest of 1 lemon
1 tbsp chopped fresh parsley
flaked sea salt
freshly ground black pepper

Scrub the potatoes well. Bring a pan of salted water to the boil. Add the potatoes, bring the water back to the boil and cook them for 15–18 minutes, or until just tender. Drain the potatoes in a colander, then rinse them under running water until they're cold.

Mix the mayonnaise, crème fraiche, capers, gherkins and lemon juice in a large bowl until well combined.

Cut the potatoes into quarters, add them to the mayonnaise dressing with the lemon zest and stir well. Season to taste with salt and black pepper and sprinkle with parsley before serving.

MASHED POTATOES

SERVES 6

1kg floury potatoes,
   such as King Edwards
   or Maris Pipers
75ml single cream or milk
50g butter
flaked sea salt
freshly ground white pepper

Cut the potatoes into chunks. Try to make sure the pieces are roughly the same size so they cook evenly.

Put the potatoes in a pan of salted water and bring to the boil. Once the water is boiling, turn down the heat and simmer for about 20 minutes or until the potatoes are soft. Warm the cream or milk in a separate pan and melt the butter. It really is worth doing this, as the mash will stay hot for longer.

When the potatoes are cooked, drain them well and tip them back into the pan. Mash them thoroughly, giving them a really good pummelling. Add the warm cream or milk and the butter and mix well, then season to taste. Serve as soon as possible.

THREE-ROOT MASH

SERVES 4

400g carrots
250g parsnips
500g celeriac
50g butter
a few gratings of nutmeg
flaked sea salt
freshly ground black pepper

Cut the vegetables into 2.5cm chunks. Put them in a large saucepan, cover with cold water and bring to the boil. Turn down the heat slightly and simmer for 25–30 minutes, or until the vegetables are very tender.

Drain the veg in a colander and then tip them back into the pan. Add the butter, grated nutmeg and lots of salt and pepper to taste and mash well. For an extra smooth mash, blend it with a stick blender until it is velvety and smooth.

ROAST PARSNIPS

SERVES 6

1kg parsnips
2 tbsp goose fat or
  vegetable oil
½ tsp dried chilli flakes
  (optional)
2 tbsp clear honey
flaked sea salt
freshly ground black pepper

Preheat the oven to 180°C/Fan 160°C/Gas 4. Cut the parsnips into similar-sized chunks. Heat the goose fat or oil in a roasting tin until it is smoking.

Toss the parsnip chunks in the hot fat or oil until nicely coated, then season them with salt and pepper. Place them in the oven and roast for about 45 minutes or until cooked and starting to turn golden. The exact cooking time depends on how big your pieces of parsnip are, so keep an eye on them.

Add the chilli flakes, if using, and the honey, then roll the parsnips in the sticky juices. Put them back in the oven for 10 minutes and continue cooking until golden. Don't leave them too long, though, or the honey will turn black and taste bitter.

CAPONATA

SERVES 4

5 tbsp olive oil
2 large aubergines, cut into
  2cm dice
2 celery sticks, sliced
2 medium red onions, finely
  chopped
3 garlic cloves, finely chopped
250g fresh tomatoes, peeled
  and chopped, or canned
  equivalent
4 tbsp finely chopped parsley
2 tbsp capers, rinsed
2 tbsp green pitted olives,
  sliced
1 tsp honey
1–2 tbsp red wine vinegar
2 tbsp pine nuts
a few basil leaves, shredded
flaked sea salt
freshly ground black pepper

Heat 2 tablespoons of the olive oil in a large frying pan. Add half the aubergines and fry them on a high heat for 3–4 minutes, stirring continuously, until the aubergines have started to take on some colour. Remove them from the pan with a slotted spoon and set aside. Heat another 2 tablespoons of olive oil and fry the remaining aubergines in the same way and set them aside with the rest.

Add the remaining olive oil. Fry the celery and red onion for several minutes until they have started to soften and are golden-brown. Add the garlic and fry for a minute, then tip the aubergine back into the pan.

Add the tomatoes, then the parsley, capers, olives, honey and half the wine vinegar. Stir, then cover the pan and leave the caponata to cook on a medium low heat for 15 minutes.

Toast the pine nuts in a dry frying pan until golden-brown. Taste the caponata for seasoning and flavour – it should be a good balance between sweet and sour – and add salt and pepper and a little more red wine vinegar if necessary. Serve the caponata as a side dish, preferably at room temperature, with the pine nuts and basil sprinkled over the top.

CAULIFLOWER CHEESE

SERVES 4

1 large cauliflower
25g butter
2 tbsp plain flour
250ml whole milk
½ tsp English mustard
  powder
200g Gruyère cheese, grated
pinch of grated nutmeg
50g Parmesan cheese, grated
flaked sea salt
freshly ground black pepper

Trim the cauliflower and break it into florets. Bring a big pan of water to the boil, add the florets and boil them for about 10 minutes until just soft. Drain and set aside. Preheat the oven to 180°C/Fan 160°C/Gas 4.

Melt the butter in a small saucepan and beat in the flour. Add the milk, stirring all the time, to make a thick white sauce. Add the mustard powder and grated Gruyère while stirring, then season with salt and black pepper.

Put the cauliflower florets in an ovenproof dish, pour in the cheesy sauce and sprinkle with the pinch of nutmeg. Sprinkle the grated Parmesan on top. Place in the preheated oven and bake for about 15 minutes or until the sauce is bubbling and the top is golden.

BRAISED RED CABBAGE

SERVES 4

½ red cabbage (about 430g)
25g butter
1 red onion
1 cinnamon stick
¼ tsp freshly grated nutmeg
1 bay leaf
150ml cider
2 tbsp white wine vinegar
3 tbsp light brown
  muscovado sugar
1 eating apple, cut into
  1cm slices
flaked sea salt
freshly ground black pepper

Remove the tough outer layer of the cabbage and cut out the core from the centre. Cut the cabbage in half again and finely slice down the longer side of the cabbage to give long strands.

Heat the butter in a large saucepan and gently fry the onion until soft, but not coloured. Add the cinnamon, nutmeg and bay leaf, followed by the cabbage, cider, vinegar and sugar. Stir well, bring the liquid to a simmer and cover the pan with a tight-fitting lid. Cook for 40 minutes, stirring occasionally, until the liquid has evaporated and the cabbage is nice and tender.

Stir the apple slices into the pan, cover again and cook for another 10 minutes. Good served with roast pork or our potato-crusted pork steaks (see p.75).

COLESLAW

SERVES 4

200g celeriac
100g white or red cabbage
1 carrot, grated
1 small onion, finely chopped
1 green apple (Granny Smith),
    cored and grated
grated zest and juice of 1 lime
100ml buttermilk
2 tbsp mayonnaise
1 tbsp soured cream
1 tsp sugar
flaked sea salt
freshly ground black pepper

Cut the celeriac into fine matchsticks. Finely shred the cabbage. Put the celeriac and cabbage in a large bowl with the carrot, onion and apple. Sprinkle over the lime zest and juice, then turn everything over well, making sure the apple in particular is covered in the lime juice to stop it turning brown.

Whisk the buttermilk, mayonnaise and soured cream together. Add the sugar and season with plenty of salt and pepper. Pour this over the contents of the bowl, then stir thoroughly.

RICE AND PEAS

SERVES 4

1 tbsp coconut or
    vegetable oil
1 onion, finely chopped
50g basmati rice, well rinsed
    and drained
200ml coconut milk
400g can red kidney beans,
    black beans or gungo peas
sprig of thyme
1 bay leaf
¼ tsp ground allspice
flaked sea salt
freshly ground black pepper

Heat the oil in a large saucepan over a medium heat, then add the onion. Cook gently for a minute or so, then stir in the rice. Pour in the coconut milk and 400ml water, then add the beans, herbs and allspice. Season with salt and pepper.

Bring to the boil, then turn down the heat to a simmer and cover the pan with a lid. Leave the rice and peas to cook for 15–20 minutes, until all the liquid is absorbed. Take the pan off the heat and leave it to stand, covered, for 5 minutes before serving. This is the traditional accompaniment to curry goat (see p.259).

This is a Caribbean recipe and people there usually refer to beans as 'peas'. That's why this is called rice and peas when there's no peas in it – just in case you were wondering!

RISOTTO ALLA MILANESE

SERVES 4

1.2 litres chicken stock
30g butter
2 tbsp bone marrow,
   finely diced (optional)
1 onion, finely chopped
300g risotto rice (Carnaroli
   is best for this)
150ml white wine
a large pinch of saffron,
   soaked in warm water
4 tbsp freshly grated
   Parmesan cheese
flaked sea salt
white pepper

Pour the stock into a saucepan, bring it to a simmer and keep it gently simmering – it must be warm when you add it to the rice.

Heat half the butter and the bone marrow, if using, in a large, shallow pan. Add the onion and cook gently over a fairly low heat, until it's soft and translucent. Add the rice and cook for a further minute, stirring continuously, until the rice is glossy from the butter and bone marrow. Season with salt and white pepper.

Pour in the wine and let it boil away to almost nothing, then add a ladleful of warm stock, and the saffron and its soaking water. Cook over a medium heat, stirring the rice continuously, until all the liquid has been absorbed.

Continue adding stock, a ladleful at a time, for at least 20 minutes, then start tasting. When it's ready, the rice should be swollen but still have a little bite to it. The sauce should be creamy – you don't want the risotto too wet, but it should not be firm either. When you drag your spoon across the bottom of the pan, the risotto should fall slowly in waves behind it.

Beat in the butter and Parmesan until melted, then serve immediately. This is the traditional accompaniment to osso buco (see p.153). You could use any leftovers to make arancini (see p.333).

YORKSHIRE PUDDING

MAKES 1 LARGE
or 12 small

150g plain flour
½ tsp salt
2 eggs, beaten
275ml whole milk
2 tbsp vegetable oil
   or goose fat

Put the flour in a bowl and whisk it lightly to get rid of any lumps, then add the salt. Make a well in the middle and add the eggs. Work the eggs into the flour, then gradually add the milk. Alternatively, put everything in a food processor and blitz until smooth. Leave to stand for an hour.

Preheat the oven to 200°C/Fan 180°C/Gas 6. Put the oil or goose fat in a Yorkshire pudding tin and place it in the oven until smoking hot. Give the batter a stir, then quickly pour it into the tin and pop it back into the oven. Bake for about 30 minutes until the pudding has risen and is a beautiful golden-brown. If you're making individual puds, use a muffin pan and bake them for about 15 minutes.

MARINATED EGGS (TAMAGO)

MAKES 6

6 eggs
200ml dark soy sauce
100ml mirin
100ml sake
50g soft light brown sugar
2 star anise

Bring a saucepan of water to the boil, then turn the heat down to a simmer. Add the eggs and simmer them gently for exactly 6 minutes. Remove the eggs from the pan and immediately plunge them into cold water to stop them cooking.

Mix the soy sauce, mirin, sake and sugar together, stirring until the sugar has dissolved. Add the star anise.

Peel the eggs and put them in a container just big enough to hold them snugly, then pour the marinade over them. If any of the eggs break the surface, weigh them down by putting some scrunched-up greaseproof paper on top.

Leave the eggs in the marinade for at least 3 hours, but preferably overnight. To serve, cut the eggs in half and add to Asian dishes, particularly ramen (see p.55).

THE LOWDOWN

We've eaten meat all our lives, but while working on the recipes for this book we realised that we wanted to know more about how meat is produced, how to buy meat and which cuts to choose.

So we went to see our old friend Peter Gott, who rears pigs, sheep and wild boar on his farm in the Lake District and sells his meat online, as well as at the market in Barrow-in-Furness and at London's Borough Market. We've enjoyed his produce on many occasions and knew that he would have the answers to our questions on everything from sirloins to sausages.

Peter's lambs roam the Cumbrian hills, while his pigs spend at least some of their time rooting in the mud, and his boar can run into the woods. He wants to give his livestock as good a life as possible and produce meat that's good to eat while still commercially viable. He's proud of his produce and wants people to enjoy it at its best. These are the questions we asked Peter.

Where's the best place to buy meat?

If you have a local butcher's shop, get to know the butchers and ask their advice. Find out where their meat comes from and which cuts they think work best for each dish. A good butcher will be able to tell you what to choose for that curry you want to make and how long to cook your Sunday roast. If you want an unusual cut, they should be able to order it for you.

These days, though, not everyone has a friendly butcher nearby and most of us buy our meat in supermarkets. If possible, head for the butchery counter, rather than the shelves of prepacked meat, and ask questions. The more the supermarkets find that people want to know about what they're buying, the more interest they will take. There are also many excellent online suppliers who will deliver their meat to you quickly and efficiently. Find out as much as you can about a supplier before ordering and don't be afraid to ring them up and ask for more information.

And then there's the old-fashioned way – markets. Farmers' markets have become more and more popular in the last ten years and if you get to know the stallholders you can buy great produce. Don't assume that everything on a market stall is good though; it's still worth doing your research.

So what's the difference between one type of meat and another?

All of us farmers have got to make some money or we can't survive. And one of the ways of making more profit is by getting the animal ready for the table in as short a time as possible. For example, you can get a commercial pig breed to 70 kilos in 16 weeks by feeding it a protein-rich diet and keeping it in a shed. For a rare breed pig it's more like 28–32 weeks so that's more feed, more expense, more time for the farmer.

Trouble is that the taste of that 16-week pig isn't quite there. It's a bit bland, a bit flabby. At about 22–24 weeks there's a pH change in the meat and the flavour starts to develop. And if that pig has been allowed to move around and live a more natural life it will taste better still. The Italians and Spanish produce a lot of cured ham, but they never cure a pig until it's had its first birthday, when the flavour has had a chance to develop. There's a very good reason why it's worth choosing meat that's come from a properly reared animal and that's taste.

What about ageing/hanging?

Beef and some game meat, such as venison, needs to be kept for a while before being sold in order for the flavour to develop. A steak that's been aged for 28 days will have much more taste than one that's been aged for just a week. The traditional way of ageing meat is to hang the carcass in a cold place for the required time – butcher's shops have special chilled rooms for hanging. There needs to be plenty of air around the meat so it dries out slightly as it hangs.

But now there's another way of ageing meat – in vacuum packs. The meat is cut up and put into vacuum bags and the air removed. People say the result is just as good, but I don't think so. It might be tender, but the taste isn't there, and without oxygen the meat develops a slightly tinny taste instead of ageing naturally. If the label on a piece of meat says 'aged' not 'hung', this is probably the process it has been through.

A third method I discovered only recently when I was visiting a slaughterhouse is to attach electrodes to the animal shortly after it has been slaughtered. The electric charges are said to change the pH of the meat and people claim that this is the equivalent of hanging it for three weeks. I might be old-fashioned, but I don't agree. I prefer the traditional way.

So what do you look for? How about beef?

First off, a bit of fat marbling the meat. I know we're all told to eat lean meat, but the little trails of fat you see distributed through a piece of meat are what give it flavour and also keep the meat juicy as it cooks.

- Aged meat – or as I've explained, 'hung' is better.
- Traditional breeds – look for British breeds such as Galloway and Dexter. These are the best.
- Colour – darker colour is generally a good guide with beef. Choose a dark red steak rather than a bright red one.
- The best beef comes from grass-fed animals kept in beef herds (rather than dairy herds).

And lamb? What's spring lamb and when is it available?

Depends on the breed – it's possible to get good lamb all year round. Spring lamb is beautifully tender and is best served pink. It has a good but not a strong flavour because it's younger.

With some of the traditional breeds, such as Herdwick and Swaledale, the lambs aren't born until April – it's too cold up in the Lake District where they live. Herdwick spring lamb is in the shops in September. But the spring lamb you see in the shops in early April will have come from lambs born at Christmas to faster-growing lowland breeds such as Texel and Beltex.

Hogget is lamb that is one year old – they say it comes from a lamb that shows a second tooth. Mutton should be three years old, but you don't see it much, as most goes to the halal suppliers. I like to cook my lamb on the bone for the best flavour.

What do I look for in pork?

You want a bit of fat cover – that's what pork is all about. And look for some marbling too, particularly in cuts such as shoulder. You can always trim external fat off once the meat is cooked. I believe pork is best on the bone.

The bone transmits heat, helping the meat cook properly, and gives flavour. Traditional pig breeds include Tamworth, Gloucester Old Spots, Berkshire and British Saddleback. I like to cook my pork pink and then leave it to rest to finish nicely, but I know this is counter to most official advice. This is not a good idea with commercial pork but with rare breed meat and wild boar, pink is good. But if you're not sure, don't take any risks.

What about bacon? What should we buy?
Bacon is pork that has been cured or brined. The cuts generally used are belly for streaky bacon or loin for back bacon.

The buzzword now on bacon is 'dry-cured'. That's what you see on fancy packets and menus and that's the traditional way to cure bacon. It is covered with salt, saltpetre and seasonings and left to cure for several weeks. Back at the beginning of the 20th century the brining method became more widely used and this worked well too. It was quicker than dry curing and more consistent – dry curing could be a bit hit-or-miss depending on the quality of the saltpetre.

Then in the 1960s chemists got involved and they discovered that if you added phosphates as well as saltpetre these held water in the bacon

so it lost less weight. (Normally in curing you lose a third of the weight.) This bacon is cheaper, but you get that nasty scummy stuff coming out when you cook it and it doesn't taste half as good. There are laws about this now, but you don't have to declare added water until it exceeds 10 per cent and that's too much for my liking.

The same applies to ham. Check the label or ask your supplier and go for ham with no added water. Ham with water and other additives has a pink slimy wet look. Proper ham is paler in colour with a drier surface.

Once cured, bacon can be sold as it is – unsmoked or 'green' – or it can be smoked over wood. Watch out for cheap bacon that just has smoky flavouring added.

And sausages?
With sausages, you certainly get what you pay for. Buy the best you can afford, as good-quality sausages will give you a much better result and they're still a fairly cheap meal. Basically, a sausage contains minced meat – usually pork although there are many variations now – plus some fat, seasoning and filler such as breadcrumbs, rusk, potato starch or rice flour. A good sausage should contain 80 per cent meat, but there are products on the market that contain only 42 per cent meat or less.

So once we get our meat home what should we do?
Meat is best kept in greaseproof or waxed paper in the fridge. If you've bought meat that's wrapped in plastic or in a poly tray, take it out of the packaging as soon as you get it home – the plastic makes it sweat. Pat the meat dry with some kitchen paper and put it on a plate, loosely covered, in the fridge. This is particularly important with pork, as you'll never get good crackling from damp pork. Always be careful to store your meat away from other foods in the fridge. Keep it in the bottom part of the fridge so there's no danger of any blood dripping on to other items.

What about freezing? Does that spoil a good piece of meat?
I'd sooner freeze a piece of meat than mess around adding lots of preservatives and additives to extend its shelf life. I believe if you freeze meat for just 4–6 weeks it can even improve the texture, as long as it's sealed properly. If meat is left in the freezer for much longer than that it can develop a rancid taste.

And what about choosing the right cuts for a dish?
Meat from the hardest-working parts, such as the muscles supporting the head and front, are full of flavour but need long slow cooking – they're good for casseroles, braises and so on. They are less expensive than meat from the middle parts, but they can't be cooked quickly.

Middle parts do no heavy work. Cuts from the middle, such as rib, sirloin and fillet, can be cooked quickly and served rare and still be tender.

Medium-worked muscles at the rear provide cuts such as topside and rump. These can be grilled, roasted or braised.

BEEF

Be sure to choose the right cut for the dish you're going to cook. There's no point slow-cooking fillet or trying to grill a piece of shin. If you can, buy good native-breed meat that has been properly hung and aged. The following are the main cuts used in this book. Locations are approximate – exact cuts depend on the animal and the butcher's requirements.

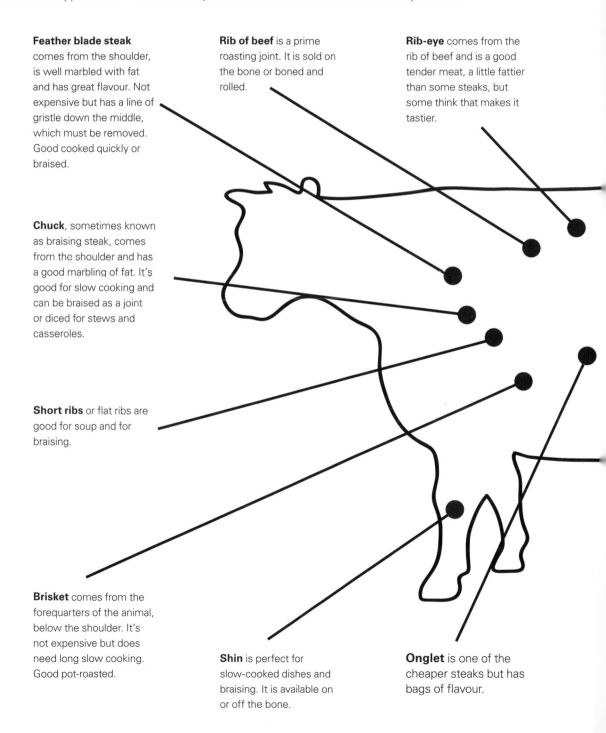

Feather blade steak comes from the shoulder, is well marbled with fat and has great flavour. Not expensive but has a line of gristle down the middle, which must be removed. Good cooked quickly or braised.

Rib of beef is a prime roasting joint. It is sold on the bone or boned and rolled.

Rib-eye comes from the rib of beef and is a good tender meat, a little fattier than some steaks, but some think that makes it tastier.

Chuck, sometimes known as braising steak, comes from the shoulder and has a good marbling of fat. It's good for slow cooking and can be braised as a joint or diced for stews and casseroles.

Short ribs or flat ribs are good for soup and for braising.

Brisket comes from the forequarters of the animal, below the shoulder. It's not expensive but does need long slow cooking. Good pot-roasted.

Shin is perfect for slow-cooked dishes and braising. It is available on or off the bone.

Onglet is one of the cheaper steaks but has bags of flavour.

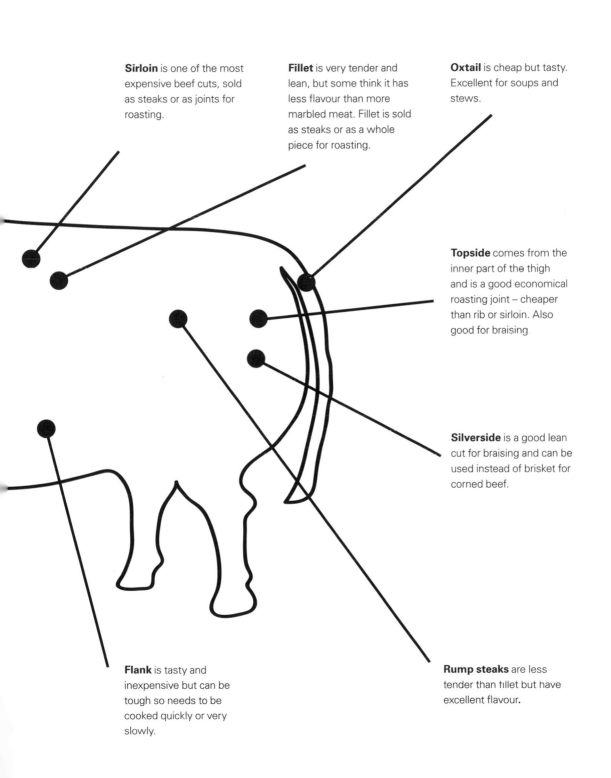

Sirloin is one of the most expensive beef cuts, sold as steaks or as joints for roasting.

Fillet is very tender and lean, but some think it has less flavour than more marbled meat. Fillet is sold as steaks or as a whole piece for roasting.

Oxtail is cheap but tasty. Excellent for soups and stews.

Topside comes from the inner part of the thigh and is a good economical roasting joint – cheaper than rib or sirloin. Also good for braising.

Silverside is a good lean cut for braising and can be used instead of brisket for corned beef.

Flank is tasty and inexpensive but can be tough so needs to be cooked quickly or very slowly.

Rump steaks are less tender than fillet but have excellent flavour.

LAMB

Lamb is much less likely than beef or pork to have been intensively reared, and in this country nearly all our lamb comes from animals that have been raised grazing on pasture. The meat, apart from the very young spring lamb, has a sweet distinctive flavour and the taste can vary according to the land the sheep has grazed on – for example, salt marsh lamb. These are the main cuts used in this book.

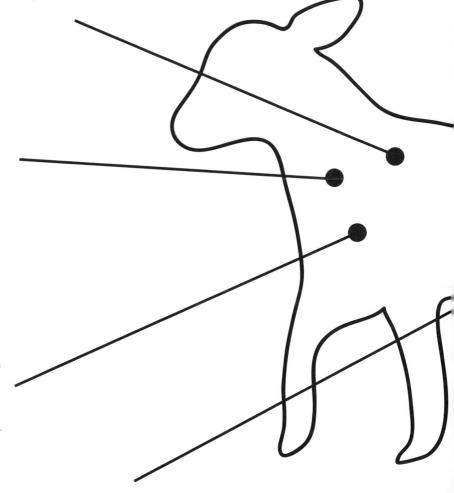

Neck fillet is a lean tender cut that is best cooked quickly and kept pink. Can dry out if overcooked.

Scrag and neck end are fairly cheap cuts on the bone that are good for stewing and have great flavour. Neck fillet comes from the shoulder.

Shoulder is good for roasting on the bone and its high fat content makes it ideal for slow roasting and casseroles, as the meat stays moist. Diced shoulder is good in stews.

Breast comes from the belly of the lamb and is a fatty but tasty cut. Best cooked slowly and ideal for stuffing and rolling for an economical roast.

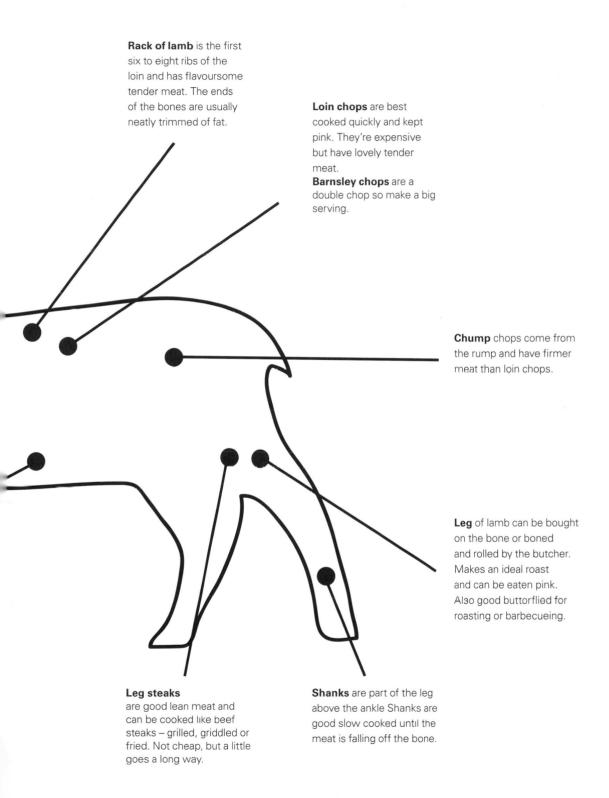

Rack of lamb is the first six to eight ribs of the loin and has flavoursome tender meat. The ends of the bones are usually neatly trimmed of fat.

Loin chops are best cooked quickly and kept pink. They're expensive but have lovely tender meat.
Barnsley chops are a double chop so make a big serving.

Chump chops come from the rump and have firmer meat than loin chops.

Leg of lamb can be bought on the bone or boned and rolled by the butcher. Makes an ideal roast and can be eaten pink. Also good butterflied for roasting or barbecueing.

Leg steaks are good lean meat and can be cooked like beef steaks – grilled, griddled or fried. Not cheap, but a little goes a long way.

Shanks are part of the leg above the ankle Shanks are good slow cooked until the meat is falling off the bone.

PORK

Buy carefully when it comes to pork. Meat from intensively reared animals will disappoint, so if you possibly can, choose free-range pork from traditional breeds and enjoy this wonderful meat at its best. Virtually every part of a pig can be eaten – including the ears and the trotters – and the meat can be used fresh (as pork) or cured (as bacon and ham). The following are the main cuts used in this book.

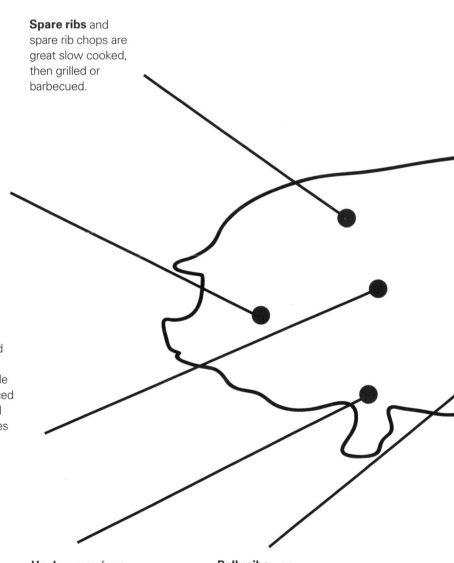

Spare ribs and spare rib chops are great slow cooked, then grilled or barbecued.

Cheeks are little nuggets of sweet tender meat and great in slow-cooked casseroles. Can also be cured.

Shoulder can be cooked on the bone, but is more often sold boned and rolled for roasting. It's affordable and full of flavour. Diced pork shoulder is good for casseroles and pies and shoulder is also used to make pork mince.

Hock comes from the part of the leg above the trotter and is perfect for soup. Also used for ham.

Belly ribs – an inexpensive cut that can be barbecued, roasted or slow cooked.

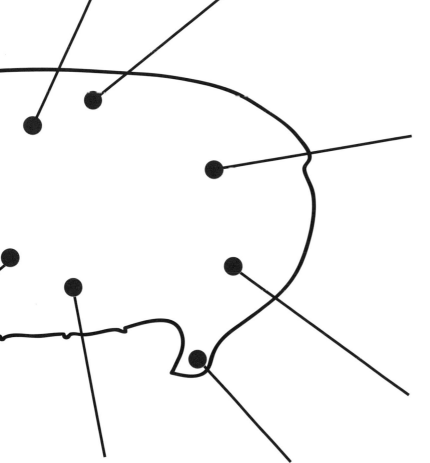

Tenderloin or **fillet** is very tender and can be grilled or roasted quickly. Tends to dryness if overcooked.

Loin comes from the back of the pig and is good roasted on the bone or boned and rolled. Can also be cut into loin steaks or chops.

Chump chops are good grilled or fried.

Leg can be roasted on the bone or boned and rolled for roasting. Leg meat is also used for gammon and ham. Steaks or escalopes cut from the leg are best beaten out, then cooked quickly.

Belly is fatty but is delicious slow roasted or braised. Good crackling. Also used in terrines.

Trotters provide great flavour and gelatine in terrines and cold meat pies. Can also be stuffed and braised.

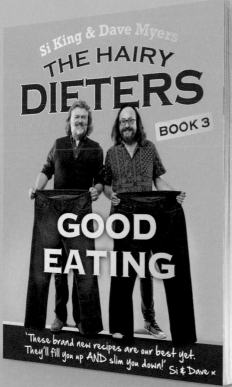

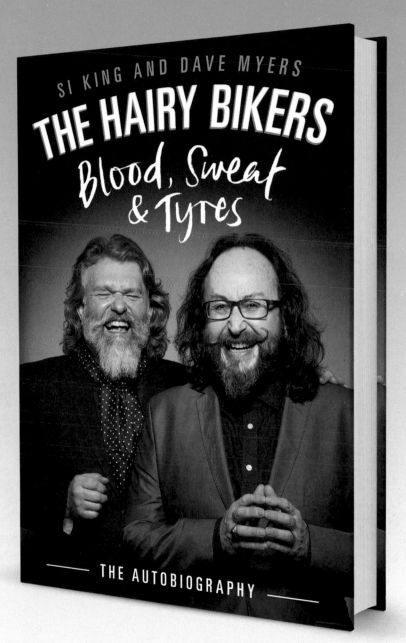

HOW SI MET DAVE

SI KING AND DAVE MYERS

THE HAIRY BIKERS

Blood, Sweat & Tyres

THE AUTOBIOGRAPHY

YOU LOVE THEIR RECIPES
YOU'LL BE AMAZED BY THEIR STORY

05/11/15

INDEX

C

T

ALSO AVAILABLE

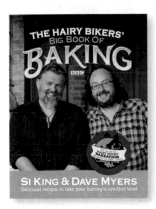

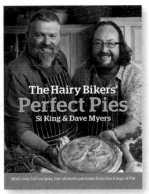

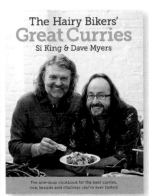

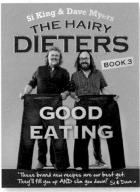

THREE CHEERS TO ALL!

We're so thrilled with this new book – yet again our fantastic Team Hairy have helped us make something we're very proud of.

Huge thanks to Catherine Phipps, who has given us loads of advice on the recipes and helped us hone them to perfection. And to Andrew Hayes-Watkins, who has surpassed himself with the photos – and what's more he's sampled every dish! Big hugs to the amazing Lisa Harrison, Anna Burges-Lumsden and their assistants for making all the food look so tempting and beautiful.

We're also very grateful to the wonderful Loulou Clark for the fresh, clean look of this book, and to tech wizard Andy Bowden and expert creative director Lucie Stericker for their valuable input. To our publisher, Amanda Harris we'd like to express our heartfelt gratitude for your never-failing support and encouragement. Also, many thanks to our editor, Jinny Johnson for putting the book together, her boundless enthusiasm and being a great mate over the years.

A very special thank you is due to our old friend Peter Gott, who runs Sillfield Farm up in the Lake District. We've been buying great meat from Peter for years and we knew he was the ideal person to go to for advice when writing this book. He answered all our questions and we've shared his knowledge with you. His meat is also available online (www.sillfield.co.uk).

And to all at James Grant Management – you are the best and we really appreciate everything you do. Massive thanks and love to Nicola Ibison, Natalie Zietcer, Rowan Lawton, Sarah Hart and Eugenie Furniss.